moving the white gaze (Hannah Black): affective
indexicality and the sensory-motor order of things

→ sensory-motor schema allow us to see the
intolerable (Deleuze, Cinema 2)
→ cliché is a sensory-motor image
→ Bergson: we perceive only what it is
in our interest to perceive in order to
continue moving (and, Deleuze claims,
avoid really seeing and knowing)
→ we do not believe in the world (Deleuze, Cinema 2)
→ we do not believe in the intolerable?
(the world has become bad cinema)
→ seeing an index of the real
does not guarantee that we
admit it into reality
→ Bergson: reality is determined by utility
→ Raengo: index is a
reality a(e)ffect, a sense (in both
senses) of its status as trace of the
real (but also, sense of reality is just that-
→ Black body as index?   felt)

you
are
sort
of
extrapola-
ting
this

→ Black: photos of Emmett Till could not
"move the white gaze from its habitual cold
calculation"

→ Cooper: "white people need to [...]
smother Black pain and outrage and
fear in an avalanche of cold-rational"
analysis. Meanwhile, minds rarely change"

INTERFACES: STUDIES IN VISUAL CULTURE

*Editors Mark J. Williams and
Adrian W. B. Randolph,
Dartmouth College*

This series, sponsored by Dartmouth College Press, develops and promotes the study of visual culture from a variety of critical and methodological perspectives. Its impetus derives from the increasing importance of visual signs in everyday life, and from the rapid expansion of what are termed "new media." The broad cultural and social dynamics attendant to these developments present new challenges and opportunities across and within the disciplines. These have resulted in a transdisciplinary fascination with all things visual, from "high" to "low," and from esoteric to popular. This series brings together approaches to visual culture — broadly conceived — that assess these dynamics critically and that break new ground in understanding their effects and implications.

*For a complete list of books that are available
in the series, visit www.upne.com*

ON THE SLEEVE OF THE

RACE AS FACE VALUE

SLEEVE

VISUAL

ALESSANDRA RAENGO

Dartmouth College Press | Hanover, New Hampshire

Dartmouth College Press
An imprint of University Press of New England
www.upne.com
© 2013 Trustees of Dartmouth College
All rights reserved
Manufactured in the United States of America
Designed by Mindy Basinger Hill
Typeset in Minion Pro

University Press of New England is a member
of the Green Press Initiative. The paper used in
this book meets their minimum requirement
for recycled paper.

For permission to reproduce any of the material in
this book, contact Permissions, University Press of
New England, One Court Street, Suite 250, Lebanon
NH 03766; or visit www.upne.com

Library of Congress Cataloging-in-Publication Data

Raengo, Alessandra.
On the sleeve of the visual : race as face value /
Alessandra Raengo.
— 1st [edition].
    p.   cm. — (Interfaces: studies in visual culture)
Includes bibliographical references and index.
ISBN 978-1-58465-975-4 (cloth : alk. paper) —
ISBN 978-1-58465-974-7 (pbk. : alk. paper) —
ISBN 978-1-61168-449-0 (ebook)
1. Blacks in mass media. 2. Visual sociology.
3. Image (Philosophy) I. Title.
P94.5.B55R34 2013
305.896—dc23   2012042090

5   4   3   2   1

To Margot.
To your resilience and your stunning beauty.

CONTENTS

ACKNOWLEDGMENTS

I do not know for sure where a book begins and ends. I know I cannot quite count the steps that took me here and acknowledge all the extraordinary mentors (Michele Marchetto and Francesco Casetti, being the first two), friends, and colleagues I have had throughout the years who have encouraged my curiosity and have inspired the style of my inquiries. I am particularly grateful to my professors at New York University who got me really started: the incomparable Bob Stam who very early on treated me like his peer, Anna McCarthy, Ed Guerrero, and Dana Polan. There are years of close conversations with Michael Gillespie which, even though not directly reflected here, have made it possible for me to even think about this type of scholarship; at the very least, the question "what is the blackness of black cinema" might have started it all.

This book is the result of a series of questions that lingered after the completion of my dissertation and were provoked by many people and circumstances along the way. My current and past advisees Drew Ayers, Michele Beverly, Kris Cannon, Melanie McDougald, and Chip Linscott have pushed this work toward deeper questions because of the bold inquiries they are developing in their work. I am grateful for the exchange and I look forward to more work together.

This project has benefited from several conversations with my colleague Jennifer Barker, whom I met as I was developing the questions that led to this book. She has changed the way I think about a lot of this. I never thought I could write about the body until she came to the Department of Communication at Georgia State University and made me immediately desire to do so. She made me mind all senses and made me want to look closer than anyone I know. Angelo Restivo has always had tremendous faith in me; I value his subtle comments, his understated brilliance, and his unique personality; Greg Smith has generously read several iterations of my attempts to explain this project and has cheered me on throughout; Nate Atkinson arrived at the tale end but was wonderfully supportive and always collected; my department chair, David Cheshier, has always demonstrated an extraordinary and unwavering support and endless generosity. I owe thanks to the many colleagues in the Department of Communication at Georgia State who have secured funding to help me out with the writing process. The incomparable Nedda Ahmed has helped with copyright clearance and made my life so much easier in more ways that I can list: Tony and Rahna Carusi gave me their readership, their intelligence, and friendship in scholarly things, and many more.

I want to thank my first set of colleagues at Ohio University, especially Marina Peterson and Andrea Frohne for "playing sports" together, and my first two advisees, Shannon Harry and Chip Linscott, for growing up together.

Thanks to the anonymous manuscript reader and to Nicole Fleetwood for her careful and passionate responses to what I was trying to do. Her suggestions have made this work so much stronger. Vinicius Navarro and Jeff Bennett read early drafts of this manuscript and made extremely supportive and gracious observations. I admire their courage in dealing with work in progress and I deeply appreciate their time and generosity.

This work has benefitted from numerous other conversations, with Eddie Chambers, for example, and Keith Harris who has the unique ability to disappear and then suddenly come to the rescue. Meaghan Sutherland and Brian Price have let me consistently overreach at their inimitable World Picture Conference, where I tried out a lot of this material, and offered me invaluable opportunities to discuss my work; and Bishnupriya Ghosh and Bhaskar Sarkar, whom I met there, have always made caring, stimulating, and constructive comments.

There are a number of friends who should be credited with keeping me sane and sometimes allowing me to get away from this all: Danielle and the whole Mikells clan, the mothers and fathers who have helped with childcare (Brandy, Janet, Heather, Marshall, Dale, Mike, and Melissa), and Chris and Pete at Inman Perk Coffee Shop for creating such a friendly and hardworking environment.

My family back in Italy has been incredibly supportive and my daughter, Margot, has been the most graceful trooper. I am stunned and profoundly touched by her ability to take stakes in this project even though she is so young and so predictably conflicted about mom working all the time.

My deepest thanks to the series editors Mark J. Williams and Adrian W. B. Randolph at Dartmouth College Press for believing in this project, and to Richard Pult for his enthusiastic response and his utter cool. I finally would like to thank the artists who kindly granted permission to reproduce their work: Kara Walker, Hank Willis Thomas, Wangechi Mutu, Glenn Ligon, Nan Goldin, and J. S. G. Boggs.

INTRODUCTION

It is as if I had been looking at a fishbowl — the glide and lick of the golden scales, the green tip, the bolt of white careening back from the gills . . . and suddenly I saw the bowl, the structure that transparently (and invisibly) permits the ordered life it contains to exist in the larger world.

—Toni Morrison, *Playing in the Dark*, 1992[1]

[handwritten margin note: fishbowl as what allows things to appear, what delimits the field of the visual]

There is a work by Glenn Ligon in which he arranges next to each other two panels featuring a life-size, black-and-white silkscreen reproduction of his full figure, wearing a white button-down shirt, jeans, and tennis shoes, and facing the camera. Underneath the image, the panel on the left bears the caption "Self-portrait exaggerating my black features," while the panel on the right bears the caption "Self-portrait exaggerating my white features." The two photographs are identical (figure 0.1). We see the same body in both panels but the captions demand that we read the same features alternatively *as* black and *as* white, thus positing the black body as a sort of duck-rabbit figure — an optical illusion. In repeating, but with a difference,[2] these two panels open a chasm in the visual field that makes apparent that seeing is always seeing *as*. It is also a chasm between, among other things, identity and identical, same and double, different and equal. With this slip-

[handwritten margin note: Deleuze - eternal recurrence]

1

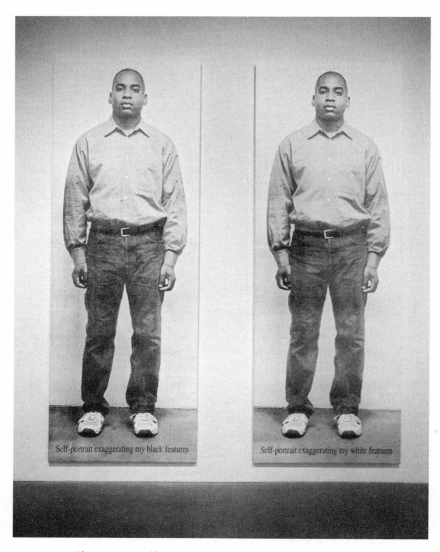

FIGURE 0.1. Glenn Ligon, *Self-Portrait Exaggerating My Black Features/Self-Portrait Exaggerating My White Features,* 1998. Silkscreen ink on canvas, two panels: 120 × 40 in. Courtesy Regen Projects, Los Angeles © Glenn Ligon.

page, Ligon makes blackness and whiteness appear as if they are coming from and leading elsewhere, to a place beyond the visible, and thus exposes the expectation that the black body would work as one sign, one perfect image.

Is this a racial image? And if so, what would make it so? When is an image "racial"? These questions posed by Ligon's *Self-Portrait* and a host of other objects discussed in this book indicate my desire to resist programmatically the conflation of the visual with visibility. Unlike the image *of* race, the racial image, I propose, is not one in which race is present as an intelligibly visible object. Instead, the racial image is where race acts as a form of the articulation of the visual — a template, an epistemology, a map, an affect, a gestalt, a medium — as W. J. T. Mitchell has most recently argued, or as Toni Morrison's image suggests, as a fishbowl.[3] In this understanding of race I join an increasing interest on issues of vision and visuality in critical race discourse and a growing commitment to race in visual culture studies.[4] Yet my focus goes beyond, or maybe underneath, their approach: I am interested in exploring the way in which the "medium-being" of race provides an ontology of the image that our supposed post-medium and post-ontology moment might have put under erasure, but is still unable to undermine.[5] The fact that visual codes of race, for which "black" and "white" constitute the paradigm, continue to secure their referent — or more problematically, but also more frequently, that they continue to be read as portrayals — prompted the guiding question for the present study: What image ontology is needed for race to (still) be read off the surface of some body? Adopting the hermeneutic straining that Morrison describes in the epigraph, I am interested in works and situations in which we can see the fishbowl as such. Not so much when and how race is visible, but what it brings to visibility and what ontology of the visual is implied by the persistence of race.

Consider the asymmetry between the two panels in Ligon's *Self-Portrait*. While Ligon's photographed body does not deliver any recognizable "whiteness," it does deliver a commonsensically recognizable "blackness," thus underscoring the constitutive imbalance between the two in the field of vision: of the two captions, only one appears truthful, plausible, and sensible. Seen through the blackness the caption both describes and conjures up, the body on the left panel appears as a perfectly intelligible, trustworthy, and transparent visual sign. "Perfect" because it is a sign where the surface bears the self-evident trace of what supposedly lies behind it. This is the visual ontology I describe as *face value*, which I think of as the possibility, the belief and, more

racial image: race brings things into view (delimits the visual)

Bergson

value inscribed on the surface

profoundly, the desire to read value (but also reference, truth, meaning) on the image's face; that is, on its visage and its surface. This image ontology is both constitutive of and constituted by the blackness of Ligon's body within a perverse circularity that keeps the black body trapped within the visual field, both proof and product of the visuality of race.[6] Consequently, the black body features in the present analyses not as the incontrovertible foundation for race, but rather as the ground for an enduring ontology of the visual — one that is modeled after that particular body.[7] This focus is not an attempt to subsume all racial experiences under the dynamic between blackness and whiteness, understood as sociological or anthropological categories, at the exclusion of many heterogeneous and complicated lived experiences of race. It is rather a means to address a fundamentally Manichean visual paradigm and to press the ontological question: what image ontology do we evoke when we say "black" and "white"?[8]

Race acts both as an agent of corporealization of the visual and an agent of abstraction. On the one hand, race is what has *fleshed out* images for us, but also what has made us like them, trust them, and want to touch them. On the other hand, race is what has enabled us to read these images. It has established and deployed a system of visual equivalences among images, and between images and the world, which we routinely rehearse in our employment of the language of "black" and "white." Race corporealizes the visual at the same time as it secures its legible surface. Thus, under the medium-being of race there is a crucial sliding of an hermeneutic practice of surface reading into an ontology of the image whereby the image's meaning and value is supposedly secured by/on its surface.[9] But what connects the "face" to value? What makes the surface perform as the repository and the expression of value?

The title of Ligon's work, *Self-Portrait,* identifies a source for the black body's troubled and troubling presence within the field of vision in the expectation that racial signs would always be read representationally as portrayals.[10] It is this demand that the black body be always both representative[11] and representational — what in relation to artistic and curatorial practices Darby English has called the "black representational space" — that charges the body's surface with the expectation that it expresses its value.[12] Thus, one of the goals of this book is to offer an alternative to a representational theory of race, which I see as the expression of an imposed system of fixed correspondences, sometimes a conflation, between face and value. In order to resist this conflation, I leverage the flickering effect and the surface tension between "face" and "value," the fact that they may seem to belong to two different ontological orders. At minimum, the notion of face value yokes together two important lines of thinking: one trajectory that pursues the phenomenology of racial embodiment, and another that understands value as an expression of the social (understood as labor, meaning, the social contract, and so on).[13]

Face value also begs the question of how the surface needs to be understood; that is, do we need to understand it phenomenologically, as "skin"? Semiotically, as a signifier? Chromatically, as a physical property? As a façade? An interface? A locus of desire?[14] And what is the surface from the point of view of the political economy of the sign? In turn, the notion of the "face" bears an inner tension because it conjures up both a body for which it provides the visage and the idea of a sheer surface. We see this at work in Ligon's *Self-Portrait*. The request that the viewer read the two photographs as evidence of different racial identities emphasizes the tension between an understanding of "face" as visage and the understanding of "face" under the condition of blackness, as nothing but a surface — the effect of exteriorization Frantz Fanon described in his account of the interpellation to which he was subjected by a French child: *Tiens, un nègre!* (Look! A Negro!) Deprived of interiority, his whole body is evacuated, divided, eviscerated.[15] As Charles Johnson puts it, his body and subjectivity are turned inside out, folded outwardly like shirt-cuffs.[16] It is this very image that inspired the title for this book, the idea that the black body is both cause and product of a visual fold whereby the body's "inside" is evacuated, turned into mere surface, and placed in full view, *worn on the sleeve of the visual.* The fold thusly understood is also what supposedly connects the face to value, by conflating them, suturing them, or fantasizing about their continuity.[17]

At the heart of this conflation there is a profound desire for race to represent difference. In *Playing in the Dark* Morrison shows this desire at work by exposing the fishbowl from within, from a place of avisuality, from the chasm Ligon makes available in his repeated photograph. She claims that the turning point that allowed her to suddenly see the fishbowl occurred when she began to read American literature as a writer; that is, with the knowledge of how an author's imagination determines her ability to fashion characters and situations. At that point, she realized that "for black and white American writers, in a wholly racialized society, there is no escape from racially inflected language."[18] Importantly, she did not read American literature searching for

the fold links surface and depth [handwritten annotation]

racial representations, but rather for the "tremors" that pervade the "white" literary utterance when it chokes what she provocatively called "the Africanist presence."[19] Furthermore, Morrison notes that white American and African American writers do not have equal access to a purportedly race-free language. "The kind of work I have always wanted to do," she writes, "requires me to learn how to maneuver ways to free up the language from its sometimes sinister, frequently lazy, almost always predictable employment of racially informed and determined chains." And then, she parenthetically adds, "(The only short story I have ever written, 'Recitatif,' was an experiment in the removal of all racial codes from a narrative about two characters of different races for whom racial identity is crucial.)."[20]

This is a brilliantly misleading statement and one that holds the key to her anti-representational approach to race. In fact, Morrison did not remove all racial codes — which, according to her previous statement is an impossibility anyway — but rather left them unattributed, handing over to the reader the task to determine who they belong to, and, even more provocatively, which codes are racial and which are not. Significantly, "Recitatif"'s critical reception has emphasized how readers search for signs of race, do not find them, and are left pondering on protocols of racial legibility. This critical reception thus accurately points out not the critical work the story performs but rather the desire it mobilizes; more profoundly, the desire to continue to think of race as a form of representation of difference.

"Recitatif" follows Roberta and Twyla, from childhood to adulthood. It is narrated by Twyla and it begins with her arrival at the New York orphanage St. Bonaventure, where she immediately "feels sick to her stomach" upon discovering that she has been put in a room with a girl of a "whole different race." The story, however, never tells us what this "other race" is but, because it expresses the characters' reactions to each other, it employs a racially charged language. Statements such as "my mother said . . . that they never washed their hair and they smelled funny," or "everything is so easy for them. They think they own the world" are easily read as racially motivated. But are they?

Despite their difference, Roberta and Twyla hit it off because they have some important things in common: for example, they are not actual orphans. Their mothers are alive, although unable to care for them — Roberta's is "sick" and Twyla's "dances all night." After this initial bonding experience over their mother's absence, Roberta and Twyla will meet again several times over the span of thirty years. At each encounter the reader is also given a new set of contradictory descriptors. For example, in the '60s Roberta has "huge hair" and she is on her way to a Jimi Hendrix concert. Twyla, instead, waits tables at a Howard Johnson's. Twyla eventually marries a fireman with a big, loud family and has two kids, while Roberta marries an IBM executive, acquires stepchildren and a wealthy lifestyle, Chinese chauffeur included. Each encounter reveals how racial strife has created a wedge between them that overrides the initial bond they had established. Their preferred mode of retaliation in these occasions where they discover they have grown apart is either a reference to the unavailability of their respective mothers ("is your mother well?" "did your mother stop dancing?"), or a reference to Maggie.

Maggie is the mute and possibly deaf woman who worked in the kitchen at the orphanage. She is as short as a child and dresses like one, with a funny hat that the older girls despise as much as they despise her. Her legs are shaped like semicircles — parentheses, as Twyla describes them — and too short and unstable for her to rely on as she awkwardly hurries through the orchard to catch her bus home. The "accident" that is mentioned at each encounter between Twyla and Roberta concerns a time when the older girls made Maggie trip and fall and they all laughed while Twyla and Roberta did not do anything to help. As the racial divide between the characters deepens against the backdrop of the '60s and '70s social unrest, Roberta begins to insinuate that Maggie was black and Twyla had kicked Maggie when she had fallen on the ground. Described as simply "sandy-colored," readers and characters are not given enough information to determine her racial identity. Maggie is not visually scripted in racial terms, but only outlined as a typographic sign that both joins and disjoins — a parenthesis.

It is around the figure of Maggie that the text builds its own dispute of the representational framework of race, and yet it is Maggie as the figure of the story's readership and textuality that has commanded most representational readings. Elizabeth Abel, for example, focuses on Maggie because she offers a *mise-en-abyme* of the text: the girls' inconclusive reading of Maggie's blackness, she claims, mirrors the readers' attempt to determine the racial identity of the characters. Thus the short story offers a useful starting point to explore how "feminist *readings* of black women's texts disclose white critical fantasies," or, as she otherwise states, how "white women's readings of black women's biological bodies inform our readings of black women's textual bodies."[21] This conflation between a biological and a textual body is precisely what Morrison is attempting to avoid. Abel recognizes that "Recitatif" renders race a "contested terrain variously mapped from diverse positions in the social landscape" by replacing "conventional signifiers of racial difference (such as skin color) with radically relativistic ones (such as who smells funny to whom) and by substituting for the racialized body a series of disaggregated cultural parts."[22] Yet, as she reads the story, she tirelessly seeks to stitch back together in a unified pre- or meta-textual figure the fragments that Morrison cunningly maintains separated. What unifying systems, she asks, need to be mobilized to finally match the right race with the right person? Is it class? Is it wealth? Education? Psychology? Politics? But how can any of these be conclusively and definitively raced?

Abel appears to be chasing the prospect of finding underneath the multiplication of (surface) readings that "Recitatif" demands a body we can understand and racially identify. In other words, we might not know who is who and what is what, but the "who" and the "what" of race, in Abel's reading, maintain an ontological thickness she is unable to challenge. Abel describes Maggie as a "*figure* of racial undecidability,"[23] but I believe that, more profoundly, Maggie turns racial undecidability into a figure — a figure with linguistic and visual integrity, with a substantial presence, with a carnality that is clearly defined, except for her racial identity — a stranger. Her semicircle legs suggest the self-containment of her body, which cannot/ does not compare to any other body around her. While Twyla and Roberta are constantly paradigmatically connected within what we can describe as a Saussurean system of differences without positive terms, Maggie is preserved from this linguistic economy and remains unattached to any paradigmatic chain. She is not only a mute woman, but a mute term as well, unyielding and inassimilable. Unlike the main characters, whom are never really described, she is given an image, but this image does not contain the key to her identity. Within the linguistic economy of the text she is more properly understood as an element of syntax, as suggested by the shape of her legs.

Trudier Harris's reading of "Recitatif" pursues a similar line of inquiry: as readers, she claims, we watch and wait in the hope that "Twyla, the narrator, will provide some clue to her racial identity."[24] We want her to slip and fall (like the characters wanted Maggie to do) and say more than the author has engineered she should say for her experiment in "the removal of all racial codes" to succeed. Ultimately, we want Morrison to fall in order to relieve us from our not knowing and attach the racial codes she so liberally employs, to the body, the mind, and the social circumstances to which they belong. In

Harris's approach, Maggie is constructed as the racially unknowable subject so that the characters themselves, whom we do not see, but who clearly see each other, can experience the temporary blindness to which the reader is also perversely subjected. In this reading, the characters become the deserving victims of the same joke Morrison is playing on us.

By seeking an answer to the riddle of Maggie's blackness, both Abel and Harris unwillingly fall into what Henry Louis Gates Jr. has called a *sociological fallacy*.[25] They appear to read racial codes as racial representations and understand these representations as implicitly corporeal: any series of signifiers, however simulacral, needs to finally land onto a body as their referent, even when this body remains unseen. Against Morrison's stated goal, both Abel and Harris struggle with the difficulty of racial attribution; yet, it is the notion of race as a corporeal attribute that they never challenge. The text, in their view, sets up a complex interplay of mirrors, so that we never have an unobstructed view of its characters. Yet, this also means that all we have to do is unravel this interplay of reflections and we will find the answer to our quest.

On the contrary, I argue that Morrison's narrative disputes this representational approach by setting up a mock specular structure only to lead the reader to discover a non-reciprocal phantasmatic chiasm that connects the two characters and the readers to the text in order to explore how both readers and characters invest with a carnal presence the space in-between. The chiasm I have in mind is the one synecdochically inflected that, building on Homi Bhabha, Lee Edelman has described as the part for the (W)hole.[26] A typographic sign, a syntactic mark, Maggie is the chiasmic X that marks the spot, the parenthesis itself that connects the whole to the hole. Maggie's textual blackness is posited to signify otherness but this otherness does not belong to her. Rather, as Homi Bhabha has repeatedly argued, it is an inscription of the "artifice" of white identity on the black's body. "The figure of colonial otherness," he writes, "is produced not by the colonialist Self or the Colonized Other but by the *distance in between*."[27] By acting as a parenthesis connecting the fiction of wholeness to its synecdochical reliance on a projected holeness, Maggie is the in-betweenness turned into a body.

She is what Sarah Ahmed would describe as a "strange body"; that is, a body with linguistic and figurative integrity that is produced by the social body in the attempt to expel what threatens its boundaries. In *Strange Encounters*, Ahmed reads a passage from Audre Lorde's *Sister Outsider* in which Lorde recalls an episode that occurred in the New York subway when she was a child. A white woman sitting next to her kept pulling her fur coat away from Lorde's snow pants. Lorde writes, "She jerks her coat close to her. I look. I do not see whatever terrible things she is seeing on the seat between us — probably a roach."[28] The child's inability to understand the woman's retreat leads her to imagine a strange body (a roach) as the cause of such horror. The white woman, instead, is seeing the young Lorde *as* a roach. Ahmed writes, "It is through a complex sliding of signifiers and bodies, that the roach becomes the black body, and the black body becomes the border which is hence transformed into an object of abjection" — a roach.[29] Similarly, "Recitatif" posits race not in any single individual, but rather in the area of contact, the connecting tissue between them, the "strangeness" that connects the hole to the whole. Race is projected onto the body of Maggie, who acts as the embodiment of the social bond that brings the characters together as well as divides them along unattributed racial lines. This is the work of race that Toni Morrison detects in American literature and whose form she reproduces in "Recitatif": the mechanism that fixates this "sliding of signifiers" into visual objects is fundamentally representational. Through the figure of Maggie, Morrison, like Audre Lorde, embodies the relationality of race in the form of a "roach," a scene of exchange between imaging and seeing *as* — the site of the chiasm that a representational framework of race forecloses from view.

In Ligon's *Self-Portrait*, instead, this chiasm is in full view. Ligon installs his own body in the chiasmic X so that his self-portrait unfolds an implied mirror stage towards the viewer who then contemplates her own mobilization of racialized protocols of legibility. Thus, Ligon shapes himself *as* a roach (within the figurative terms just described) to corporealize not simply what lies between the two photographs, but what lies between the work in its totality and the viewers' stubborn desire to see race represent difference.

The figure of Maggie stages the work of race from a position of avisuality.[30] Maggie is a textual figure generative of the visual ontology of race, but she is not in herself visible in Morrison's text. Ligon's *Self-Portrait* instead leverages the fact that, perpetually caught in between hyper- and in-visibility, the black body offers, by default, both the terrain and the vantage point from which to outline the very boundaries of the visible. The photograph leverages this in-betweenness through mechanical repetition and by having photography, as the medium and the epistemological deliverer of transparency, become, instead, a locus of instability and opacity. In this, Ligon confirms what Frantz

Fanon had already noted: the process of racialization is analogous to the photographic process of photochemical fixation, whereby the body is fixated in the field of vision, like a photochemical imprint is fixated by a dye.[31] By folding the visual onto its outside and then triggering the fixation of this fold, the black body offers both nourishment and pretext for a photochemical imagination that, I argue, lingers across the digital divide. In keeping with Fanon, here *photochemical* does not strictly refer to a specific medium or technology of image production, but rather to the referential affects and a cultural logic of investment in the continuity between the world and photographic images. A lot of these affects have congealed around the continuing reflection on the indexicality of the photographic image that has re-proposed the ontological question in a changed, now predominantly digital, visual culture: whether the index as a sign function remains relevant with digital images and can still ground their truth claims, or whether maybe digital images (as well as the practices of which they are part and our response to them) have finally uncovered for us that the index is more fundamentally and more foundationally an *affect* — an investment in a certain idea of referentiality that the black body has historically delivered. Said otherwise, as the paradigmatic visual sign, as the sign that wears its value on its surface and its ontological status on its sleeve, the black body is both product and trigger of an *effect* and *affect* of reality, a reality a(e)ffect.[32]

LOOK MAMA, A PIPE!

Ligon's *Self-Portrait* withholds the suturing between seeing and saying, seeing and touching, seeing and believing that the black body is supposed to deliver. "Somewhere between these two photographs," writes Nicholas Mirzoeff, "there should be a color line, but it is elsewhere."[33] This "color line" that lies "elsewhere" marks this missed suturing even though the terms "black" and "white" used in the captions still make us search the surface of the body for their possible reference, even though the repeated photograph lets us know that the referent will not be found inward where we would want to locate it. Ligon's *Self-Portrait* too, therefore, opens up a place of avisuality — the space in between the repeated photographs; and just like "Recitatif," it does so by leveraging the conjuring power of "black" and "white."

The tension between seeing and saying, suturing and severing that Ligon's work puts in place is foundational to the image ontology of face value. One of its primal scenes is the oft-quoted passage from *Black Skins, White Masks*: "Look! A Negro!" There Fanon outlines a dialectical movement between the attempted closure of racialization and its irreducible openness and unstoppable slippage as it unfolds around the sight of a black body.[34] By resisting this attempted closure, Fanon also resists a representational concept of the visual in order to dislodge the black body from its central position as the paradigmatic visual sign. Fanon conceptualizes blackness not as a visual property, but rather as a visual relation, which becomes a thing only as a consequence of the moment of fixation. When Fanon's narrator is singled out by a frightened child he is given back an image of himself that is available to no one — not to the child who has projected it, nor to the narrator who can only see its reflection onto the child's reaction to it. This black *imago*, this haunting presence of a phantasmatic blackness, is a visual relation that never coincides with a visual object. Suspended between reflection and projection, Fanon locates "blackness in the place between the interpellator and the interpellated."[35] He accounts for blackness as formed *in*, not simply *as*, difference, an "uncomfortable suspension" between a negated recognition as Self and the impossibility to identify as Other.[36]

However, it is only Fanon's critical response to this interpellation that makes available the indeterminacy of blackness. From the child's perspective, instead, the Martinican constitutes a perfectly contained, fully intelligible visual object, a perfect sign that benefits from the synergy of iconic and indexical functions. The slippage between the terms *nègre* Fanon uses in this passage and the term *Noir* he employs more often has the ability to suture language and vision, seeing and saying, to suspend the awareness that, as Michel Foucault puts it, what we see is never contained in what we say.[37] While critical theory revels in this gap, this chasm that Ligon's *Self-Portrait* makes so whimsically available, it too acknowledges the desire for referentiality that undergirds the idea of representation. In critical theory a primal scene of recognition of this desire is found in Foucault's reflection on the infinite relation between seeing and saying in his famous analysis of Velasquez's *Las Meninas* and even more in his reading of René Margitte's *La Trahison des images* (*Ceci n'est pas une pipe*, 1929), (figure 0.2).

What happens when we read these two scenes together: Look mama, a pipe! This expression, a graft that puts *en-abyme*, while mocking, two separate and preexisting grafts (the *nègre/Noir* and Magritte's painted pipe) describes the "retinal pop" triggered by the sight of the black body (Look!).

FIGURE 0.2. René Magritte, *La Trahison des images (C'est n'est pas une pipe)*, 1929. Oil on canvas, unframed canvas, 25 ⅜ × 37 in. © ARS, NY. Purchased with funds provided by the Mr. and Mrs. William Preston Harrison Collection (78.7). Los Angeles County Museum of Art, Los Angeles. Digital Image © 2009 Museum Associates/LACMA/ Art Resource, NY.

But it also triggers a series of referential affects prompted by the way the black body fulfills the need for a referential closure: the sight of corporeal blackness appears to always deliver "the black." Reading together Fanon with Foucault and Magritte can help us appreciate that what both Magritte and Fanon manage to estrange — the way of seeing and saying that confuses the object with its representation, visual with discursive knowledge — is precisely what black bodies make difficult to do. Indeed, the transparency of the visual object is what Magritte satirizes by staging it as its face value. At first sight, claims Foucault, Magritte provides us with an image that "is as simple as a page borrowed from a botanical manual: a figure and the text that names it."[38] Similarly, the statement "Look! A Negro!" describes Fanon's body as the appearance of a figure and its name, a Negro. The black body, Fanon shows, is a visual object that appears to prevent reflection on the way of seeing and saying that constitutes it as immediately transparent and directly accessible. It commends precisely the statement that Magritte attempts to estrange — "This is a pipe!" Yet, while the latter can satirize the desire for the suture between seeing and saying, the former speaks from a position in which that suture has already occurred.

Foucault's analysis is well known, and it has been deployed also by W. J. T. Mitchell to conceptualize his notion of "metapictures."[39] These two analyses read Magritte's painting as a meta-argument about vision, naming, and representation, and the desires undergirding them; as an instantiation of what Mitchell expresses with a Wittgensteinian argument — specifically that naming is always naming *as*, and seeing is always seeing *as*. Whatever the interpretation of the referent for Magritte's *ceci* (the drawn pipe, the statement "this is not a pipe," the painting itself, etc.), its deictic properties — the pointing finger that it supposedly directs outside the painting to the pipe itself — do not allow for the definition of a "meta" perspective "that would let us say that the assertion is true, false, or contradictory."[40] On the contrary, in Magritte's second painting, *Les Deux Mystères*, the desire for that perspective has become a floating pipe, impossible to anchor either to its original image (now satirically framed within a didactic context of the blackboard), nor to any statement we might want to make about it (figure 0.3). This floating makes visible the desire that representational codes (whether racial or not) would land somewhere where they supposedly belong — on the blackboard, on the canvas, onto a surface that might secure that this image is indeed a fold from the real. Instead, not only does Magritte succeed in creating a wedge between resemblance and affirmation, but he ignites a crisis into the distinction between figurative and literal uses of language. Magritte's caption, as Mitchell points out, short-circuits common sense because it is literally true (that indeed is not a pipe, but the picture of a pipe), but figuratively false (when asked what that picture is, we would say, "it's a pipe").[41] It also succeeds in yanking both linguistic and visual levels of representation from the servitude of reference and locates them instead in what Foucault defines as the ontological plane of similitude, "the indefinite and reversible relation of the similar to the similar."[42] In his *Self-Portrait*, Ligon further complicates this relationship between resemblance and similitude: "Resemblance has a "model," an original element," writes Foucault, while the "similar develops in series that have neither beginning nor end. . . . Resemblance serves representation, which rules over it; similitude serves repetition, which ranges across it."[43] In withholding delivery of any conclusive referent, *Self-Portrait*

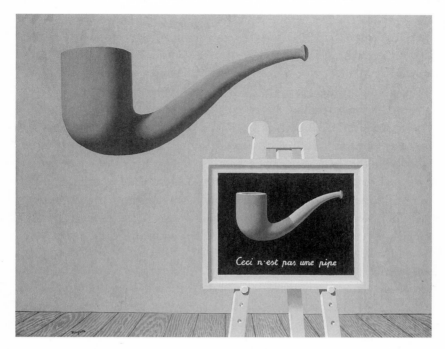

FIGURE 0.3. René Magritte, *Les Deux Mystères (The Two Mysteries)*, 1966. Oil on canvas, 65 × 80 cm. © ARS, NY. Private Collection. Photo Credit: Banque d'Images, ADACP/Art Resource, NY.

stages the dilemma of Magritte's painting as a form of seeing *as,* where the mockingly accessible pictured body occupies the place and performs the role of the *as.* Here it is Ligon's photographed body, not the pipe, that performs the function of the unraveled calligram, posing as the shape, so to speak, not the referent, of the terms "black" and "white" used in the caption.[44]

Known primarily for his text paintings, Ligon's work often occupies both visual and verbal registers at once and capitalizes on its location "inside a conflict between looking and reading."[45] In the case of *Untitled (I Am an Invisible Man,* 1994), Ligon committed to the canvas the text of the opening prologue of *Invisible Man,* a novel that theorizes a perverse fold in the visual field whereby the black subject is invisible because of its body's hypervisibility. Ralph Ellison's text becomes progressively illegible as Ligon's stencil marks become thicker and thicker and the painting slowly transforms back into an object to be looked at, while our ability to see is frustrated by the inability to make out the words it is supposed to represent. Ligon shows the desire that propels the representational impulse by rubbing together looking and reading. As Darby English notices, this is a way in which Ligon's work wrestles with the problem of the surface, refusing its function as locus of identity and instead repurposing it as a site for "a crisis of apprehension."[46]

Unlike his text paintings, here Ligon embraces photographic presence and the "closed form" of his body to mock the demand for its perfect legibility. As much as we want to read it, his caption underscores the irrelevance of this operation. The surface, which is central in his work, is here again charged with the expectation to represent while it is also withheld as an ending point to our hermeneutic effort. It slides back, into an infinite recess, into the place of blackness that Barthes postulates for the viewer of photography.[47] English says that Ligon "paints *in spite of the surface*, treating its hallowed ground as a beginning rather than an end."[48] A beginning that, despite its full photographic delivery, is short-circuited by the caption and does not lead anywhere. Here, the blackness of the body does not deliver the black. Rather, the black body has become intransitive: a pipe is a pipe is a pipe is a pipe.[49]

IN THE FISHBOWL

Chapter 1 introduces the imbrication between race and the photochemical imagination by reading together Fanon with Barthes. I turn to Fanon because his realization that the process of racialization in the visual sphere takes the form of photochemical fixation makes him a particularly astute reader of the relationship between blackness and the affects and desires of a photochemical imagination. I turn to Barthes because of his investment in the photographic connection as an embodied experience and his troubled and troubling relationship with the iconicity of blackness.[50] This chapter focuses on the affects associated with indexicality by discussing the "photographic" as a state of the image that, sharing the same semiotic structure as the black body, has reinforced the sense of the materiality and referentiality of race.[51] It does so through a close reading of a lynching shadow, an oxymoron, from the standpoint of photographic ontology. Because the blackness of the shadow does not coincide with the blackness of the body while still being tethered to it, this image challenges the photochemical imagination that supports a racial reading of it. As a result, rather than a structure of referral, this shadow suggests that photography can be instead understood as a structure of deferral. This racially agnostic but visually black shadow offers also an alternative to the representational paradigm still dependent on a Platonic/mimetic conception of the image as *mirror*. Whereas the paradigm of the mirror focuses on the authenticity and truth-value of racial representations — that is, on the extent to which they adequately (or not) portray black people — the paradigm of the shadow locates blackness not *in* bodies but *in between* them. The shadow is an image state that emphasizes connection rather than representation. In this tension between images that can be trusted because of how they "look like," and images that can be believed because they are tethered, we discover that the representational framework that sustains the photochemical imagination would like to have it both ways: images that are as tethered as shadows and as faithful and recognizable as mirror reflections.

As a following of chapter 1's focus on fantasies of suturing signifiers with referents, the shadow with the black body, chapter 2 focuses on the attempted suturing of seeing with saying implied by the term "black." I read it through the trope of catachresis — the attribution of a name for something that supposedly does not have one — and I attend to its phenomenological and aesthetic implications, which show how the process of racialization functions as a "distribution of the sensible."[52] The language of black and white, obviously, carries the visual with it, and with the visual, it also carries a series of promises, assumptions, and fantasies about what "black" should deliver. Black describes a visual attribute, a quality, a pole in the color spectrum, but the place of blackness, as Ellison expresses in *Invisible Man*, and Morrison does too with Maggie, is a place of avisuality.[53] To suture the visual and the avisual, catachresis grows a body that fills the gap. The case study here is PRECIOUS, which is the way I signify the catachrestic conflation between the body of the actress Gabourey Sidibe, the character Clareece Precious Jones, and the title of Lee Daniels's film, *Precious: Based on the Novel "Push" by Sapphire* (2009). My analysis shows that the filmmaker anticipated this conflation in the film's reception and reflexively addressed it through a series of effects of *mise-en-abyme*. Yet, there is a desire of the main character that the film cannot fully address. It is the desire to *cut a figure*, to claim a face from the depth of the visual field. I, therefore, turn to artist Wangechi Mutu's collages to show how this is possible and how catachresis can be brandished as a surgical instrument to cut through a flattened and overgrown visual surface. Through her cuts, Mutu turns the muted, pathologized, overembodied native woman, the eroticized vessel for colonial nostalgia, into a posthuman, Afrofuturist, biocybernetic female warrior.[54] Her aesthetic choices suggest another possibility for photographic practices to challenge the photochemical affects, that is, photography's ability to perform as excision of what processes of racialization have produced as an ectopic growth.

Chapters 3 and 4 are concerned with the way in which both photography and race pass through capital to gain exchangeability. They do so because they share the same hermeneutics of the surface — the hermeneutics of face value. Mostly preoccupied with avisual objects, chapter 3 offers a detour onto the relationship between face and value through an analysis of the political economy of the racial sign. Under this analysis, which leverages Marx's semiotics of value as one in which the body of commodity A acts as the mirror of the value of commodity B, value acts as a counter-concept to the notion of indexicality. Value, Marx says, does "not have its description branded on its forehead."[55] Yet, it is the ability for blackness to act as an exchangeable surface that is crucial in this case, its performance as the signifier of exchange. My guide in this investigation is the concept and the aesthetics of blackface, which I regard primarily as the dramatization and reification of blackness as face value. I begin with a joke that stand-up comedian and civil rights activist Dick Gregory published in 1962: "wouldn't it be a helluva joke if all this was really burnt cork and you people were being tolerant for nuthin'?" Through this scenario of reversibility between black skin and burnt cork, Gregory calls attention to how these signifiers function as tokens of exchange and, therefore, to blackness as currency. The rest of the chapter examines blackness as a commodity "form"; that is, as the principle of visibility, the *face,* of commodity status. Building on a reading of Spike Lee's *Bamboozled* and of photographer Hank Willis Thomas's work, the chapter asks, "what type of commodity is the one for which blackness acts as principle of visibility?" The analysis of a contemporary work of cyber art — Keith Obadike's *Blackness for Sale* — in which blackness is conjured as the manufactured product of a transaction that the work itself initiates shows a continuing process of de-corporealization of blackness. These works testify to blackness transitioning from being the signifier of a corporeal property to being the signifier of speculative value, from being a bodily index to a market index. They suggest that blackness has become a phantasmagoria; that is, it has come to signify a moment in which an increasingly simulacral status of the visual has developed its own, independent, social materiality. They finally allow us to understand the current moment as another phase in the journey of blackness from the surface of the body to the surface of material culture to where it is now — *on the sleeve of the visual.*

Chapter 4 maps photography onto race and capital through the concept of the Long Photographic Century. In pursuit of an analysis of the hermeneutics capital, photography, and blackness share — the hermeneutics of face value — chapters 3 and 4, respectively, look at race and photography as the *money of the real.* This view of photography has a long history, one that I build on in order to claim that it is the photochemically fixated black body that has generalized the money form of the visual sphere. I show this at work in Scott McGhee and David Siegel's 1993 film *Suture* about a case of mistaken identity between two characters played by a white and a black actor. The film handles blackness and whiteness only iconically, as sheer surfaces, in order to outline an economy of exchange that, the film makes us realize, has been fully naturalized. But why is that so? Whereas chapter 3 mostly concerned with the way in which capital generalizes a hermeneutics of the surface rehearsed (applied, extended, perfected) in the understanding of the black body during the Long Twentieth Century, chapter 4 focuses more strongly on objects that recapitulate the history of visuality produced by the bolting of race to capital, which I call the Long Photographic Century. I then explore the implications of the lingering photochemical imagination across the digital divide. The objects examined here — Hank Willis Thomas again and Kara Walker's post-cinematic silhouettes — show how the ontological and sensible partition introduced by race is not challenged by the digital image but in fact reinforces and perpetuates the photochemical imagination.

Finally, the book's conclusion returns to my initial question: what is a racial image? Throughout the book, I pursue an understanding of race that resists the conflation between the visible and the visual and the expectation that racial images would perform as mirrors of a supposed racial subject. Thus, at the end of the book I return to the NAACP shadow as offering a possible way to unhinge blackness from the body. Seen from the perspective of this shadow, race appears to more prominently inhabit the state and not the content of the image.

The methodology employed throughout is interdisciplinary and eclectic, but each chapter privileges a set of disciplinary frames over others. Chapter 1 mobilizes mostly film studies, and theories of the photochemical and digital image. Chapter 2 dialogues predominantly with rhetorical theory, aesthetic theory, art history, and scholarship on black cinema. Chapter 3 relies heavily on Marxist theory and on what I consider to be the intimate connection between visual and material culture. In this chapter I read one through the lens of the other. Chapter 4 and the conclusion return to visual forms and, therefore, bring the theoretical work of the book back to bear on the ontology of the visual.

Each chapter deals with a different aspect of the photochemical imagination and explores the possibility for photography, understood as a state or passage of the image, to act in ways that resist the ontology of face value, which is grounded in two movements, one toward the inside and the other across the surface. Each chapter examines various kinds of bodies — photographically rendered bodies and rhetorically rendered bodies (like Maggie and Audre Lorde's roach), visible bodies and avisual bodies, bodies that are phenomenologically fleshed out and bodies that instead matter only as pure surfaces, bodies that suture and bodies that sever. Furthermore, in each of the chapters these bodies perform different actions: they cut; they vanish; they appear when conjured up; they overflow their boundaries; they grow in unexpected places; they are iconized and made exchangeable; they are abstracted and eviscerated. Virtually all of the objects described perform an act of pivoting in the visual field by turning its racially sanctioned relationship between surface and depth inside out.[56]

ONE
THE PHOTOCHEMICAL IMAGINATION

In the NAACP files at the Library of Congress I found a highly unusual lynching photograph: an extremely high angle of a seemingly endless crowd crossed diagonally by the elongated shadow of a hanging body (figure 1.1). Descriptively titled "Crowd of people, with shadow of man hanging from tree superimposed over them," the photograph is undated, although it is estimated to be from between 1920 and 1940, and anonymous.[1] It was probably a published professional photograph since the only inscription it bears is thought to indicate the size of its publication. Arguably, it might have been produced as part of the massive anti-lynching campaign the NAACP mounted in those decades,[2] a campaign that had been successful in first reducing and then virtually eliminating the spectacle lynchings this photograph re-creates by superimposing the shadow of a hanging man onto the crowd.

Unlike most lynching photographs, made for and representing the point

FIGURE 1.1. NAACP Photograph—Photographic Print, Title: [Crowd of people, with shadow of man hanging from tree superimposed over them]. Created/Published: [between 1920 and 1940]. Courtesy of Library of Congress Prints and Photographs Division Washington, D.C. The author wishes to thank the National Association for the Advancement of Colored People for authorizing the use of this image.

of view of the murderers, this rare image directs the gaze away from the object of the spectacle — the lynching itself — and focuses it instead onto the spectators, thereby framing as spectacle the formation of a white constituency that must contemplate off-frame the necessary condition of its own making. This photograph demands a multiplicity of readings: on a first level, we read it in relation to other photographic lynching tableau, as offering other comparable scenes of the crime.[3] In this first reading we analyze its visual field. On a second level, the photograph is also part of a larger visual culture delimited on the one hand by what Nicholas Mirzoeff has called the "hooded archive" of race; that is, the covert and secretive (in Jacqueline Goldsby's eloquent phrase) circulation of lynching images and, on the other hand, by the public relation efforts the NAACP mounted to dissipate this secrecy and mobilize support for anti-lynching legislation.[4] Within this visual culture reading we appreciate the photograph's different cultural logic and its weakened evidentiary power (from a forensic standpoint).[5] Yet, the photograph's effectiveness lies in its formal properties. It is because the scene of the crime is rendered *this* way — through a superimposition that announces on its surface the extent to which it is an art*efact* — that the photograph is capable of showing the transparent structure of Morrison's fishbowl.[6] By redrawing so radically the conventional lynching tableau, this photograph shows us Toni Morrison's fishbowl: "the structure that transparently (and invisibly) permits the ordered life it contains to exist in the larger world."[7] I understand race to be such structure: a visually rendered social contract, a meta-image, a world picture, a structure of visuality, and a medium.[8] Even though we don't have a direct view of the body; that is, even though we are deprived of the ultimate site/sight and signifier of race, race still inhabits this picture. In figuring out why and how that is the case, we can understand how "race" avisually structures our visual field, visual culture, and how, through the black body, race corporealizes the ontology of the image. Building on this, I am interested in exploring how this shadow challenges and complicates the imbrication of race and photographic ontology — what I describe as the *photochemical imagination*.

The visual field this photograph establishes is unique among lynching photographs because the photographer's unusual angle institutes a theater of gazes that offsets and reverses conventional relations of looking. Whereas in most lynching photographs the white mob is both spectator to the lynching and consciously addresses the photograph's anticipated viewers — thus acting as a stand-in for its own audience — here, the crowd we see looking at a lynching does not look back at us. The crowd does not acknowledge our presence on the other side of its anticipated photographic repetition and does not claim a clear position within the social field. This photograph, then, twice bypasses the ethical dilemma facing contemporary viewers: the dilemma of *looking without seeing* the violated corpse, and, for white viewers specifically, the need to disidentify with the all-too-visible perpetrators and to disavow the interpellation to participate in the construction of whiteness fostered by their look into the camera.[9] By deviating from conventional looking relations this photograph allows us to enter the lynching tableau from a different angle — one that emphasizes how lynching photographs are also celebrations of a paradoxical type of social visibility, one whereby the perpetrator's visibility is obscenely detached from their accountability. Lynching itself is sustained by a double denial: it is the social (in)visibility of the perpetrators and the shift of investment from the body *of* evidence to the (black) body *as* evidence. Thus, while the disavowal of what is visually available — that is, the possibility of recognizing the perpetrators — establishes a wedge between the visual and the social field that sustained white unaccountability, this very same wedge is sutured by the central position of the black body as evidence, as metaphysical presence that spectacularly and panoptically organizes the visual field within which the social ritual of lynching takes place.[10] As a constant threat, or in Richard Wright's words, as a "conditionally commuted death sentence,"[11] lynching enacts a regime of surveillance by "inscribing visibility everywhere."[12]

From a formal point of view, Robyn Wiegman has noted that "operating according to a logic of borders — racial, sexual, national, psychological, and biological, as well as gendered — lynching *figures* its victims as the culturally *abject*," which is visualized in the identifiable aesthetics of the lynching tableau: "monstrosities of excess whose limp and hanging bodies function as the specular assurance that the racial threat has not simply been averted, but rendered incapable of return."[13] The image of a body that has lost "integrity" of form and intentionality signifies the fantasy of a successfully expelled abject object. This aesthetics also functions in the exemplary role of lynching in that it sets an example to reaffirm a white supremacist order, while its synecdochic structure, quite literally, reifies the idea that one black is as good as any other to signify the entire race, and by extension, the entire social order.[14] Yet, none of this is present in the NAACP photograph. We don't see a dismembered body. In fact, we don't see a body at all, only its shadow. For this reason, this is one of the few lynching photographs we can actually look at. We are repulsed by it, not because we are looking at a violated body, but rather because it brings into stark relief a picture of whiteness as terror and terrorizing.[15]

The photograph offers no direct visual assault: visible here as mere shadow, we comfortably see the crowd through the hanging body. The actual body could be located somewhere outside the frame on the left, the direction in which the entire crowd is looking. Yet, signified by a *trace of its elsewhere*, the precise spatial location of the body cannot be conclusively identified. Rather, it appears instead to be "hanging." The shadow marks almost equally the body's projection and our viewing position: placed just like the victim, at a very high angle, in a sense, we give our eyes to him, so that he can return the gaze and see the crowd's reaction to the spectacle of his death. On our part, we are both "there," hanging with the body, and safely outside the scene.

What visual field is being drawn by the paradox of the lynchers' impunity in the face of their photographic visibility and the blacks' hyperpresence before the law but impossibility to be represented by it, their skewed anonymity, their matter-of-fact interchangeability?[16] What visual field is created by the fact that, as Jacqueline Goldsby puts it, lynching victims become invisible by virtue of their very appearance in the field of vision? The lynching tableau inhabits this paradox through a specific figure-ground relation that in this photograph is made abstract by the impossibility to identify the victim, as well as made concrete through a sharply drawn formal relationship between the hanging shadow and the crowd. This shadow opens up a space of suspension between projection and conception: the shadow is the projection of the body but it does not "spur" from the diegetic situation of the photograph. Between fixation and duration, the shadow has been photographically captured, but it is in itself a fleeting sign between presence and absence, then and now. Through these effects of suspension, the shadow also destabilizes the notion of blackness, which can no longer be seen as an attribute of the body, but rather only as a visual effect.

By affording a purely formal reading of the visuality of lynching through a consideration of multiple figure-ground relations, this shadow sutures the wedge that lynching creates between the social and the visual sphere. The image then not only literalizes Goldsby's thesis that the spectacle of black murder has organized early mass-produced and mass-circulated visual culture, that it has "secreted" American modern visual culture, but also that race theorizes more generally the visual field. By literalizing the role of the black body in arranging the scope of the visual field and in outlining its boundaries, through a shadow that, although superimposed, acts as the pivot of the photograph's *mise-en-scène*, this image affords the possibility of reflecting on the inescapable racialization of the visual. Even though it is overlaid on the surface of the image, the shadow seems to come from within, just like racial blackness is deposited on the epidermal signifier as it is understood as an indexical trace of the body's genetic and biological "inside."

Because it foregrounds a blackness that does not coincide with the blackness of the body, this picture allows one to behold, paraphrasing Charles Mills, the *partitioned* social ontology of a racial world as it expresses itself in the visual field.[17] Race, this photograph suggests, is not the exception that needs to be explained, but rather the foundation of the social bond that continually renews itself across the visual terrain. It is not the exceptional character of a handful of pictures, but it is the meta-image that corporealizes (and, therefore, seemingly gives and is given substance by) the way we still understand visual relations.

LYNCHING AND THE CORPOREALIZATION OF THE INDEX

Leigh Raiford has claimed that, as a disciplinary ritual that returns race to the body, lynching re-creates the same type of coincidence between skin and race that marks the auction block. The rush to secure strands of hair, body parts, and scraps of clothes from the victim — that is, fetishes and mementos of the lynching — further sanctioned this metonymical operation. The more or less conspicuous circulation of these memorabilia attests to the existence of a segregated consumer culture. In lieu of mementos, photographic documentation of a lynching served as the next best thing: "[I]f lynching was a return to the slave block, a reinscribing of the black body as commodity, then lynching photographs functioned as the bill of sale and receipt of ownership."[18] Thus, as Mirzoeff concludes: "The lynching photograph became, as it was intended to be, that which made the index of race adhere to its object. It created another still more shadowy, even *hooded* archive of race, housed in the mantelpieces and in the desk drawers across the United States."[19] This "hooded archive" indexes race epidermally, as well as socially and politically. Lynching images disclose the color line unambiguously: they display a very specific distribution of the sensible by returning "everyone to his or her corporeal essence, to the 'racial' truth that is only skin deep."[20] Furthermore, in lynching photography the materiality of the referent and the materiality of the photograph double each other. The NAACP photograph, however, cannot perform the same social function as the lynching relic because it doesn't have enough evidentiary value. It cannot circulate as a substitute object for the body itself; rather, it is fully and deliberately an artefact that works on and over the traditional lynching photograph, understood both as a genre and as an item of material culture. By doing so, this shadow exposes at the heart of the photochemical imagination an investment in the indexicality of the photographic image facilitated by its analogy with the black body.

A number of scholars have already established how photographic indexicality has been enlisted to create the effect that race is equally indexical, therefore turning the epidermis into a writing pad.[21] As Coco Fusco observed, epidermalization lies at the roots of the social functions of photography, which was "marshaled to document the 'fact' of racial difference [and, in the process] produced race as a *visualizable fact*."[22] This is so when photography and race are both primarily conceived as indexes in the sense of traces. Not only do race and photography share a similar semiotic grid, but they have given each other substance: photography has lent materiality to race because it has provided a visual technology that has further sutured race to the body.[23] Providing a transitive surface that points inward to its meaning and its truth, the black body, in turn, has offered a way to conceive and sustain the ontological claim that, in David Rodowick's repetition of Stanley Cavell's formulation, unlike painting, photography is not a world, but it is rather *of* the world.[24]

What I want to emphasize here is that the relationship between the photochemical imagination and race is mutually energizing: just like the epidermal signifier brands the body with the marks of race and indexes the body's location within a visual archive that trades in surface signs, so the photographic trace brands the real with a regime of image-ness that lays claims to an ontological connection between its surface existence as a visual object and the historical depth — the "reality" — from which it was seized.[25] Both photography and the black body are understood as offering a continuous surface of legible information. They share similar processes of exteriorization and, following Frantz Fanon, also of "overdetermination from the outside," which he described with an image that recalls the chemical processes involved in photography: "the Other fixes me with his gaze, his gestures and attitude, the same way *you fix a preparation with a dye*."[26]

This moment is as foundational to the photochemical imagination as the other primal scene, "Look! A Negro!" has been to critical race discourse and the understanding of the visuality of race: Fanon explained the alchemy of race after the chemical basis of the photographic process because photography, for him, describes an image state that fixates and fossilizes — a Medusa effect. Fanon's metaphor effectively describes a photochemical fantasy, one *[margin handwritten note: index as a(e)ffect of continuity with the world]*

that suggests indexicality guarantees that the photographic image exists in continuity with the world. The NAACP photograph, instead, challenges these a(e)ffects of continuity: all we see here is a shadow, which dematerializes the index as *trace* and mobilizes instead more prominently the function of the index as *shifter*, as a finger pointing simultaneously in two directions: toward the lynched body and toward the body politic.[27]

A STRUCTURE OF DEFERRAL

Formally speaking, this photograph overlays various forms of non-coincidence, introducing a structure of deferral that is unique among lynching photographs. First, our view of the body does not coincide with the geographical location it occupies. The function that Shawn Michelle Smith identifies as normally performed by the corpse, usually displayed front and center, as "the negated other that frames, supports, and defines a white supremacist community" is here performed by a shadow.[28] Thus, this indirect view of the corpse does not afford the suturing of the Lacanian mirror stage, where, as Smith argues, the pleasure of white misrecognition as wholeness is achieved by *projecting* a split between self and image only for the black subject, allowing the white one to remain blind to the suturing effects of its own fundamental misrecognition. On the contrary, as the *other* than the body and stretching across space beyond the body's boundaries, the shadow *figures* instead the unbridgeable wedge between self and image. Second, since it has no evidentiary value, the photograph offers no documentary information regarding the specificity of this lynching. It testifies to a (recurring) occurrence, but not to its historical specificity. It functions rather as what W. J. T. Mitchell describes as a metapicture, capturing how lynching photographs "simultaneously make visible and proclaim invisible the lawless privilege of whiteness."[29] In this photograph the only evidentiary value the shadow maintains is as an indexical trace attesting to *a* body to which it belongs. Fixated through the photographic process, filed in the NAACP's archives, and then again at the Library of Congress, this shadow also takes responsibility for the body it signifies, making it present, recording its death — an unclaimed death, like so many others — and inscribing its trace and instituting an ethical space, a bookmark, within American visual culture. Third, the blackness of the shadow does not coincide with the blackness of the body. In fact, we are not given any visual clues to determine the racial identity of the victim. Instead, if we think of the victim as black, it is only because we have attributed racial identity based on historical and cultural context, on the archive to which it belongs, and on the racialized social geography that the photographer's chosen angle visualizes. Just like the shadow is superimposed on the crowd, we map "race" onto the picture because it is a lynching photograph and it shows a regime of racial repression carried out through panoptic and spectacular means. Fourth, since the shadow's blackness is not a mark of racial identity, it functions as the visualization of a place of difference. It offers a point of view inside the picture: we see the crowd through the shadow; we are hanging, like the shadow is, and come to occupy the same place of suspension. Ultimately, this shadow acts as a meeting point between seer, seen, and scene.

The blackness of the shadow acts most prominently as a figure of spatial deferral because it cannot, other than ideologically or contextually, be connected to a body's pigmentation: it signifies the presence of a body that is elsewhere and yet joined at the hip, so to speak, to the signifier of its (spatially removed) presence. In general, the shadow indexes temporal presence (the shadow is here as long as the body is here) but spatial removal (but the body is not here, in this shadow. Rather it is *there*, where the shadow comes from). Therefore, on the one hand, the shadow always has a clear point of origin that temporally coexists with it, on the historical-existential plane. On the other hand, the shadow is the trace of a body's extension beyond itself by means of light. The body is not in the shadow, in its projection, and yet the shadow doubles the body, extending its reach, and locating it in two places at the same time.

This doubleness — this being in two places at the same time, this being the "same, but not quite" — is one of the properties of the shadow that Homi Bhabha invokes to characterize the colonized subject. The colonized, Bhabha writes, is the "tethered shadow" of Western man.[30] It is the colonizer's irremovable profile and inseparable Otherness. It is not something that the colonizer faces, but rather something that sticks to him. This doubleness also reveals a tension that is intrinsic to the indexicality of the shadow, which signifies both as a trace and as a shifter. The NAACP shadow, in particular, turns the photographic structure of referral into a process of deferral. Even more radically, it wears photography's already existing, but often disavowed, structure of deferral on its own sleeve.

In a special issue of the journal *differences* devoted to the assessment of the contemporary discourse on photographic indexicality, Mary Ann Doane reminds us that despite the still-enduring mythology of the index as trace, Pierce conceived of the index both as a trace and as a shifter—a sign produced by contiguity and contact, but also a pointed finger gesturing always beyond itself. She writes:

absence,
emptiness:
"we" or
"you" as
index

> As photographic trace or impression, the index seems to harbor a fullness, an excessiveness of detail that is always supplemental to meaning or intention. Yet, the index as deixis implies an emptiness, a hollowness that can only be filled in specific, contingent, always mutating situations. It is this dialectic of the empty and the full that lends the index an eeriness and uncanniness not associated with the realms of the icon or symbol. At times, the disconcerting closeness of the index to its object raises doubts as to whether it is indeed a sign, suggesting instead that the index is perched precariously on the very edge of semiosis.[31]

index
as
absence
and
presence

As shifter, the index is a "hollowed-out sign"; it has no content; "the index asserts nothing; it only says "There!'"[32] When understood as trace, the index implies "the reproducibility of a past moment," it is a "witness to an anteriority," but when understood as deixis the index is instead linked to presence and signifies a *remaining gap* between sign and object.[33]

The index is part of the semiotic structure of photography but it has also been regarded as a "formal logic"[34] of "indication and connectivity." The index's purpose is "to suggest 'the mute presence of an uncoded event.'"[35] The shifter, Rosalind Krauss argues, is "that category of the linguistic sign which is "filled with signification" only because it is "empty."[36] While the NAACP shadow is obviously the indexical trace of a body that has cast it, it is not the indexical trace of that body's skin. Beyond the tension between trace and shifter, the mythology of the index, Doane points out, is also fraught with tension between the iconic and the symbolic. On the one hand, the trace (footprint, death mask, photograph) partakes of the iconic because the sign often resembles the object. On the other hand, the shifter partakes of the symbolic in that its content might be conventional and arbitrary. We see this tension clearly in the indexicality of the Turin Shroud, the photogrammatic trace *par excellence*, which shows that "[i]f the index's powers are spent in the verification of an existence, the icon and the symbol . . . work to extend and prolong the aura of that indexical authenticity."[37]

These notions of indexicality suggest that the index implies, at the very least, a particular social and cultural geography of the sign (contiguity), specific temporal structures (continuity), and an identifiable notion of the relationship between nature and culture.[38] It also implies, or at least mobilizes, a way of understanding the relationship between the seeable and the sayable. If the index is the "natural" sign *par excellence* indeed, if it is the "writing of nature," especially when thought in relation to photography, then how does it also become its picture? In other words, what is the primary mode of the index? Is that mode discursive or visual? It is an assertion of existence (there! As in "there you have it!"), but one that is in itself empty of content.[39] The index affirms without knowing what it affirms, but because it claims a physical or existential connection to its source, resemblance or likeness supply the supposed content to a connection that is already intractably there.[40]

The retention of indexicality in discussions of the ontology of the image — both by scholars that claim it is lost in the digital image and those who argue that the digital too can be seen as indexical, those that seek the index in the image and those that seek it in the mind — often expresses apprehension over the loss of truth value of images, fear of a disconnection from the world, anxiety over simulation, manipulation, and so on.[41] Following increasing scholarship that, rather than focusing on what the index is, reflects on why we care so much about it, photographic indexicality emerges more and more as an affect rather than a sign function that can lay claims on the real.[42] The index emerges as a reality a(e)ffect. Following Massumi's idea that some indexes can be affectively constructed — for example in the political manipulation of the semiotics of fear following 9/11 and the war on terror, threats are born retroactively so that the smoke precedes the fire — or taking Greg Hainge's suggestion that photographic fixation is analogous to the process of constitution of normative bodies, we might find particularly insightful Fanon's indication that it is the moment of photochemical fixation that carries the affective ability to construct the visual truth of what in reality is a discursive moment.[43] The moment of fixation is fundamental for the sense of presence and materiality that photography entails. Vivian Sobchack describes it so: "Abstracting visual experience from an ephemeral temporal flow, the photographic both chemically and metaphorically 'fixes' its ostensible subject quite literally as an object for vision. It concretely reproduces the visible in a material process . . . Furthermore, this material process results in a material form that can be objectively possessed, circulated, and saved."[44] Seen through race, and specifically through this

Fanonian theory of the photographic image, the photographic represents a certain faith on the index and thus offers a map of the visual that, in its claims to materiality, considers successfully resolved the question of reference.[45] For my purposes, what matters most is the fact that the notion of the index as trace, rather than shifter, has most strongly been mobilized to secure a closure of the visual field — a folding of the real onto visual representation. This privileging of the trace and its folding of the real onto visual representation has paradigmatically occurred at the expense, and on the ground, of the black body because the "truth" it displays on its surface is supposedly connected, like an indexical trace, to the "truth" of its genetic makeup.[46] In other words, the black body — the photographic object *par excellence* — doubles in a different scale the photographic map of the visual; that is, the sense of a phantasmatic and affective continuity between essence and appearance, inside and outside, identity and image.

Here, I consider three traits of the photochemical imagination that congeal around the moment of photographic fixation before I suggest a non-medium specific and more flexible notion of photography as a state of the image. First, photochemical fixation has the capacity to bestow an excess materiality to its referent; second, by leveraging the idea of the index as a shifter and, therefore, a pointing finger, the photochemical fixation expresses a fantasy of touching the profilmic world; third, as Fanon explains, the moment of fixation can produce an effect of evisceration of the body, which is evacuated of its interiority and is folded onto the outside like shirt cuffs.

ANIMALIA: THE INDEX AND THE INSECT

Peter Geimer's essay, "Image as Trace," offers an extraordinary dramatization of the a(e)ffect associated with the moment of photochemical fixation: a fly caught by the photosensitive plate in one of Antonio Beato's 1870 Cairo photographs. During the long exposure required to photograph Egyptian monuments, a fly entered his camera and remained trapped by the collodion coat. From the point of view of the photograph's composition, the fly appears monstrous because its scale does not match the landscape behind it. But from the point of view of photographic ontology, the fly is even more monstrous because it is of a different ontological order than the photograph on which it has been caught. Its presence and "liveness," even as a corpse, compete with and exceed that of the photograph. The fly is, in some sense, the only "living" thing in an essentially mummifying picture.[47] The fact that the fly has recorded itself directly, immediately, and photogrammatically on the surface of the photograph offers an intractable testimony of the fly's existence that competes with any sense of the Intractable the photograph might hope to deliver. The fly is not a shadow, copy, or trace, but (comparatively) the "thing itself," delivered "without mediation," as Barthes would say,[48] without inscription, a natural photogram within a photograph: "The fly collided with the photographic shot. It brought something from the real world into the reproduction and transferred it to the picture in the form of a trace."[49] The fly becomes the trace of the photographic process. In a sort of accidental *mise-an-abyme*, the fly reproduces the photographic process in an ontologically augmented form while it seemingly provides material substance — a body of evidence — to the idea of the photographic index as trace.

Even though it does so in a different and totally accidental context, Antonio Beato's photograph presents the supplemental materiality that is also at work in the consumption and circulation of lynching images, especially the not-uncommon practice of gluing a curl of hair onto a photograph or a postcard. This supplemental material trace would be understood as evidence of someone's personal witnessing to the lynching. Beato's fly also performs as this trace. In similar fashion, the fly performs as ontological augmentation and accidental *mise-en-abyme* of the compound indexicality of the lynching photograph itself. Whether it takes the form of Beato's fly, or a strand of hair, or a scrap of cloth, this supplemental materiality embodies the understanding of photographic connection as trace and photography's ability to put us in the presence of, in touch with, that which the photograph has seemingly "captured." The fly or the hair function as loci of desire, but also lenses through which to appreciate, through similar mechanisms of supplemental corporeality, the way the photographic has lent materiality to race.[50]

THE TWO FINGERS

Considered alongside the NAACP shadow, Antonio Beato's fly and the lynching relic attached to a photograph present various forms of photographic embodiment that differ in degree. All three are products of a deliberate or accidental superimposition; all three "supplements" pose or act as ontological and affective augmentations of the photographic connection. The lynching shadow brings the corporeality of race and death to bear upon a picture of a white crowd, but it is in itself a disembodied form. In that sense, the shadow performs deictically, as a shifter, a pointed finger — a function that introduces another form of embodiment, that of the body politic.

In lynching photographs the deictic quality of the index is made visible by the white mob's deliberate address to the camera. Sometimes, as in Lawrence Beitler's 1930 photograph of the double lynching of Thomas Shipp and Abram Smith in Marion, Indiana, the indexical function of the pointed finger is literal (figure 1.2). There, as Shawn Michelle Smith observes, the pointed finger "invites viewers to read the photograph as an object lesson."[51] The lynching tableau, as it has been often noted, is a photographically imagined scene: the onlookers are staged and perform for the benefit of the photograph's audience, establishing — with their direct look at the camera or with their pointed fingers directing the gaze to the corpse — a paradoxically highly studied "*punctum*." In apparent antithesis to the way Barthes distinguished the *studium* from the *punctum*, lynching photographs pierce not with their unexpected qualities (the casual detail, for example), but with their formality. It is the *form* of the lynching photograph that most strongly pricks the viewer, forcing a corporeal alignment on either side of the color line.

Furthermore, in these images the finger that points stages, within the photographic field, the social function performed by the finger that clicks: the photographer's action on the camera shutter that Barthes fetishized as the ground for photography's claim to sharing the same historical space with the event it purportedly records. The formality of the lynching tableau, in other words, indexes in two directions: it points toward its own connection to the lynching scene, and toward its own connection to its photochemical reproduction and secret(ed) circulation. Thus, the finger that clicks performs as the "umbilical cord" that Barthes found at the heart of photography's essence.

In the NAACP photograph, instead, there is no pointed finger but rather a shadow that, uniquely, points toward the crowd, thus reversing the traditional direction of the gaze toward the corpse. Hence, by implication, the crowd, not the lynched body, is framed as the object. As the stand in for the finger that clicks, the shadow doubles the photographic process within the photographic field, just like Antonio Beato's fly, but this time in a disembodied form. Like the fly, the shadow has collided with the photographic process — a photogram within a photograph. Unlike the fly, the shadow does not deliver a

FIGURE 1.2. Lawrence Beitler's photograph of the double lynching of
Thomas Shipp and Abram Smith in Marion, Indiana, 1930. Courtesy of the
Indiana Historical Society.

carnal body but only the signifier of one — a signifier that, like photography,
is produced by a play of light.

The shadow as pointed finger thus creates a counter *gestalt* not only to
the conventional lynching photograph, but also to the relationship between
blackness and photography. Whereas the added scrap of clothes or hair in
the conventional lynching photograph would reproduce the photographic
process in corporeal form, in this photograph the only blackness we see is
that of the cast shadow. We do not see a corporeal attribute, but a viewing
position, a placeholder for the viewer within the lynching scene. Yet, because
the shadow is also the projection of the lynched body, its placeholder amongst
the crowd, the blackness of the shadow is also the space where the viewer and

the victim finally touch. The shadow itself provides the membrane through which viewer and victim inter-*skin*.[52]

In the literature that insists on conceiving indexicality solely as trace, but also, and more strikingly, in the discussion surrounding the loss of indexicality with the digital turn, it appears that, to be thought as truthful, the photograph needs to allow us to touch the profilmic world.[53] In other words, it is ultimately the possibility to understand the photographic itself as a form of embodiment (not only of the photographed object but also of the viewing subject and, more importantly for my purposes, of the object-subject connection as well) that grounds the photograph's supposed truth value.

There are two forms of photographic embodiment that are relevant for the present discussion. First, the continuous sensuousness of the world grounds the possibility to leave a trace. Second, photography itself is a bodily membrane because, as Akira Lippit, Jonathan Auerbach, Brian Massumi, and Vivian Sobchack, and others have argued in various ways, the ultimate photographic archive is not the filing cabinet (as Allan Sekula posits in his discussion of Alphonse Bertillon), but rather the human body.[54] In *Atomic Light*, for instance, Lippit shows that early cinema is but one of the three phenomenologies of the *inside* coming together in 1895, alongside X-ray photography and psychoanalysis. In distinct and yet interconnected ways, all three "figured" new and phantasmatic surfaces, producing images of three-dimensional flatness simultaneously cast and projected onto a screen.[55] Furthermore, cinema, X-ray photography, and psychoanalysis transformed the structure of visual perception from phenomenal to phantasmatic, from perceived to imagined visuality, from visual to avisual, and in so doing constituted another shadow archive — the avisual archive of a new phantasmatic visuality — to be placed alongside the one identified by Sekula. "What constitutes, defines, determines the *thereness* of the X-ray?" asks Lippit, "[w]hat is *there* in the X-ray, depth or surface, inside or out? What is *there* to be seen? A *thereness*, perhaps, that is avisual: a secret surface between the inside and out."[56] Freud described both the ego and the body as surfaces in which we are projected, and he conceived of psychoanalysis as a search for depth on the surface of things. In the meanwhile, both X-ray and the cinema introduced a mode of radical photography marked by a profound superficiality. X-ray photography flattened the inside and outside of the body into one common screen/surface turning the vantage point of the spectator-subject inside out, while the cinematic screen provided an impossible order of deep space dramatized by a plethora of images of movement across the screen, such as arriving trains or receding subways. Cinema, argues Lippit, is a series of planes that expand and contract in what Deleuze described as a metaphysical surface.[57] As he further argues, the profound superficiality of these phenomenologies is possible because, in psychoanalysis, X-ray photography, and the cinema, the skin and the screen are conflated onto each other: the skin acts as a surface of projection while the screen functions as a metonymy of skin.

If the human body is the primary archive for the image state of photography, then what happens when the body is raced? If the epidermal signifier is read as a trace that race leaves on the body, then what kind of materiality is supposed by this interpretation? What is the "matter" of race?

Again, I am drawn toward the NAACP photograph because the blackness of the shadow does not coincide with the blackness of the body. Yet, the superimposed shadow offers the means whereby the lynched body "touches" the white crowd. Through its own metaphorical skin the shadow offers a figuration of the reaching of the lynched body beyond itself even as it does not have, in itself — that is, apart from the affects connected to the compound indexicality of lynching photographs — an embodied materiality. Rather, this shadow is racially over-embodied (both in the sense of being burdened with an excessive carnality and in the sense of being embodied *over*; that is, through a superimposition) because of how race presses onto the picture both from the inside and the outside.

STATES OF THE IMAGE

The imaginary associated with "photography" has obviously changed now that images proliferate in other, mostly digital, forms so that it is now possible to distinguish a photochemical logic (invested in the index that touches) and a digital logic, invested in resemblance and computational equivalences. Mary Ann Doane has talked about the "photographic" as a desired "logic" of indexicality, which has intensified with (and has been incorporated by) the digital. While the indexical exudes a fantasy of referentiality, the digital exudes a fantasy of immateriality. The continued discussion of Roland Barthes's *Camera Lucida*, furthermore, indicates a remaining interest in addressing a series of affects and investments linked to the photochemical imagination Barthes expressed so effectively.[58] These two "logics" are not tied to the technological mode of production of images, but they articulate changing notions of indexicality, materiality, and embodiment, as well as movement and stillness, life and death, and, I argue, race and blackness as well.[59]

The exploration of the photochemical imagination requires an understanding of photography that is non-medium specific, one that also offers the possibility to resist this fixation on photographic fixation.[60] I follow Raymond Bellour's attempt to, once again, isolate the specificity of the photographic way of understanding these relations in the context of the other "arts of the image." The double helix is the form Bellour has chosen to express the connection between the arts' ability to convey movement (whether it is a movement primarily of the "soul," as in photography; that is, a movement that belongs to the viewer, or whether the movement belongs to the image, as in the cinema) and the amount of analogy the image can sustain — analogy understood as the power of the image to resemble and represent. It is impossible, or at least undesirable, argues Bellour, to discuss the arts discretely, because the history of images "has become an indication of our own history, a sign of the impressive accumulation of images." As there are increasingly less Image(s), and "we know less and less about the nature of *the* image, *an* image, or *the* images," he argues, it is more appropriate to talk about "passages of the image."[61]

In "Concerning the Photographic," Bellour writes: "'The Photographic,' as I imagine it, is not reducible to photography even while borrowing part of its soul and the fact of which we believed photography to be the guardian. The photographic exists somewhere in-between; it is a *state* of 'in-betweenness': in movement, it is that which interrupts, that paralyzes; in immobility, it perhaps bespeaks its relative impossibility."[62] The notion of the *passage* or the *state* of the image suggests not only the in-betweenness that Bellour is after, but also an affective movement or charge that is intrinsic to the image itself. A "state," as the *Oxford English Dictionary* says, is "a condition, manner of existing; a combination of circumstances or attributes belonging for the time being to a person or thing"; thus images can be understood to be in a particular state, in a chemical, but also in an emotional, sense. "State," therefore, is a way to indicate a picture's mode of existence as precarious, sensitive, volatile, and unstable. The "state" is the temporary form an image assumes as it *passes*, through and to. Within this framework, the index can be regarded as one type of passage of the photographic image that attempts to counteract its volatility: the photographic passes through the index to acquire a measure of quasi-chemical "stability." This is the reason that prompts

Barthes to claim that photography is the child of chemistry. This stability is not at all simply a technological product, but it is also supplied affectively when the indexical connection is experienced, as it happens in Barthes's account of the photographic, as an umbilical cord.

Thus the understanding of the index as trace and the consequential elevation of the photographic as the state of the visual that can most securely deliver reference and truth value, doesn't rest solely on a specific semiotic theory, but it also implies specific notions of materiality, presence, contiguity, connection, and embodiment. In fact, as Sybille Kramer observes, "what makes it possible to leave traces and to read them is the material continuity, physicality and sensuousness of the world."[63] Building on Bellour's notion, the photographic/photochemical is thus a "state" that the visual assumes when it posits itself in existential and material continuity with reality, regardless of the specific technology of image production. Because of its underlying theory of embodiment, the photographic is also the state of the image that has most sanctioned and secured the effect of the materiality of race. With each reiteration, the photographic image thus conceived rehearses the racial fold.

THE SHADOW

What happens, though, when we regard a shadow, rather than a fly, as the site of concentration of photochemical affects? The NAACP shadow reproduces the process of racialization, but it withholds closure, reference, and permanence not only because of Talbot's characterization of photography as the art of "fixing the shadow," but also because of the *condition* of the visual they both share. Such a condition (or is it an affliction?) is first of all the idea of the indexical image as trace. But what kind of image is the shadow?

From an ontological standpoint, the shadow is not a picture and yet it pictures.[64] In its impermanence, it is not a durable sign, but the potentiality of one. Its indexicality aligns it most strongly with photography, its iconicity with the pre-photographic form of the silhouette, and its constitutive becoming with the cinematic. Because of its phenomenological capability to extend beyond the body, the shadow figures both the process of photographic impression and the dislocation and doubleness of the projected image. It thus presents itself as a "state" in-between the two — photographic "fixation" on the one hand, and cinematic becoming on the other. Thus, on the one hand, infinitely more than photography, the shadow's fleeting contingency and in-betweenness is a passage of the image. On the other hand, as Victor Stoichita has argued in other respects, the shadow is the prototype of the inalienable sign and, therefore, a sign of permanence because it "is undetachable from, that is, coexistent and simultaneous with, the object it duplicates."[65]

More importantly, the shadow offers one of the two paradigms that in Western art have determined the ontology of the image alongside the paradigm of the mirror. The history of the shadow, Stoichita writes, begins with Pliny the Elder's account of the origin of the plastic arts in the myth of a young Greek woman who draws the outline of her lover's shadow as he is about to depart for war.[66] According to the Plinian tradition, then, the first pictorial image is not the result of direct observation but rather the capturing of a body's projection.[67] The first image entertains an individualized indexical connection with its source. It is somebody's image: it doesn't simply resemble but also belongs to the person whose image it is.

The paradigm of the image as shadow has been historically concurrent with, but also dialectically opposed to, the Platonic understanding of the image as a mirror. In Plato's cave, in fact, pictorial representations are not the result of an act of love that finds a way to make a durable re-presentation of the lover's trace. In Plato's cave visual activity is understood merely as the equivalent of cognitive activity. For Stoichita, Plato equates artistic images to mirror images in order to underline "the nothingness of mimesis" — the fact that "the painted image, like the specular reflection, is pure appearance (*phainomenon*), devoid of reality (*aletheia*)."[68] The mirror image has no substance, hence no truth. This equation of reality/substance with *aletheia* (truth) is what turns the mirror into the model for epiphenomenal representations in Western art, which has overwhelmingly used the notion of the mirror, rather than the projection of interposed bodies, as the vehicle for mimesis. In the tradition of Western visual arts, the shadow remains in a dialectical relationship to the mirror image: the Plinian tradition understands images indexically — in contiguity with the real, as its cast shadows — and has remained in a dialectical relationship with the Platonic tradition that conceives of images iconically, as purely apparent beings linked to the real by their mirrorlike resemblance. If "in the Plinian tradition, the image (shadow, painting, statue) is *the other of the same,* then in Plato the image (shadow, reflection, painting, statue) is the same in a copy state, *the same in a state of double.*"[69]

What concerns me the most, as I follow Stoichita in this brief recounting of these two paradigms of the visual in Western art, is first the implied frontality of the mirror image, and second the relationship between trace and resemblance. The paradigm of the mirror establishes a frontal relationship with its source; hence, the ontological claims it makes are dependent upon the mirror image's resemblance or likeness to that which it mirrors. The paradigm of the shadow, instead, manifests itself in the profile and its ontological claims are based on its existential relationship to the model — a relationship that is contiguous, but oblique. Thus, Stoichita suggests, while the Lacanian mirror stage involves primarily the identification of the *I*, the shadow stage involves the identification of the other.[70] The shadow is not a likeness of the self, but rather something that has emanated from it. While we face the mirror, we don't face the shadow. The shadow, in fact, is fleeting, semi-autonomous, oblique, and pragmatic; that is, sensitive (and subjected) to the circumstances of its formation.

Race has often been euphemistically described as a shadow, but usually in metaphorical or allegorical ways. "Shadow," for example, indicates the ghost in the machine, the way in which race cuts across the American screen, the return of the (racial) repressed, the doppelgänger, and the Other of the self.[71] "Shadow" was also a term used to indicate photography, one that, when applied to photographs of black bodies, makes evident to contemporary eyes the semiotic transference of the blackness of the shadow to the blackness of the black.[72] However, rather than lingering on a vaguely allegorical association of the shadow with racial blackness, a reading that remains located within the Manichean visual template I am trying to complicate, I believe it is more important to investigate the alternative paradigm it offers, the structure of deferral it makes available, the different relationship between surface and depth it implies, and the model of photographic embodiment it provides.

PHOTOGRAPHIC EPIDERMALITY

Even though it is superimposed, the NAACP shadow still reads as coming from a contiguous offscreen space. Such are the spatial relations that the photograph establishes at its face value. We read this shadow as somewhat contiguous because, no matter what the circumstances and the location of its formation, *this* is some*body*'s shadow; it is tethered to the lynched body that has cast it. Thus, from a more strictly formal standpoint, the NAACP shadow institutes a variable figure-ground relation between the body offscreen and the crowd, coming forth as "figure," when regarded as the indexical trace of the body offscreen, and as the "ground" on which the white constituency stands. In this variable relationship, the shadow brings two bodies to this image — the lynched body offscreen and the body politic gathered around this scene of the crime.

In the shadow, a certain state of the visual is caught in suspension — put *en-abyme*. The shadow, in fact, is not fixed, but rather travels through space; it doesn't have mass, but it is the projection of a mass. The shadow needs a surface to become visible, and when it casts itself over a surface its empty blackness equalizes textures, masses, and rank. Thus, visually, it is ruthlessly democratic and abstractive: everybody's shadow is black.

Consider the textural contrast in the NAACP photograph. On the one hand, there is a smoothness resulting from the way the difference between materiality of the body, the pole, and the rope are equalized in the shadow's blackness; on the other hand, there is the coarse texture of the crowd, which registers like an oppositional (resistant?) background. While the overall texture of the image encourages a tactile engagement, what do my fingers know when I look at the NCAAP photograph?[73] What do I touch when I touch its blackness? This shadow challenges the relationship between figure and ground, inside and outside, and my haptic relationship to it. I am sensorially engaged by the crowd, which I feel I can touch, but sensorially withdrawn from the shadow, which, instead, flaunts its untouchability. Nothing comes back to me as I extend myself toward it. I could move across space forever without ever reaching that shadow. Thus the blackness of the NAACP shadow figures (and yet it simultaneously undermines) the very process of superficialization of epidermality insofar as it is a contingently produced surface turned into a sign. Otherwise put, the shadow wears its blackness on its sleeves.

The shadow's blackness figures the sociohistorical constitution of a supplemental corporeal border; that is, pigmentation and its effect — what Fanon has called the "epidermal schema" — on photography itself. Because the shadow's blackness figures, but does not deliver, skin pigmentation, the shadow also figures the epidermis of photography's ghostly membrane.[74]

For Fanon, photography and the epidermal schema are both phenomenologies of the surface. Indeed, they share the same phenomenological structure of a profound superficiality that Akira Lippit has found in psychoanalysis, early cinema, and X-ray photography. Teresa De Lauretis makes the connection explicit. She argues that Fanon shows how Freud's body-ego ("the projection of a surface") is over-inscribed by an epidermal schema, which the child's gaze has the ability to fix like a dye.[75] The corporeal schema, which Fanon describes in terms that are very close to Maurice Merleau-Ponty, is not indexical; rather, the schema is a "sedimented effect without a stable referent or predictable content."[76] When the body enters in relation to the world, it does so through its sensate border — having sense and making sense — which then acts as a "skin." Fanon shows how, as a consequence of its interpellation, the child's body schema is overridden by an epidermal schema — an outward body image that does not correspond to that of the subject. While the bodily sense of the self occurs through the folding of proprioperception and perception, self and other, seer and seen, sensible and sentient, the child's interpellation interrupts the possibility of this folding by "freezing" and fixating it into a fully exteriorized frontality. Seen from the outside by the other, the body becomes "epidermalized"; that is, fully externalized (to the other looking, but also to the self who now sees himself from the outside) and deprived of interiority — "the body Fanon describes is all surface."[77] When this happens, explains Charles Johnson, "[a]ll I am, can be to them is as nakedly presented as the genitals of a plant since they cannot see my other profiles." "My subjectivity," he continues, "is turned inside out like a shirtcuff."[78]

If from a phenomenological standpoint the skin is the border that feels, the visuality of skin; that is, its pigmentation, institutes another border, at the same time deeper (lodged in the genetic makeup or in an "interiority") and more superficial (epidermal) in between bodies in the social space. Pigmentation triggers a figure-ground relationship between touch and sight that can work against the folding of self and other. As a chromatic property, pigmentation can elicit a "retinal pop" that foregrounds and isolates vision from the remainder of the sensorium: "*Maman*, look a Negro; I am scared."[79] As a tactile border, however, it can also project a surface of desire, a desire to touch, possess, or "eat" the Other.[80]

In the NAACP photograph, the black shadow superimposed onto the crowd institutes a place of enfolding that the frontality of the traditional lynching tableau violently denies, thus showing the constitutive interpenetration between the lynched body and body politic. Beyond that, the NAACP shadow is a figure for the "skin" of the visual as the border that feels (from both sides), a surface of impression and expression, a containing but also releasing membrane, a seal and a face.[81] Otherwise said, in this shadow the visual appears as the "mode" in which bodies inter-skin (rather than inter-face), as the terrain in which bodies touch and constantly redraw their boundaries.

Roland Barthes's *Camera Lucida* remains arguably the most influential account of the phenomenology of the photographic surface as a complex and shifting figure-ground relationship between the tactile and the visual. Not epistemologically rigorous but existentially and rhetorically audacious, *Camera Lucida* offers a still-relevant description of the state of the photographic image even beyond the digital turn. In fact, photography emerges from the book as an image state just as nervous, conflicted, and passionate as the book's author.

What draws me to *Camera Lucinda* is Barthes's commitment to exploring photography's ability to connect rather than represent. Photography, for Barthes, is a corporeal medium, in the spiritist sense, a body that functions as a vehicle for a necrophilic encounter: it is a corpse through which we touch other corpses. And yet, photography is also a womb, a return to the inside of the mother's body, the only place where we know we have been before. Barthes's notion of photographic connection pivots around his idea of indexicality as a sort of "umbilical cord" and his description of light as *a carnal medium*, "a *skin I share* with anyone who has been photographed."[82] But what does "skin" mean in the context of a lynching photograph? What does it mean here for *this* lynching photograph?

The connection Barthes describes as an umbilical cord is an affective one. Barthes privileges photographs that "prick" him. He seeks the essence of photography ultimately in the photograph of his deceased mother because of how it invites him in, in its "space," in its "bosom." Photography is for him a space of habitation — a place where he wants to live, a dirt road that he remembers his body having traveled a long time ago. He is drawn to photographs that are not obvious, not studied, not composed; that is, nonrepresentational. His interest is not so much "to see" but rather to "be there" — hence his elaboration of the affects associated with the realization that the noumenon of photography is its "having been there." These affects, as it is well known, congeal around his notion of the *punctum* — a quasi-tactile realization of the awakening and circulation of one's desire — as the site and the occasion in which we are startled by our sudden experience of photography as a connection. As Kenneth Calhoon observes, for Barthes "the finger, not the eye is the photographer's true organ, and the *punctum* . . . connects the finger that points to the wound it indicates."[83] The *punctum* is the place where the index is experienced as a pointing finger, a shifter, to be sure, but one that also touches that which it indicates. Crucially, Barthes' *punctum* is also experienced through the mediation of the black female body.

Barthes invokes the notion of skin primarily to describe the photographic connection with a tactile language. Yet, if it is clear to any reader of *Camera Lucida* that Barthes understands the photographic connection as a form of inter-embodiment, it is less noted how the pigmentation of the skin we supposedly share with the photographed subject can, in fact, undo such a connection.[84] That is, while Barthes invests in the continuity that photography affords us with the physical world, he instead divests and retracts when looking at bodies that are black. This is to some extent ironic, especially given that, as Fred Moten observes, blackness marks the spectatorial position in *Camera Lucida*, and particularly Barthes's refusal to show his mother's photograph,[85] as well as the place of death. He insists that the photograph is the corpse of an event. Barthes protects his "ontological desire" to inquire into the essence of photography, clouding both its addressee (the Mother) and its representation (the Winter Garden photograph) in blackness. Thus blackness is the sign of the maternal, which Barthes considers as the only fundamental and universal metonymical connection we can claim: the umbilical, the carnal. It is the sign of a temporal structure that connects the origin (the womb) with the destination (the mother's death), and thus institutes a complex dynamic between interiority and exteriority — blackness as skin versus blackness as space, blackness as a physical attribute versus blackness as the mode of an interaction.

Most commentators interested in the role of blackness in *Camera Lucida* observe that Barthes introduces the concepts of *studium* and *punctum* when discussing Van Der Zee's photograph *Family Portrait*. Barthes introduces it as an example of a most studied photograph (and most naively studious subjects) which, nevertheless, and against what we can imagine to be the intention of the photographer, pricks Barthes for its vulnerable details — affectation in dress, jewelry, and posture — all elements he can "sympathize" with. Barthes uses *Family Portrait* to explain the distinction between *studium* and *punctum*, but his account confuses the two. The *studium* is patronizingly found in the desire to embody a higher social class that the sitters manifest by supposedly mimicking white people and in the paternalistic and shocking description of the woman in the back as a "solacing Mammy." That to Barthes this description appeared neutral and benign is startling. Barthes is obviously not interested in the cultural and social valence of African American portraiture and, even though he might have known Van Der Zee's *The Harlem Book of the Dead*, as Olin suggests, he took this photograph and the description of its *studium* from a special issue of *Le nouvel observateur*.[86] The imagination of the standing woman as a "mammy," even though (or maybe because) she reminds him of an aunt of his, is troubling and propels an interest in his handling of family connections and blackness throughout the book.

Barthes describes the photograph's *punctum* again a little later in the book when explaining how the *punctum* works in supplementarity — it is something we bring to photographs, he claims, but also what is nonetheless already there — and its utter subjectivity, its existence in memory, its ability to "work" on the viewer. So as he recalls the Van Der Zee photograph, Barthes misremembers and misrepresents the woman's necklace, and he describes it as a "ribbon of gold" because he is more interested in conveying that he feels pricked by this detail for how it reminds him of an old, unmarried aunt of his. As Shawn Michelle Smith observes, what is really disturbing about Barthes's faulty memory of the black woman's jewelry "is not the erasure of a pearl necklace for a gold but the effacement of an African American woman) [who happens to be Van Der Zee's own aunt] under the sign of Barthes's aunt. One is left to wonder whether this erasure, effected by the *punctum*, is in part a result of the *studium*, a racist paternalism that disregards an African American woman's self-representation as trite."[87] Ultimately, as both Fred Moten and Carol Mavor point out, Barthes is "nursed and nourished by the blackness of the Van Der Zee woman — the black twin (at least in his mind) of his Aunt Alice." As Mavor summarizes, "Barthes's novel(esque) *Camera Lucida* is a story of a desire for the maternal that is nurtured by photography, whose very texture tells the story of the nourishment of race."[88] Overall, in *Camera Lucida*, blackness marks the location of a private, intimate, and familial encounter, except when it "belongs" to the body that Barthes faces in these photographs. As much as Barthes thinks about photography as a space of habitation, he instead describes photography as Intractable when discussing encounters with black bodies, which he tellingly reads as exemplary of both the mask and the fact of race.

The first photograph of a black subject is Richard Avedon's *William Casby, Born a Slave*, which Barthes discusses in relation to the capacity of photography to visualize a *mask* — a word, he says, that Italo Calvino uses to indicate the perfect intelligibility of a socially constructed meaning (figure 1.3). Cap-

FIGURE 1.3. Richard Avedon, *William Casby, born in slavery, Algiers, Louisiana March 24, 1963.* © The Richard Avedon Foundation.

FIGURE 1.4. Richard Avedon, A. *Philip Randolph, founder,*
Brotherhood of Sleeping Car Porters, New York, April 8, 1976.
© The Richard Avedon Foundation.

tive of the mystique of the Other, Barthes sees in the Avedon's photograph the "essence of slavery" laid bare. But what is it about this photograph that makes Barthes hold it as perfectly intelligible, as a mask (that which "makes a face into the product of a society and its history"); that is, as conforming to socially constructed protocols of legibility?[89] Barthes reads the "essence of slavery" in William Casby's face: we are left to wonder whether such essence is a feature of Casby's self (a slave by essence?), or whether his face is conceptualized as the writing pad for a specific social and property structure, as bearing the inscription of what Bill Brown calls the "historical ontology of slavery."[90] But what is it, other than Avedon's complicit title — offered as a testimony of the history of the photographic subject — that prompts this reading? Or is it Casby's sheer blackness and his age-worn face sufficient in itself to conjure it up? Is his blackness the writing pad? What is it about this photograph that makes Barthes feel in the presence of, and in contact with, its history? "The mask is the meaning," he writes, "insofar as it is absolutely pure."[91]

Other photographs of blacks appear in *Camera Lucida,* most notably Avedon's 1976 portrait of Philip Randolph, which Barthes uses to illustrate his notion of the air ("a kind of intractable supplement of identity),"[92] the *animula* — the bright shadow, the spectral image of the soul that good photography is supposed to capture (figure 1.4). Again, this photograph of a black subject offers no space of habitation, but rather the attempt to show an essence as an image. "If the Photograph cannot be penetrated," he writes, "it is because of its evidential power."[93] When photography testifies, it is flat and "I can only sweep it with my glance," stay on the surface, on the outside. I cannot touch it, only face it. Importantly, Barthes appears to recognize the superficiality of photography, its exteriority, mostly in relation to the blackness of the photographic subject, as if the skin of the sitter had already performed a labor of superficialization for him. And also a labor of humility, as the two "masks" (now understood in a broad sense) he identifies — that is, William Casby and Philip Randolph — either show the essence of slavery or an "air of goodness (no impulse of power: *that is certain*)."[94]

This tension between the merely visual and the haptic properties of blackness surfaces most strongly when Barthes discusses the photograph of a slave market (a magazine clipping) he used to have as a child. The photograph, he claims, both fascinated and horrified him because "there was a *certainty* that such a thing had existed: not a question of exactitude, but of reality, . . . slavery was given without mediation, the fact was established *without method.*"[95] In this unexpected return to his earlier positions (that of regarding photography as a "message without a code"[96]), Barthes's horror is a byproduct of the realization that the photograph places slavery in the same historical continuum as the viewer, that the referent has, so to speak, stuck to it. As Susan Sontag puts it, the Intractable of images of atrocities is what puts our privileges "on the same map" as the suffering we see.[97] Or, if we are to take seriously Barthes' carnal theory of photography, photographs of atrocities put him in the same body of the suffering he sees, and that body — the body he touches, the skin he is invited but might not want to inhabit — is, paradigmatically, black. Ultimately, Mavor summarizes, for Barthes "the fact of blackness is as stubborn as the photograph's link to the referent."[98]

Barthes's attitude toward the photographic is both *necrophilic* and *negrophobic*. In my view, Barthes describes his experience of the photographic connection in terms that are very close to Vivian Sobchack's description of the cinesthetic subject — the subject that, through a sensual catachresis, experiences the nonhierarchical reciprocity and figure-ground reversibility of "having sense" and "making sense."[99] The cinesthetic subject is the one that "feels his or her literal body as only one side of *an irreducible and dynamic relational structure of reversibility and reciprocity* that has as its other side the figural objects of bodily provocation on the screen."[100] But Barthes's photographic connection has a crucial difference from Sobchack's cinesthetic subject: Barthes's imagined or projected chiasmatic relation is not occurring with a film's living body but rather with a corpse: still photography, a dead mother.[101] While Barthes insists that the encounter with a photograph produces movement, that the *punctum* pricks him and awakens him, that he animates and is animated by certain photographs, the reciprocity and fluidity Sobchack finds in the film experience remains in Barthes fundamentally one-sided. Ultimately, Barthes understands the photographic connection as raced, because he embraces what Sobchack describes in relation to cinema, as the "figure-ground reversibility between 'having sense' and 'making sense'" only when in the photographic presence of certain bodies and not others. Barthes avows this connection only when it translates into a heightened and intensified experience of his own sensorium, not when this experience of reversibility heightens and intensifies the experience of his sensorium as another's. When facing black bodies Barthes rejects and disavows the catachrestic process, because of, paraphrasing Sobchack, his sensual retraction from race's sensible figuration. The black body "makes the skin crawl" and thus interrupts the chiasmatic structure of reversibility with an obtuse materiality — one that, importantly, is instituted by the process of interruption itself. It triggers an investment to remain on his own side of his body — to avoid, rather than seek, tactile contact.[102] Barthes's example shows how a fixation on photographic fixation troubles the relationship between vision and the other senses.

The complex indexicality of the NAACP shadow has allowed me to reflect on the imbrication between race and the photochemical imagination and the *affects* and *effects* it sustains — a(e)ffects of reality, materiality, tactility, continuity, contiguity, and corporealization. Even though, and maybe because, it is fabricated, the NAACP photograph brings awareness to affective investments: for instance the desire to follow the pointed finger like a yellow brick road and reach the body, whether to mourn or witness. Yet, what happens when on the surface of the image we find a shadow, rather than a fly? The shadow withholds closure and, instead, puts the photochemical process *en-abyme*. Photography emerges as a structure of deferral rather than referral, and we see how the umbilical cord is affectively supplied and how much the black body is instrumental to delivering a referent to its image.

TWO
ON THE SLEEVE OF THE VISUAL

[T]he word "nègre" acting like some kind of
chemical dye convert[s] epidermal surface into imago.
— David Marriott, *Haunted Life*, 2007

In the previous chapter I showed how the NAACP shadow redraws the phenomenological experience of the lynching photograph by reversing its visual field and dissipating its expected corporeality. In this process, the photograph also redefines photography as the state of the image most invested in the indexical trace, as well as confounds the experience of visible blackness, which no longer coincides with a visible object, but is rather signified obliquely by the shadow, and, because of the tension between its optic and haptic properties, it also reconfigures the very notion of "skin." By skin I mean the skin of the viewer, of photography, and of the picture. With this reconfiguration, the NAACP photograph offers new ways to experience the relationship between racial and photographic epidermality and a way to begin to think about how race projects a sleeve onto the visual, how it creates yet another surface to the image, another skin, an outside layer we think we can trust.

In the epigraph, David Marriott shows how the black body licenses this fold: the Fanonian moment of photochemical fixation is triggered by the word *nègre*. The black body is folded like shirt cuffs through a rhetorical move, a catachresis. I take Marriott's fold as the starting point for the present chapter in terms of the way in which, by suturing together seeing and saying, racialization shares the rhetorical, phenomenological, and aesthetic structure of catachresis. In order to introduce the concept of catachresis — the trope whereby a name is assigned to something that supposedly does not have one — I first briefly reread previously discussed objects and show how they led me to the realization that catachresis is one of the central structures of race discourse. I then provide an overview of how this trope has been discussed primarily in rhetorical theory and phenomenology. This enables me to outline the aesthetic theory underlying catachresis as having the tendency to corporealize the unbridgeable gap between seeing and saying by fashioning objects (or scenarios, or fetishes) that sit in between the two. My ultimate interest is the possibility to consider aesthetic practices that in turn leverage catachresis's ability to close this gap in order, instead, to burst it open.

The object I discuss as exemplary of this strategic "guerrilla" mobilization of catachresis is Lee Daniels's film *Precious* (2009). I suggest that *Precious* performs the same function as Magritte's imagined pipe; that is, it is an object that is rhetorically conjured as if existing and fully embodied in order to fill the unbridgeable gap between seeing and saying, in order to deliver a perfectly intelligible and fleshed out representation. Because of its ability to "breed pipes," catachresis offers the opportunity to see the work of resemblance as it is taking place, to appreciate how likeness acts as the ground and the vehicle for exchange.[1] I show how *Precious* occupies the chiasmatic position catachresis is supposed to mediate and how it turns that function inside out. For this very reason, *Precious* occupies the midpoint of the chapter, allowing me to transition to a discussion of an oppositional use of catachresis as a materialist aesthetic practice in the collages of Wangechi Mutu. In Mutu's work, catachresis becomes visible not only as a technique of dismemberment but also as a process of folding the already-eviscerated black body onto the outside, thus projecting a second and troubling sleeve on the visual. Mutu's cuts and her use of preexisting photographic materials suggests the possibility for photography to act *stylistically*, understood etymologically — from the Latin *stylus* — as an instrument of incision and separation, capable of excising the overembodiment catachrestically produced. Finally, I deploy catachresis as an additional lens to explore how the NAACP photograph meta-pictures the photochemical affects it mobilizes. I look at the shadow as a figuration of the chasm that Ligon introduces with his repeated and yet separated panels or the critical use of the missing body Fred Wilson adopts in his installation *Cabinet Making 1820–1960* (1992–1993). Having focused on the phenomenological, rhetorical, and aesthetic moves that are made to fill this empty space, I finally introduce a notion of photography as ectopography — as the possibility for photography to excise, rather than suture, what it recognizes as an ectopic growth.

In previous pages, I identified a series of objects that present radical challenges to a representational theory of the visual. Antonio Beato's fly, Audre Lorde's roach, and Toni Morrison's Maggie all indicate that the visual is not only or necessarily the realm of representation, but it is more precisely the realm where bodies (individual and collective bodies, bodies natural and bodies politic) inter*face* and inter-*skin*, where skin is understood in a phenomenological sense as the sensate border of the body in the world, a hinge between the material and the phantasmatic, the physiological and the psychic, the present and the absent.[2] Following Sara Ahmed, the skin is a surface that is produced in the act of reading it, and "bodies take the shape of the very contact they have with objects and others."[3] The fly, the roach, and the mute woman with legs like a parenthesis, can achieve this effect because they are structured like a catachresis — a concept I employ in its widest sense, spanning the fields of rhetoric, phenomenology, and aesthetics — a mechanism capable of producing an excess, an exteriority, a grotesque growth that sits on the outside like a red wart on the tip of a witch's nose. At its most basic, catachresis is the trope that accounts for the paradigmatic terms we use to talk about race: black and white, in fact, are not terms that have a counterpart in nature, but they are rather names catachrestically applied to "something" that supposedly does not have a name. Furthermore, as they are employed in a naming capacity, they suture the infinite relation between seeing and saying that both Magritte and Fanon attempt to reopen by rhetorically asserting *this is NOT a pipe*.

CATACHRESTICALLY BLACK

Again, from a tropological standpoint, catachresis is the attribution of a name for something that supposedly does not have one — *the legs of the chair* or *the foot of the mountain*. Catachreses are literally false — chairs don't have legs and mountains don't have feet — but figuratively true.[4] Literality is the realm of their performance, while figurality is the realm of their epistemological function, the level at which they produce knowledge. When we examine Fanon's primal scene through Foucault's reading of the Magritte painting, we can appreciate that Fanon simultaneously captures and attempts to undo the rhetorical process whereby a figural blackness is sutured to his body through a performance of literality; that is, by performing *as* literal and being seen *as* such.[5] Black and white are therefore the outcome of a process of "seeing *as*" — what Wittgenstein described as "aspect seeing" — which for Paul Ricoeur lies at the roots of the catachrestic process as well.[6] As Foucault observes, the place where the figural and the literal are peeled apart in Magritte's painting is the shifter *ceci*, which acts as a pointing finger that allows us to pass from the place where we say to the place where we look. Yet, as he also remarks, what we see is never contained in what we say, except, so it seems, when we call someone "black."

A shifter lies at the heart of the Fanonian primal scene as well: "Look!" is a deictic verb which, like a pointing finger, institutes a field of vision, commands a certain trajectory of the gaze, and then fashions an object within this field of vision, which is identified and immediately named by its chromatic properties — *un nègre*. Ultimately, Fanon's "blackness" acts as a switch point that allows a metaphorical impulse (seeing dark skin *as* black) to operate catachrestically as a proper name — *a black*. Even though "black" does not describe actual skin color, it still functions as a figure of substitution that has become fully naturalized, perceived as literal, just as the expression *the legs of the chair* in its common usage has lost memory of the metaphoric impulse that has established it in the first place. This is because it supposedly describes what we see, even though it is more properly the outcome of seeing *as*.

As already mentioned, W. J. T. Mitchell connects his notion of the metapicture to the duck-rabbit figure Wittgenstein relied on to advance his theory of aspect seeing. Metapictures are not representational. Rather, they are pictures that tell us/show us/stage for us the *as*. They are scenes of exchange that unravel the "dawning of an aspect." But in doing so, they also compile the traces of the transaction, the shift, the reorientation that is achieved by the modifier *as*. Toni Morrison's "Recitatif," for instance, compiles the traces of incessant transactions across the racial line that dead-end in the character of Maggie, which, I argue, is textually "black" by the very fact of being located at the ending point of this series of exchanges.[7] Rather, like

Magritte's *ceci,* "black" points and names, deferring to a place where seeing and saying will supposedly coincide: Look! A Negro!

Sometimes catachresis is a necessary act — when we find we have to name something for which no other name exists — and it thus performs a generative function: naming brings something to existence. Other times, however, as the Latin term *abusio* suggests,[8] catachresis can be regarded as an abuse of language, as the outcome of a violent act of displacement because it presupposes a void to be filled on the basis of a resemblance between entities (in function, in purpose, in behavior, etc.), which is instead an effect of discourse.[9] As Foucault suggests in his reading of Magritte's work, likeness is instituted by the linguistic act, rather than simply sanctioned or described by it. Thus, catachresis can show how an act of naming might retroactively project a void in the very act of filling it.

In other words, an act of naming is not necessarily an act of charity. As Robyn Wiegman eloquently puts it, calling the African "black" reduces race to the binary structure of vision, which in turn grounds the possibility for race to act linguistically as a visual language of social relations. The black-as-body is constituted in the colonial representation not only as different but also as the sign of difference. Even more profoundly, the term "black" utters an ontological division into being — what Charles Mills calls a "partitioned social ontology" that, drawing a line between white and non-white, institutes the ontological category of the sub-person. The sub-person, Mills further specifies, "is not an inanimate object, like a stone, which has . . . zero moral status. Nor is it simply a nonhuman animal." Rather, it is an entity that "because of phenotype, seems human in some respects and not in others. Even though [an] adult, is not fully a person."[10]

Yet, because of its generative possibilities, catachresis has been connected to the possibility of social change, especially in Ernesto Laclau's political theory.[11] For Gerald Posselt, this tropological economy of catachresis points to a performative theory of resignification, whereby the name constitutes the identity of what is named, but only and always provisionally. Because it implies the possibility of a new proper sense, catachresis creates the suspicion that there "has never been an original proper sense at all."[12] In its performativity, catachresis has been called the queer trope.[13] What interests me about catachresis is this intrinsic hybridity. Catachresis is the site of a tug-of-war between what Bruno Latour has identified as the two expressions of the modern project — the work of purification and the work of translation — the first performed by erecting hard epistemological and disciplinary divisions between subject and object, nature and culture, and so on, and the other made necessary to mediate between these segregated realms.[14] Catachresis is a Latourian figure of hybridity because its queerness bears the traces of its own failed figurality. With catachresis, the most hybrid knot in the chain is put in charge of the border, so to speak. Catachresis is a scene of exchange between different orders of signification, but also different ontological orders, and disciplinary orders as well.[15]

Whether it bestows a name to something that does not have it, or whether it has the capacity to attribute traits that do not belong (for instance, legs to a chair, or feet to a mountain), catachresis, it is generally recognized, is a radical trope. With catachresis something erupts, something is being triggered. But with catachresis something might also grow unexpectedly and in improbable directions so much so that many descriptions of the trope, even the most positive ones, are couched within a gothic imagery. Take Paul de Man, who writes, "something monstrous lurks in the most innocent of catachreses: when one speaks of the legs of the table or the face of the mountain, catachresis is already turning into prosopopeia and one begins to perceive a world of potential ghosts and monsters."[16] Not accidentally, ghosts and monsters appear also in Thomas Keenan's account of catachresis as the tropological structure of the commodity fetish. For now, though, I am more interested in the fact that de Man's appeal to prosopopeia suggests that these monsters and ghosts are conjured up by catachresis's ability to *carry voice* or to *give face*.[17]

If *La Trahison des Images* is a metapicture of the work of resemblance, which suspends its suturing effect, then the catachrestic moment would rather look like Magritte's *Decalcomanie*, where the man with the bowler hat has been seemingly transferred laterally leaving in its wake a cutout curtain (figure 2.1). As Foucault observes, in *Decalcomanie* we witness "a displacement and exchange of similar elements, but by no means mimetic reproduction."[18] *Decalcomanie* suggests that catachresis has the ability to effect a redistribution of the sensible, whereby the moment of replacement is always already in excess of the void it supposedly fills, especially when we focus on the slim overlapping of the curtain, the fold that doesn't quite match the void. Or, even more provocatively, catachresis would look like Magritte's *La Philosophie dans le Boudoir* where catachresis performs a sideways substitution between the fetish and that which it covers over. Here, breasts and feet that have grown — literally — on the sleeve of the fetish, have facialized

FIGURE 2.1. René Magritte, *Decalcomanie,* 1966.
© ARS, NY. Private Collection. Photo credit: Herscovici/Art Resource, NY.

it as a result,[19] in a theoretically loose, but aesthetically gripping, application of prosopopeia. From an aesthetic point of view, catachresis develops indeed a *sleeve* — one that gives face (albeit sometimes a monstrous one) to that which did not or was not supposed to have one. I understand this process of facialization as a case of what Kathryn Bond Stockton's analysis of the figure of the queer child describes as sideways growth, one that doesn't just grow meanings but also bodies.[20] Catachresis is carnal and capable of producing growths that, like barnacles, stick to the surface and populate it.

Both Morrison's Maggie and Audre Lorde's roach are examples of a cata-chresis that is generative and queer, because, as it grows sideways, it has the ability to corporealize the in-betweenness of the social bond. In the case of Maggie's blackness, catachresis is found in her parenthetical status as that which connects the whole with the hole. Her corporeal presence, her abso-lutely mute presence as nothing but a body (given her lack of access to any linguistic and discursive order beyond her syntactical function) gives her the role of Audre Lorde's roach, which is also the product of a catachrestic process that begins with the white woman regarding young Audre *as* a roach, as the "strange" body that triggers her withdrawal and a postural and subjective realignment. With both rhetorically constructed "roaches," catachresis functions as a form of aspect seeing, what I would describe as catachresis as *kaleidoscope* because, like in the duck-rabbit figure, one can behold two figures present in the same space. Catachresis, I found, is also the figure for a corporeal growth — catachresis as *pimple,* as *barnacle.* Blackness operates catachrestically in both senses of the term: within our image ontology, when understood as a property of the body named by the term "black," blackness produces a growth, an excess of corporeality, an overembodiment that might take the form of an "insect" sitting uncomfortably between, for instance, a little child's skin tone and an older woman's sense of the violation of her own bodily boundaries. This corporeal blackness is also what fills the lynching shadow with the corporeality of a body off-frame. Not only that, as Fanon (and DuBois before him) show, this apparently mute and liminal corporeality is also the site for an unacknowledged point of view onto the suturing process itself.[21]

"Black" is a catachresis that has the capacity to continuously erase the traces of its own violent making because it is also an iconic sign and, as such (that is, as a sign that signifies by resemblance), it is primarily invested in its circulation. Unlike the index, which can be regarded as a mark of individuality and singularity, the iconic is instead a vessel of circulation and exchangeability. Icons are signs that hold together a myth of transparency (whereby the sociocultural origin of the "resemblance" they display with the referent is often ignored) and a demand to function as currency; they combine a need for recognition with an affirmation of authority. Thus, the iconic also brings to the fore the process of semiosis that makes a catachresis "feel like" a proper name.

Catachresis implies also a phenomenological structure that performs a crucial role in Fanon's account. In his account, the transition from seeing and saying is achieved through a catachresis that is simultaneously rhetorical and sensorial, both visual and tactile. As already mentioned in relation to Barthes's *Camera Lucida*, catachresis is central to Vivian Sobchack's description of the phenomenology of the cinematic experience — a specular structure whereby one's own lived body is mirrored on/by the screen.[22] For Sobchack, this phenomenological structure is both literal and figural. The ambivalence between "real" and "as-if-real" sensual experience is phenomenologically grounded in the "nonhierarchical *reciprocity* and figure-ground *reversibility* of 'having sense' and 'making sense.'"[23]

The chiasm Sobchack discusses is fundamentally an empathic structure, which, as we have seen, is what malfunctions in Barthes's case. Barthes endorses this chiasm only in relation to the possibility of getting in touch with his own place of origin and maternal nourishment, as well as the place of death. Blackness is the mode of this very personal experience in that it marks the site of the chiasm. At the same time, we have seen how Barthes suspends this structure of reversibility when he is instead facing some*body*'s blackness. Blackness in this case interrupts the desire for reversibility Barthes had previously nourished. When pigmentation exteriorizes the photographic image to the point that it no longer offers a desirable tactile and fleshy encounter the image becomes Intractable, with its "blackness" standing as the *face* or mask of an incontrovertible truth. In Barthes's reaction we see the ability for blackness thus understood to fashion a body in-between, a "strange" body that makes the skin crawl.

SO BIG . . . SO BLACK

Throughout the various meanings of catachresis (rhetorical, sensorial, political), two properties continue to come face to face: on the one hand, catachresis has the ability to corporealize by performing as a graft, an implant, and a prosthesis; on the other hand, catachresis has the power to abstract, etherealize, and exchange. Furthermore, catachresis offers a redistribution of the sensible (what I have half-jokingly described as catachresis-as-barnacle) and, when it functions as a kaleidoscope it performs a rearrangement of the visible that introduces vantage points in new and unexpected places.

The first sense of catachresis as barnacle and ectopic growth describes the popular and critical reception of Lee Daniels's 2009 film *Precious: Based on the Novel "Push" by Sapphire*. The film registers precisely this collapsing of distinctions between representation and represented, which takes the form of a conflation between the film (*Precious*), the character (Claireece "Precious" Jones) and the actress (Gabourey Sidibe) — all of them are PRECIOUS. As I write PRECIOUS — in all caps — I want to call attention precisely to the film reviewers' difficulty to peel them apart and Daniels's strategic embracing of this conflation in order to flaunt the difficulty of fashioning an artistic language for a subject that is still too often critically located within the purview of sociology or natural history. That is, Lee Daniels preemptively adopts the work of catachresis in order to read it against the grain and ultimately fold it inside out. Casting choices, framing, effects of *mise-en-abyme* achieved by the fantasy sequences imprison the film/character/actress within an intransitive visual field that yields nothing outside itself. Thus, PRECIOUS provides both the "retinal pop" that seemingly delivers "the pipe" and the visual short circuit whereby "a pipe is a pipe is a pipe." Ultimately, it fashions a spectatorial position as an embodied in-betweenness, where the spectator is placed in the position of having to catachrestically fill the gap, complete the chiasm, deliver "the thing," or alternatively to embrace the body that marks the spot — PRECIOUS.

A sixteen-year-old overweight and illiterate girl, who is bearing her second child by her father, abused by her mother, and HIV positive, Claireece "Precious" Jones, critics agree, is a veritable social and human nightmare; the character is hardly the subject matter for a film with artistic aspirations. *Precious* was therefore an "impossible" film to make. From the start, it was destined to be received as contributing to a continuing history of pathological and pathologizing racial representations. In fact, the press condemned the film as a "gallery of horrors," a "freak-show," and a "porn flick," and Precious and her mother Mary (played by Mo'Nique) are described as "biological monsters."[24] What these reactions display is the critics' inability to see that *Precious* is, among other things, an intervention into the critical discourse that is still distracted by the content of the image rather than paying attention to the artistic utterance as a whole; the critical discourse that focuses solely on, in Morrison's words, "the glide and lick of the golden scales," but misses the fishbowl entirely.

This *New York Amsterdam News* review of the film is exemplary of some of the critical difficulties with the film:

> Gabourey "Gabby" Sidibe is not Precious, the character that has catapulted her into overnight superstardom in Lee Daniels' critically acclaimed film *Precious: Based on the Novel "Push" by Sapphire*. The title character in the movie is an illiterate, neglected and abused teenager trapped in a 1980s Harlem version of hell, who fantasizes about a better life filled with dashing red-carpet appearances and preening photo shoots. Gabby, the vivacious 26-year-old Harlemite who plays Precious, lives that dream.[25]

But does she? That the reviewer feels compelled to spell out the differences between the actress and the role is, in itself, revealing. The assumption is that that difference will not be at all apparent, because, so it seems, there is no available gap between the black and the image. Precious is a pipe and Lee Daniels's role is to "un-pipe" her. To challenge this tendency, the filmmaker incorporates the critics' myopia — their seemingly incontrollable impulse to see through the film's form rather than look at it — in order to reflect on the representational demands that still afflict nonwhite artists. *Precious* is a provocatively and deliberately overembodied film. It has the "thereness" of a botanical manual, to recall Foucault's description of the relationship between text and image in Magritte's first pipe painting — a gallery of horrors, a freak show as it has been described in the press — and yet its goal is to put this "thereness" *en-abyme*. Still, many critics reacted to PRECIOUS as if it was a specimen, nakedly available to scientific scrutiny, or, alternately, as exploitative race pornography. Thus, it is not surprising that several critics preferred the appeasing and uplifting John Lee Hancock-directed film, *The Blind Side* (2009), which was released at the same time as *Precious*. This is possibly because *The Blind Side* has no qualms about delivering a specimen — an unthreatening, needy black character seen through a romantically inflected anthropological imagination. As one perceptive critic observes, the film treats Leigh Anne Tuohy's (Sandra Bullock) visit to Michael Oher's (Quenton Aaron) old neighborhood like Margaret Mead landing on Samoa. "It's as if Erin Brockovich had been given charge of E.T.," he further claims.[26] As ethnographic subjects, Michael and Precious have a lot in common. They are, paraphrasing Wolf Blitzer's pornotroping comments about Katrina victims, "so poor, so black."[27] Additionally, they are very big.[28] Yet, while, according to *The Blind Side,* Michael Oher's size and protective instincts become an asset in the football field, Precious's size cannot be redeemed. On the contrary, it is a constant reminder of her multiple abuses. While Oher, as the same reviewer notices, looks like "a Buddha statue transplanted to Tennessee," Daniels gives Precious a complex living body. Throughout the film she starves, she eats, she throws up, she aches, she breastfeeds, and so on. Her body is always at risk of being dismembered, caught in a tug-of-war between self-determination and various forms of social and domestic abuse, between overeating and throwing up, being force-fed and being starved, between being penetrated and being slapped, abused from the inside out and the outside in — pulled in opposite directions that constantly threaten to dismember her.

By focusing on the life of the flesh of his main character, Lee Daniels in turn *fleshes out* and ultimately restores interiority to a body that would have otherwise existed only externally, fully contained, and pacifying as Michael Oher's Buddha—a mute presence tucked in the depth of the visual field. Instead, Precious's interiority is anticipated in the film's credit sequence in which the agency that struggles to come to visibility as a speaking voice (the mark of recognizable personhood since the slave narratives) is rendered through incomplete, hesitant words and a tentative font, and is reaffirmed by the title character's voice-over narration throughout the film.[29] Furthermore, Precious's living, breathing, and aching body offers the model for the way Daniels organizes the film's body, as well as the way in which it interacts with the body of the spectator. Rather than setting out to document a sociological problem, *Precious* performs an ethical gesture in that it constructs an experience of racial embodiment in which the three bodies of/in the film (the text, the character, and the actress) slide and rub against each other and against the spectator's own body as well.

Adapted from the novel *Push* by African American poet Sapphire, the character of Precious is very deliberately and at its origin a textual figuration—a narrative voice, more specifically—that metonymically stands in for a number of students Sapphire encountered in her years working as a New York City schoolteacher. That we have to leverage framing devices to understand the film is obvious from the start: the film begins with a fantasy sequence. An elegantly dressed African American woman on a runway puts a red scarf on Precious's shoulder—a symbolic token of her right to fantasize. Then the film fades to black. After the title, "Harlem 1987," the voice-over narration begins: "My name is Claireece Precious Jones. I wish I had a light-skinned boyfriend with really nice hair. I want to be on the cover of a magazine. But first I want to be on one of those BET videos. Mama says I can't dance. She says who wants to see my big ass dance anyhow?" This last statement poses an uncomfortable and not-at-all rhetorical question, which also anticipates and incorporates the expected shortcomings and dilemmas of the film's reception—the fact that, predictably, Gabourey Sidibe ended up on the cover of *Ebony*'s March 2010 issue, but did not "fit" on the cover of *Vanity Fair*'s Hollywood issue. Just like the fantasy sequences offering access to alternative modes of visualizing Precious's embodied blackness, this question demands that viewers confront, test, and experience the limits of their own integrationist imagination and the extent to which they want to make room for PRECIOUS in the visual culture of mainstream America.[30] As if to test these limits, the fantasy sequences show Precious dancing quite a bit, showered with attention, glamour, and fame. Yet, these fantasies offer an entry point into the film's exploration of racial embodiment because of how they are chiasmatically grafted onto episodes of abuse.[31] The frames within frames Daniels carefully sets up through these sequences do not fit neatly inside each other; rather, the frame layers grow sideways and ultimately overflow into the sensorial space of the viewer.

The sequence following the school principal's discovery that Precious is pregnant for the second time begins with the principal's question: "Is something going on at home? If there is something going on at home I want you to tell me right now." The camera is on Precious's blank stare and then cuts to Precious at home, tilting up over her body in a close-up as she stands at the kitchen sink, washing a frying pan. Her mother, barely distinguishable in the background on the right, asks Precious if she has bought cigarettes for her. Met by a negative answer, she throws the remote control and hits Precious in the head, sending her falling forward. A cut in mid-motion shows Precious falling not on the kitchen floor, but rather backward onto a bed. The film cuts very rapidly between a close-up of a man taking off his belt, bed springs contracting under pressure, a pan of frying eggs, a jar of Vaseline, a man's waistline, and then the full figure mounting her, a mewing cat, the rape again but this time showing her mother witnessing it the background left, a close-up of Precious, and then, from her point of view, a close-up of a crack in the ceiling which bursts open as the camera moves through it and finds Precious in a fantasy sequence. On "the other side" of the crack she is exiting the premiere of her latest film, followed by her light-skinned boyfriend, and surrounded by photographers. She claims the film was fabulous and she feels great. Then she hears thunder, looks up, and is immediately splashed in the face, not by rain coming from the sky, but rather by her mother, back in the kitchen, dumping a bucket of water on her face.

The sequence combines two backward and forward movements to effect a paratactic transition — a structure that Daniels also employs to great success in *Shadowboxer* (2005)[32] — that sutures together various forms of abuse and fantasy, various forms of fleshiness and materiality (the cut to the frying egg which frames Precious's flesh as meat), food and semen, meowing and moaning, top and bottom (the bed springs and the ceiling). Precious's body is placed in the middle, at the site of the chiasm, in between what Sobchack

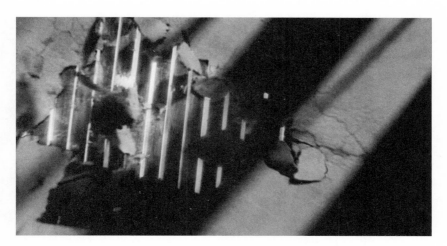

FIGURE 2.2. "Catachrestic passage." *Precious: Based on the Novel "Push" by Sapphire* (Directed by Lee Daniels, 2009, Lionsgate/Lee Daniels Entertainment), frame grab.

describes as our *cinesthetic* movement toward the screen and the film's movement toward us.[33] These are movements we would be prone to complete if they did not lead to unexpected destinations — either unrealizable fantasies or unspeakable abuse. Because the movements carry Precious and the spectator to unexpected destinations, they also lead one to hesitate before, rather than invest in, the film's sensible figuration.

Daniels's editing accounts for this awkwardness later on in the film. For example, in the dog who licks Precious's ear as she is lying facedown on the sidewalk, pushed by teenage boys who had been catcalling her, while she is imagining her light-skinned boyfriend kissing her on stage. Here it is the sensorial similarity between the two actions that acts as a pivot for Precious's body's extension across the chiasm between spectator and screen. In her fantasy, she is kissed on the right-hand side (in foreground) by her boyfriend, but in reality the dog is licking her left ear in the background, while her body fills the space in between. The sensorial stimuli that come from, and pull, in opposite directions (the boyfriend's kiss on the right ear and the dog's lick · on the left), do not suggest that she mistakes one for the other, but, rather that they coexist at all times. Like her, we too are no longer just on one side of our body, facing the screen, or the world,[34] but we are rather located at the scene of another more profoundly troubling chiasm — the chiasm that connects, in a reversible relation, pleasure and abuse.

The labor of putting Precious *en-abyme* so that she is not as nakedly present as "the genitals of a plant"[35] runs contrary and yet complementary to the labor involved in deglamorizing Mariah Carey, who plays the part of the ultimately compassionate social worker Ms. Weiss. "They totally changed me," she told the press, "I didn't want to look in the mirror. It was beyond dressing down because Lee Daniels loved to torture me. He really wanted me to not just look plain, he wanted me to look homely." Dressing down, looking homely, is described as torture and Lee Daniels is the abuser presumably so that Carey would develop the adequate amount of sympathy for Precious. But the detail that remains the most difficult for Carey to assimilate, the one she is determined to let people know it's only make-believe, is the fake moustache. "I'm not very hairy," Carey claims, displaying her forearm on which not a single hair could be seen. "I've never had that issue."[36]

Apparently, this impertinent growth is rhetorically and sensorially necessary for Carey to experience her character from the inside out. However, unlike Carey, Gabourey Sidibe cannot use her own body off the set to show the extent of the uglification she had to undergo to play the part. As Daniels said, Gabby would not "take off her suit" after the end of the shoot. Or, as Mo'Nique also remarked, "we are fat girls — we have had training [in abuse]."[37] Carey, on the other hand, was careful to explain: "Now I see why [Daniels] wanted it because people didn't recognize me and he didn't want me to take people out of the movie because they were seeing Mariah Carey."[38] On the contrary, I believe that Daniels used celebrity casting — including Lenny Kravitz in the role of nurse John — as a framing device to foreground the film's formal properties and counteract the effect of transparency the film's subject matter would unavoidably produce. A recognizable celebrity, in fact, underlines the precarious distinction between the film's inside and outside, thus marking the film's own skin. Moreover, by casting Mariah Carey, Daniels was able to productively oppose bodies that "perform" and bodies that "stick" — in this case a fake mustache or actual body fat — the figural and the literal, and ultimately and more radically, he fashioned a body — PRECIOUS (again, understood as the body produced by the conflation of the film, the character and the actress) — that grows sideways, overflows its boundaries and, with its excess corporeality, tests the audience's ability to hold it and embrace it.

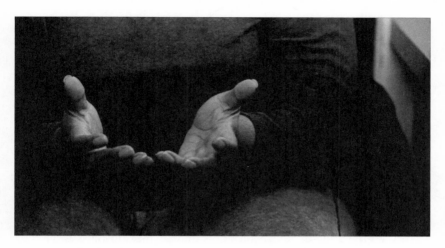

FIGURE 2.3. "Both of 'em." *Precious: Based on the Novel "Push" by Sapphire* (Directed by Lee Daniels, 2009, Lionsgate/ Lee Daniels Entertainment), frame grab.

Finally, consider the film's closing sequence at the welfare office, where Precious's mother, Mary, is confronted about her knowledge of the abuse that was occurring in her home. As she talks about her "bresses" and how she bottle-fed her daughter but breastfed her boyfriend, Daniels again offers an image of *both/and* and *crossing over*. The abuse started one day when Precious, then three years old, was lying down on her pillow in the big bed on one side of Mary, with Mary's boyfriend Carl lying on the other side. At one point he *reached over* to Precious. Mary explains her complacency as the camera is fixed on her close-up: "I had a man and a chile . . . ," but, as she adds, "and I had to care for both of 'em," the camera closes in on her hands, stretched out, palms facing upward, as they seemingly carry the unspeakable weight of the confession she has just made (figure 2.3). These hands are themselves unable to cross over, to perform the movement that Carl made, Mary allowed, and eventually sealed Precious's fate. Unlike the previous instances of flashbacks and fantasies, the film no longer cuts away from the scene, but rather ends with two hand*fuls* — first, the hands that Mary did not use in Precious's defense, and then Precious's own hands, carrying her two children, as she walks away from the welfare office and into the New York City subway.

The importance of unpacking the work of race through the lens of catachresis lies in the possibility of undoing the suturing between seeing and saying that ultimately triggers the construction and proliferation of PRE-CIOUS as Magritte's pipe. If "black" sutures the infinite relation between seeing and saying; if, from a sensorial standpoint, the "work of race" fashions strange bodies, insect bodies, that materialize the in-betweenness, then what moves are available to counteract the suturing and over-embodying logic of "black" and "white"? Or, when is the black not the pipe? One aesthetic strategy I would like to consider can be read as a response to the suturing and abusing effects of racial catachresis. Specifically, catachresis's ability to rhetorically sever and rearrange the very texture of reality to establish a wedge between the "thing" and its representation; indeed, to redraw the terms by which we encounter either. Brandished as a surgical instrument, catachresis can work aesthetically against its own rhetorical function and allow the flattened subject to pierce through the visual field. Paraphrasing Richard Powell, catachresis makes it possible to "cut a figure."[39]

Cutting a figure describes the way in which the African American subject of portraiture makes a visual claim to subjectivity. The cut indicates an act of carving a *face* from a canvas of invisibility.[40] Cutting a figure is a sort of *Kunstwollen* — a will to form[41] — the desire to cut through the surface in order to gain a face, a visage, a recognized and legible outline of personhood. The human figure cuts through the visual field when, resisting its flattening into a "silent world of inanimate bodies" it presses against the photographic surface, with ostentation, deliberation, and style. Here, I understand style etymologically — from the Latin *stylus* — as connected to photography through the concept of writing. The word *stylus* describes a writing tool, an implement used for etching or engraving, and, etymologically, photography is writing with light. In relation to Powell's notion of cutting, I am interested in the ability of the photographic to act stylistically as a writing tool, which, as the notion of engraving suggests, can also be an instrument of incision and separation. More broadly, for Powell, cutting a figure opens the performative aspects of portraiture to reveal "the whys and hows of a modern and composite human design."[42]

Alongside this notion of the cut, I also want to pursue de Man's idea that figuration is a form of giving face and, by extension, that collage is a strategy of facialization, and catachresis is the master trope for this operation. Thus, I employ Powell's idea of cutting a figure as a way to discuss the faciality of the figure and to explore the relationship between this notion of the face — understood as the locus of perception and expression, the site where the body communicates the most — and the cut; that is, between what sits *on* the surface of the visual and the visual *as* surface. It also offers the possibility to explore the ability for the photographic to act "stylistically"; that is, as a tool of both inscription and separation in order to bring rupture to the catachrestic process that underlies the ontologizing affects of the photochemical; that is, the ability of race to suture itself to the surface of the body.

Collage capitalizes on the formal agency of the cut. Through collage, the photographic, as a style of presence, as a technology that has written race onto the body, and as the state of the image that affectively considers resolved the question of reference, can be put at a remove. Its ideological charge can be cancelled out in the moment of reassemblage according to a modernist (in fact, in Romare Bearden's case expressively post-cubist) *mise-en-scène*.[43] As the point of contact between photography, writing, and race, but also as a point of possible reversal of their historically sanctioned relationships, the cut holds the possibility of folding the visual field inside out so that what sits silently and invisibly within its depth can acquire agency and come onto the outside, acquire a visage and, with it, interface the viewer.

Bearden's work offers an important impulse for Powell's development of the notion of "cutting a figure" and the way in which Bearden's collages succeed in embedding a multiplicity of viewing positions — eyes that stare out and relentlessly engage the viewer — has a lot to do with this.[44] In this scrambling and reassemblage of the visual field around the pivotal element of the eye, Bearden lays the foundation for a catachrestic aesthetics — one that slowly unravels, unstitches, and shreds to pieces the suturing process catachresis performs. In this foundational artistic move, Bearden is a crucial precedent and inspiration to contemporary collage artist Wangechi Mutu, for whom catachresis can be seen to characterize her aesthetic project. Her chosen technique, the dominant aesthetics, and the imaginary she employs in her work excavate and confound the implants that are rhetorically necessary for her main object to be only and just a pipe; that is, the native woman as colonial fiction; to be, as Charles Johnson puts it in his commentary to Fanon's passage, "as naked as the genitals of a plant."[45] In particular, Wangechi Mutu's work displays a productive tension between the function of catachresis as a forced and unequal exchange, the violence embedded in the work of resemblance, and catachresis's function as a growth, which in her work takes the specific form of a surgical implant. In fact, in her work, catachresis is ultimately ectopic. Just like Romare Bearden before her, she performs a vanishing act in which the body is first vacated and then precariously reconstituted in a myriad of mosaic-like surfaces that are no longer available as the anchoring visual evidence of race. By radically exteriorizing the body, making it untouchable and unfixable, these works cut through photography understood as a functional model built on a specific correspondence between the outside and the inside of the body. They cut through it because they leave incomplete, unfulfilled, and unaccomplished one of its fundamental expectations, which is the fact that racialization would deliver a perfectly contained and recognizable visual object.

CATACHRESTIC CUTS

A Kenyan artist educated at Yale, currently working and living in New York City, Mutu's signature work is a series of female figures created through a combination of collage and watercolor. Some of these figures, as in the *Pin Up* series, are archaic and yet futuristic, often mutilated, trans-ethnic and trans-species females. They are created by gluing extremely heterogeneous magazine clippings onto the outline of a human figure in pinup pose painted on Mylar, a semitransparent polyester film. Later series, however, apply collage on integral preexisting pictures: postcards from Kenya in the *Ark Collection* and colonial gynecological texts in *Histology of the Different Classes of Uterine Tumors.*

Mutu's choice of technique and of supporting materials, ranging from the acrylic film-like Mylar to the preexisting medical texts, allow her to slow down, unpack, and flesh out the process that instead pornotropes the colonial subject by suturing and invisibly overlaying it with its representation. Predictably, the artist herself has been caught up in this process and has been conflated with her work: her figures have been read as "abstract self-depictions." "Viewers often find it impossible to separate me from my subjects," Mutu tells Gerald Matt. She continues, "I have rarely heard a European white artist asked if the Caucasian-looking characters or figures in their work are a projection of themselves."[46]

The claim that collage is catachrestical might seem obvious and, therefore, theoretically not very productive. Yet, catachresis accounts not only for how collage grows sideways, through a material process of assemblage of incongruous preexisting materials, but also how it sheds light onto the productive function of the cut — the cut *from*, the cut *away*, and the cut *to*.[47] As practiced by Mutu, collage straddles the line between the literal and the figural. The line is that between a material cutting and gluing to which the artist is particularly attached versus a more metaphorical "cut" which has to do with the recontextualization, removal, recombination, and citation of a subject — for example, the native woman, which, like PRECIOUS, is captive of generic forms, such as the scientific text, the ethnographic account, the pornographic image, or the romanticized postcard, to name just a few, that conflate her with her representation.[48]

Furthermore, Mutu's figures constantly refer back to the materiality of her chosen technique because they are amputated, mutilated, and pieced together through an array of incongruous prostheses. Her figures stand or crouch on limbs collaged from magazine clippings of a variety of consumer fetishes, such as motorcycles and stilettoes, which function as artifactual extensions of the body itself. In *I Shake a Tail Feather* (2003), most of the female figure is rendered through watercolor, except for the shoulder and neck abruptly removed from an erotic context, judging from the way the head is cocked, but here only suggesting a body that is perpetually contorted and unstable (figure 2.4). The smoothness of the photographed skin contrasts with the mottled watercolor pattern of the rest of the body and creates ambiguity as to whether a flesh and blood woman has cannibalistically ingested this futuristic, yet animal-like figure, or whether the opposite has occurred. One arm is stretched behind the back or missing; on the other arm, the hand is held firm inside a stretcher while the woman's legs end in bird paws. Tendrils grow throughout her body — in the back as a tail, and on her hips, knees, and waistline. An oversized glittery broach decorates her right hip and she wears a silver bracelet on her arm. She is taunted by a creature whose body is made of human limbs, possibly the body of a male dancer with legs spread wide open, pearls covering his genitals, a dinosaur head, and a long reptilian tail. Blood sprouts out of both the head and the tail, but she appears unaffected.

Typically, the facial features of Mutu's figures are rendered through clippings of limbs, animals, and oversized, alluring mouths usually taken from porn magazines. She claims to be drawn to the materiality of magazine pictures, rather than digital images, because magazines "are our collective

FIGURE 2.4. Wangechi Mutu, I Shake a Tail Feather, 2004. Ink, acrylic, collage and contact paper on Mylar, 66 × 42 in. Courtesy of the artist and Susanne Vielmetter Los Angeles Projects.

psyche's waste. Looking through them is like sifting through elephant dung to find out what the animal ate, where it came from, what state of health it is in."[49] Her investment in the use of found objects (in part influenced by David Hammons) stems from her commitment to a materialist historiography of the predicament — but also the possibilities — of the postcolonial subject. A materialist historiography that, evidently, holds that our imaginary is best found in our collective feces.

This commitment to materiality manifests itself also in the series of mutilations, amputations, and prosthetic growths her pinup figures are made from. For her, collage is a technique of dismemberment and re-memberment — an effect that, formally, occurs over and across competing scales. Often the larger subject's facial features are rendered through collaged photographic magazine pictures of full bodies and even group scenes, as in *Blue Eyes,* where the mouth of the subject on the right is rendered with a clipping of the back of two males hunched to perform some manual task. The eye sockets and the eyebrows of the bust on the left are made by human arms, while the nose is rendered through the full figure of a crouching "African" man lying across and looking up toward the forehead. At least two motorcycles are embedded in the figures' chests and one dangles from the ear, their chrome hardbodies shining against the watercolor background. Other features are made of flowers, petals, and two fairy-like females dressed *as* flowers next to a colorful parakeet that mingles with their dresses.

As she articulates in her short film, tellingly entitled *Cutting* (2004), in which the artist manically hacks with a machete what looks like an animal's carcass as if to mold it into something, Mutu understands her art as a process of amputation but also as monstrous prosthetic surgery — simultaneously defacement and portraiture. For her, cutting necessarily entails mutilation, a forceful pushing back, which she understands as a strategy of survival and adaptation. The female body, she argues, is always already chopped by processes of fetishization: "As a woman, that deep and wonderful churning connection and disconnection with your body is very real and often extreme. It is for this reason that *I turn the body inside out*, extending and reconfiguring it."[50] The woman's body is always and already mutant, forced to adapt, sever dead limbs, contort, lose its fluids, and so on.[51]

Here, again, Mutu straddles the line between the literal and the figural. For her, the way the female body is read in the public and transnational space is already an experience of amputation, which can only be rendered by juxtaposing synecdochical reminders of the spheres in which these mutilations occur — that is, ethnography, pornography, anthropology, medicine, to name a few. In a conversation with Barbara Kruger, she explained she decided to render the violence that this brings to the subject as a series of "body injuries or mutilations or malformations or exaggerations or prostheses, as a way of talking about the need to extend, perforate, change, or shape-shift your body in order to exist."[52] Furthermore, she also understands her entire artistic process as an investment in mapping and remapping her own body: "I think one of the things about being an artist is that your brain is in every part of your body that you use to create."[53]

Collage provides a technique whereby proximity can create resemblance. Because of the nature of that proximity — that is, the fact that it is the result of a material relocation of materially existing objects — collage is a technique that necessarily raises ontological questions about its "matter of expression"[54] and about the iconic order of signification; that is, how "likeness" is constructed and maintained and on what grounds. Yet, just like Kara Walker (who I discuss in the final chapter), Mutu uses figurative art to frustrate the representational expectations her work unavoidably poses in certain quarters (that is, who is the model for this? Or, as Angela Stief's essay in the eponymous exhibition catalogue eloquently puts it, *In Whose Image?*), and poses instead an ontological question: what are these figures? Where do they come from and where do they live? Mutu's portraits break free from the generic expectation of approximating a model and instead embody processes of identity *assemblage,* whose expected fictional unity is mockingly projected onto the hyperbolically and artificially smooth surface of Mylar. This allows her to mock portraiture's underlying humanism by composing her figures out of a catachrestic series of grotesque acts of exchange (figure 2.5).

In the *Ark Collection*, Mutu addresses the complicity between the exotic and the ethnographic by having them materially interact as separate layers within the same picture so that one acts as a frame and a lens through which we see the other. The collection is made from images of black models taken from porn magazines, glued over postcards that are reproductions of photographs by Carol Beckwith, an American photographer and amateur ethnographer who lived with the Masai of Kenya and Tanzania beginning in the 1970s (figure 2.6).

These doctored postcards are then arranged inside four vitrines as if they were themselves specimen. Mutu cuts the top layer in such a way that the

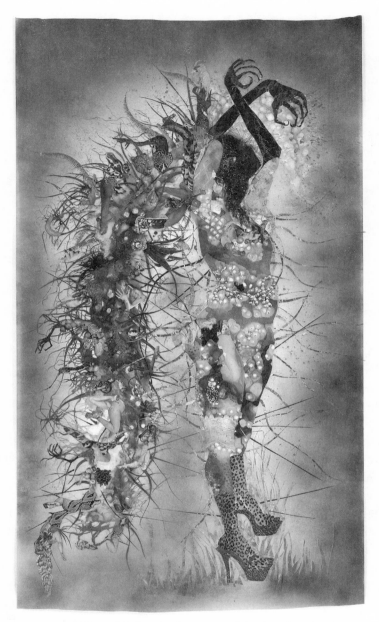

FIGURE 2.5. Wangechi Mutu, *Lockness*, 2006. Mixed media ink and collage on Mylar, 95 ¼ × 54 in. Courtesy of the artist.

FIGURE 2.6. Wangechi Mutu, "The Ark Collection: Highland Woman, Muslim Woman, Konso Woman, Muslim Woman, Ogaden Market, Hamar Woman, Hamar Couple, Somali Woman," 2006. Collage on postcards, vitrine, 40 × 62 × 23 in. Installation view. Courtesy of the artist.

background comes through to fill in the missing body parts or to complete gestures initiated in the porn image. Often the erotic movement of one female figure is arrested, deflected, and defaced by the presence of the other. The place of the genitals or the breast in the pornographic image is often occupied by the gaze of the ethnographic subject coming through and looking back from its objectified and silenced position in the picturesque postcard. The pornographic poses remain evident, but instead of delivering voyeuristic revelation, the genitals are usually covered, "playing lust and prohibition off against one another."[55] Obviously, Mutu reacts against the exoticization of the African woman, but also against representations of the native as a scientific specimen and what Fatimah Tobing Rony indicates as one of the ideological underpinnings of colonial anthropology — that is, the fact that "the exotic is always already known,"[56] that cognition is always already recognition, and repetition as well.

In the series titled *Histology of the Different Classes of Uterine Tumors*, the original illustration of the colonial medical text elides the colonial woman, who is violently fragmented in a conflation between the pathologies the text illustrates and her pathologized otherness. Spread open, flattened out, only her "abnormal" insides are visible. In this case, Mutu again glues porn magazine clippings on top of the original page.[57] Removed from their titillating context, these body parts now embody the peculiarly colonial dialectic between erotic attraction and fear, multiplicating, while also literalizing, the woman's orifices. In *Indurated Ulcers of the Cervix*, the collaged bust of a woman from a porn magazine masturbates: her arm is directed toward the vagina in the medical text underneath, but it ends in a mechanical grip that has seemingly chopped off her hand. Collaging a woman's face on top of the original page offers Mutu the possibility to facialize the medical text. In *Uterine Catarrh*, Mutu builds a face around the original text's illustration of a vagina so that it occupies the position of the Third Eye, which is instead an organ of second sight (figure 2.7). For Tobing Rony, this is the organ through which the native returns the gaze from within the visual field and "pierce[s] through the veil of the imagination of whiteness."[58] As much as colonial discourse constructs the native woman synecdochically *as* a vagina, Mutu empowers that bodily opening with an inquisitive, challenging, and knowing look. She institutes a violently grotesque interchangeability between bodily orifices, a vagina becomes an organ of sight or sometimes a mouth, an organ of speech.

In both the *Ark Collection* and *Histology of the Different Classes of Uterine Tumors*, one picture performs concretely as the material lens through which we see the other picture. Collage allows Mutu to commingle them, turning the looking relations of the original material inside out. Thus the act of exchange, the catachrestic process of substitution, occurs not only between the organic and inorganic, human and natural, made and found, unpredictable body parts, metal and textile, optic and haptic, micro and macrocosmic and so on, but also between the seer and the seen. Contiguity creates violent and revealing associations between types of fetishes. Importantly, each of these fetishes harbors a point of view, which further fragments Mutu's work in a kaleidoscopic mosaic of trajectories of looking. Once relocated to outline the contours of an eye or the feature of a face, a limb that belonged to a porn image is no longer mute flesh, but appears instead capable of seeing, of understanding its new circumstances, its new purpose, and its belonging to

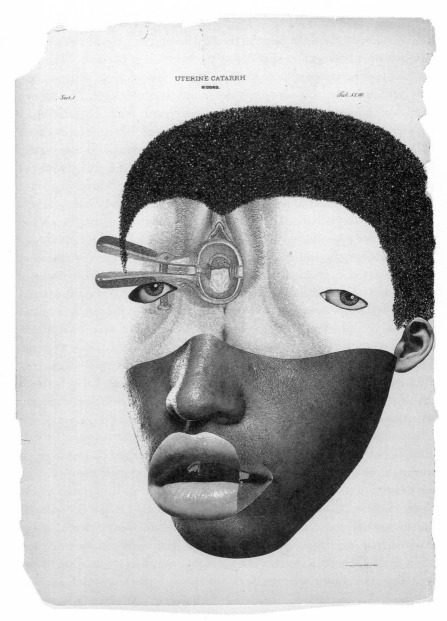

FIGURE 2.7. Wangechi Mutu, *Uterine Catarrh*. From *Histology of the Different Classes of Uterine Tumors*, 2004. Glitter, ink, collage on found medical illustration paper, 18 × 12 in. Courtesy of the artist and Susanne Vielmetter Los Angeles Projects.

something larger, more nuanced, and more exciting. As we piece together the human figure, aided by the outline created through watercolor, the viewer's gaze is always attracted and pierced by the eyes — clipped from magazines, hence recognizably human — which both act as passageways to the "other" side of the image as well as effecting a return of the gaze. Because of this ability of fragments to convey a point of view, in Mutu's work synecdoche triggers processes of *mise-en-abyme*. Viewers are put before their own rules of legibility as they are forced to determine for themselves the boundaries of what constitutes the human.[59] Standing before the artwork, viewers too are cutting a figure.

As a redistribution of the sensible, catachresis operates also in the haptic properties of Mutu's work by producing a receding surface that frustrates the possibility of a visual unity and a consistent and satisfactory tactile engagement. The choice of working on Mylar creates what Jennifer González characterizes as a semiliquid surface, which "seduces her viewers with a festering image of exploitation and erotic desire syncopated in a warm rhythm of flesh on flesh."[60] On the one hand, the use of watercolor on Mylar echoes the sleek and glossy aesthetics of the modern-day fetishes and the tactile pleasure of these images resides in their shiny patina. On the other hand, tactile stimulation is sought literally with the application of organic materials such as rabbit fur so that it acts as materialization of a desire for a tactile encounter with the porno/ethnographic Other that was already present, but also disavowed, in the glossy aesthetics of the female figure of pornography or advertising. Yet, as much as Mutu's surfaces are seductively glossy, they are also exceptionally moist: splattered with blood and other bodily fluids coming from improbable places and received with improbable pleasure by the subjects in the works themselves.[61] These different densities, genres, and haptic stimulations further augment the tension and the flickering between the ethnographic and the pornographic, thus offering a tactile and visual experience that cannot give way to the work of empathy underlying what Hartman has identified as the scene of subjection.[62] We are in awe of her figures. They cannot be pitied.

The surface of her work recedes also in consequence of manipulation of scale. Facial features, just like anatomical parts, are only visible as a result of a hermeneutic effort that has to reconcile their material and generic heterogeneity and incongruous scales of vision engaged in the same space. Not only are the facial features of her bodies made of collaged limbs, but also of full human figures, and even groups of people, landscapes, animals, textiles, and commodities within a larger figure. For example, *This You Call Civilization?* (2008) functions as a "host" organism to the slime, trash, and waste of our culture. The same female figure can be host to the micro and macrocosmic which sometimes patterns her skin (as in *Riding Death in My Sleep*, 2001), just as she is precariously distinguished from the natural world surrounding her. Mutu's bodies grow in all directions. They display protruding flesh, or barnacles, but they also sprout roots onto the soil; they grow tails, feathers, tendrils, that draw complex circular patterns into their surroundings.[63]

Mutu's use of organic imaginary and materials denotes the collapsing of the divide between nature/culture, thus exposing that the object that had been erected to guard the border between nature and civilization; that is, the native woman, is instead a more profoundly and more spectacularly hybrid one.[64] Her hybrid border positioning stems primarily from her function as a receptacle of colonial fantasies that consign to the Other what cannot be successfully and cleanly assimilated onto the unified vision of the Western self. Additionally, the native woman introduces a temporal structure that is simultaneously projected toward the past and the future. As most commentators observe, Mutu's female figures appear to inhabit competing temporal frameworks, at once primitivist and posthuman, ancestral and postcolonial, futuristic and archaic. She participates, for example, in a taxidermic imagination similar to the one Tobing Rony sees spectacularly captured by Merian Cooper and Ernest Schoedsack's 1933 film *King Kong*. This tension between the original and the derivative, the man-made and the natural, manifests the same chronological structure as catachresis, whereby the (synchronically) derivative has historically (diachronically) occurred first.[65] In other words, in Mutu's work catachresis acts also as a chronotope — a specific aesthetic arrangement of the relationship between time and space.[66] Her *Alien* series is a case in point. Imbued with melancholia, their diaphanous heads tilted upward towards the sky, Mutu's figures seem to look at a long lost distant future searching for the resources to voice a past that has not yet come to full representation. As she states, "My work is reclaiming an imagined future."[67]

Predictably, the terminology used to describe Mutu's work is highly ekphrastic in an attempt to convey the violently incongruous and yet alluring associations on which it relies. For Okwui Enwezor, her work is "at once grotesque and elegant, paratactical yet hybridized."[68] It pursues the "abject sublime."[69] At stake is the production of a spectatorial gaze that cannot rest on any one clear position. Or consider the highly evocative and hybrid lexicon employed by Michael Veal:

> These women appear at times conjured from a fantastical realm of nocturnal toadstool reveries and at other times, fabricated from the rotting remains of open sewers, garbage heaps or toxic waste. Alternately engaging in mutual frolic or ecstatic disfiguration, their glorified orifices bestow life-giving fluids and anoint the land with toxic elixirs. It is ironic and telling, however, that a good portion of the oozing in Wangechi's art is not done via the usual body parts; rather, liquid pours as frequently from bodily punctures and ruptures. Which is to say, this is an *ecstatic aesthetic of trauma*.[70]

"Ecstatic," in particular, is a recurring term used to characterize Mutu's figures. Contained within the idea of ecstasy is the notion of the body beside itself. And her bodies are precisely so, not only for their poses and the organic, enmeshed relationship to their natural surroundings, but also because their photographic implants are ectopic, they come from — and lead — elsewhere. Mutu suggests that photography can be thought of as ectopography.

The idea of photography as ectopography; that is, capable to effect a cut that excises an ectopic growth, comes from Henry M. Sayre's discussion of Nan Goldin's photograph *Ectopic Pregnancy Scar, New York City, 1980* (figure 2.8).[71] Sayre regards Goldin's photograph as a representation of the fact that photography works simultaneously as a suture and a cut, a joining, but also a hole, and a passageway. An ectopic pregnancy is an abnormal pregnancy that occurs outside the uterus. It is a growth that is out of place: most commonly the fetus implants in the fallopian tubes, or in an ovary, the abdomen, or the cervix. None of these areas has as much space or nurturing tissue as a uterus for a pregnancy to develop; hence, as the fetus grows, it will eventually burst the organ that contains it. The fetus is misplaced and displaced and it needs to be removed to avoid rupturing its surroundings.

In Goldin's photograph the surgical incision and the scar it has produced are traces of this threat from within to the very integrity of the human figure. Additionally, they perform a *mise-en-abyme* of the vaginal opening. The "thereness" of the vagina competes with the "thereness" of the scar, which seems to want to normalize the photographic cut as well. As the photograph (at least affectively) severs a subject from a historical/material continuum, the scar for the ectopic pregnancy attempts to institute a scene of healing

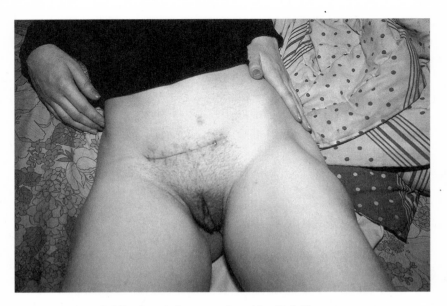

FIGURE 2.8. Nan Goldin, *Ectopic Pregnancy Scar, New York City,* 1980.
Cibachrome, 20 × 24 in., 51 × 61 cm. © Nan Goldin, courtesy of Matthew
Marks Gallery, New York.

that stitches the cut back together. The "cut" in this case is both that of the
scar and that of the photograph, which has violently chopped the woman's
body by framing it so that the eye can only really focus on the two "cuts."[72]
Yet, one is stitched and the other is open; one is the outcome of a corrective
measure toward an out-of-place growth, while the other is the appropriately
located anatomic configuration. Writes Sayre: "This photograph disfigures
pornography because it negates its figures, it deforms and defaces the scene of
the pornographic — that is, the body — just as the scar disfigures the subject
in Goldin's photograph. Disfigurement leaves scars. Scars trace disfiguring's
violence. But scars mark, as well, the scene of healing."[73] This photograph
does keep in play the irresolvable tension between photography's ability to
connect — grounded, for some, in its embeddedness in the very texture of
reality — and its capacity to sever, but also its capacity to write, inscribe,
and script.

When we compare Goldin's photograph with Mutu's *Ectopic Pregnancy,*
we appreciate that the native woman in the original medical text is already
and helplessly spliced open in the way she connects biopolitics to practices

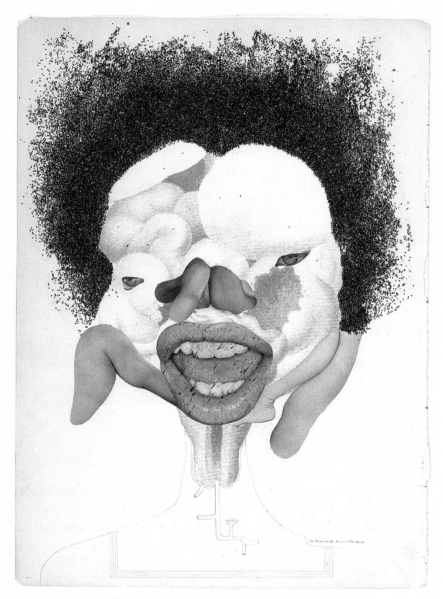

FIGURE 2.9. Wangechi Mutu, *Ectopic Pregnancy,* 2004. From *Histology of the Different Classes of Uterine Tumors.* Glitter, Ink, collage on found medical illustration paper, 18 × 12 in. Courtesy of the artist and Susanne Vielmetter Los Angeles Projects.

FIGURE 2.10. Fred Wilson, *Cabinet Making 1820–1960. Mining the Museum: An Installation by Fred Wilson, Maryland Historical Society, 1992–1993*. Installation view. *Photograph from the Museum Department. Courtesy of the Maryland Historical Society.*

of governmentality (figure 2.9). Mutu literalizes the opening of the original image and places a mouth and spread legs on the underlying drawing of the uterus. She implants blue eyes on the ovaries, glues together limbs for a nose and black glitter all around to suggest a bushy hair (and pubis). The resulting face evokes one of the totem objects of Victorian culture — the Elephant Man — with monstrous growths on the face. The mouth is splattered with blood, revealing an incision, or cut, that has occurred just off-frame, but still sprays inside the open orifice.

Photographic ectopography, as practiced by Mutu, is that in which indexicality performs as a pointed finger gesturing toward the promise of a suture between the image and its referent that will occur elsewhere or that we need to supply with our affective investment in it. Yet, this affective investment does not deliver the emphatic identification triggered by what Saidiya Hartman has described as a "scene of subjection," which, in an abstract sense, is a witnessed or imagined scene in which the emphatic substitution of the suffering makes that suffering comprehensible only to the extent that it can be identified as one's own. When that occurs, subjection is compounded rather than lifted because, "in making the other's suffering one's own, this suffering is occluded by the other's obliteration."[74] Ectopography denies the object of identification because it recognizes that, as it is catachrestically produced, that object is always already ectopic — out of place and out of whack.

PHOTOGRAPHY AS ECTOPOGRAPHY

The NAACP lynching photograph is equally ectopic because it withholds a direct view of the object that is supposed to suture the visual field and stabilize its semiosis. In this withholding, it shares the critical use of the missing body Fred Wilson puts in play in his installation *Cabinet Making 1820–1960* (1992–1993). Part of *Mining the Museum* — an exhibition Wilson installed at the Maryland Historical Society in 1992 using pieces from the institute's permanent collections — *Cabinet Making* consists of a group of nineteenth-century Victorian chairs facing Baltimore's whipping post, which was in use in Maryland until the mid-twentieth century[75] (figure 2.10).

The chairs are arranged in such as a way that the spectacle of black pain is on display,[76] staging "lynching as a kind of living-room leisure sport."[77] Yet the body that organizes it is conspicuously missing. The empty spaces foster the work of the imagination and demand a spectatorial complicity in re-creating the scene. The objects bare the traces, the memories, of their past usages in that that bodies of the users and victims hover over the scene so much so that we are invited to take up the position of the missing body ourselves.[78] "Who occupied these fine furnishings," asks Jennifer González, "who left their sweat and blood in the wood grain of the whipping post? Although no black body or white body is present, the dynamics of optical domination resonate with a history of racial encounter."[79]

Not only do these objects define the type of subjection and subject-formation available to the raced subject, but they function both "as metaphorical signs [and] also as indexical links to a larger social history of people and things."[80] Both a conjuring object and a scene of the crime, *Cabinet Making* registers the bodies of its users as a "latent presence."[81] While in *Cabinet Making* this contact occurs physically because of the history of the material objects that make up the installation, in the NAACP photograph this contact occurs vicariously through the image state of photography — thanks to the referential affects it triggers — particularly in relation to the compound indexicality of the lynching photograph. There the body's latent presence is figured as a "lingering shadow." Both works leverage the logic of indexicality as trace. Through the fantasy of a past contact, both reenact the "dance with things" people make to produce race but they also both act ectopographically to make this contact ultimately unavailable and, in so doing, foreground the affective labor that the viewer needs to perform to connect the indexical trace to its source.

THREE
THE MONEY OF THE REAL

Wouldn't it be a helluva joke if all this was really burnt cork and you people were being tolerant for nuthin'?
—Dick Gregory, *From the Back of the Bus*, 1962[1]

In his essay "The Shadow and the Substance," Nicholas Mirzoeff discusses a *carte-de-visite* titled *Emancipated Slaves* (figure 3.1) featuring a group of slaves — adults and children alike — of various skin tones. Produced and circulated within abolitionist propaganda, the photograph relied on the whiteness of the children's skin to argue for the end of slavery. Their whiteness exposed the evil of the institution because the "wrong" people were being held captive.[2] Mirzoeff notes that one of the slaves behind the children is branded in the forehead, a place that could not be concealed, which means that he was probably an apprehended runaway. Juxtaposing the light-skinned children with the branded dark-skinned slave, the photograph mobilizes multiple and competing forms of racial indexicality: the brand on the man's forehead performs as an indexical trace of the property structure of slavery, which duplicates and compounds the indexicality of his blackness.

EMANCIPATED SLAVES BROUGHT FROM LOUISIANA BY COL. GEORGE H. HANKS.

The Children are from the Schools established by order of Maj. Gen. Banks.

WILSON CHINN.   MARY JOHNSON.   ROBERT WHITEHEAD.
CHAS. TAYLOR. AUGUSTA BROUJEY.   ISAAC WHITE.   REBECCA HUGER.   ROSINA DOWNS.

Entered according to Act of Congress, in the year 1863, by GEO. H. HANKS, in the Clerk's Office of the United States for the Southern District of New-York.
Photographed by M. H. Kimball, 477 Broadway.

FIGURE 3.1. Myron Kimball (fl. 1860s), *Emancipated Slaves*, 1863. Made in New York City. Albumen silver print from glass negative, 13.2 × 18.3 cm. (5 ³⁄₁₆ × 7 ³⁄₁₆ in.), oblong oval Mat: 19.9 × 25.2 cm. (7 ¹³⁄₁₆ × 9 ¹⁵⁄₁₆ in.). Gilman Collection, Purchase, The Horace W. Goldsmith Foundation Gift, through Joyce and Robert Menschel, 2005. The Metropolitan Museum of Art, New York, NY. Image © The Metropolitan Museum of Art/Art Resource, NY.

The whiteness of the children's skin, however, does not bear the trace of their racial identity. Instead, it indexes that whiteness is an asset, a color capital, and a property, which grounds a claim to something other than captivity.[3] These children, the photograph argues, are entrapped by slavery where their appearance determines that they do not belong. Rather than indexical, their whiteness is an iconic representation, one that signifies by resemblance, and thus attends to a fundamentally social semiotic process.

I am interested in reading this image also from the point of view of the political economy of the sign. From this point of view, *Emancipated Slaves* shows a scene of exchange in which the bodies of the darker slaves function as the mirror of the value of the lighter ones. Yet, rather than illustrating the formal equality that is presupposed by commodity exchange — the same formal equality that prompts Gayatri Chakravorty Spivak to claim that there is "no *philosophical* injustice in capitalism"[4] — the photograph testifies to the intrinsic violence of capitalist exchange. The black slaves cannot exchange, circulate, and move the way the light-skinned slaves can. Overall, this image illustrates how the black body becomes both vehicle and signifier of exchange and thus generalizes the *money form* of the social sphere. It does so by putting in play two ways in which the photochemical imagination is imbricated with race. The first, which was discussed in chapters 1 and 2, is the investment in the indexicality of the trace, the idea that the visual is in continuity with the real as its outward fold. The second, which is introduced in this chapter, is the understanding of photography as the *money of the real*. On the one hand, this *carte-de-visite* enlists the effect of photographic transparency to reinforce the idea of the transparency of race; that is, the coincidence between the photographic and the racial index. On the other hand, it stages a scenario of both desired and failed exchange, while, as a material culture object, it acts as a token of exchange for a projected emancipation.[5] It also holds in tension the indexicality and iconicity of blackness, which manifests itself in the way some slaves' bodies express the value of others. In this, the *carte de visite* presents the semiotics of value Marx outlines in *Capital*; that is, the relationship whereby the body of commodity A acts as the mirror of the value of commodity B.

This chapter offers a reflection on the notion of face value from the point of view of the political economy of the racial sign. In chapter 1, I argued that the image passes through the racial index to acquire a certain measure of (affective, semiotic, symbolic) stability. In chapter 2, I approached photography first as a suturing and carnal catachresis and then as ectopography — a structure that, wielding catachresis against its own grain, is capable of excising ectopic growths. Here I am concerned with the way in which photography passes through capital to gain exchangeability. This is what scholarship in film and visual studies has described as photography's ability to function as the money of the real[6] — the fact that, regardless of their aesthetic stance, all photographic representations partake of the logic of the commodity form — "the exchange abstraction that haunts the culture of capitalism."[7] Whereas the two previous chapters focused on the ability for photography to produce reality a(e)ffects, in the last two chapters of this book I focus on exploring the money form of photography. The claim I make here is parallel to my earlier claim: race stabilizes both photography's ability to connect to, or produce, the real, as well as photography's ability to exchange for the real. The iconicity of the (photochemically fixated) black body, I contend, generalizes the money form of the visual sphere. My goal in these last two chapters is to show that blackness and photography share the same hermeneutics — the hermeneutics of *face value*.[8]

I have decided to characterize face value through the notion of the Long Photographic Century, which I explore in chapter 4, in order to graft the image state of photography onto the Long Twentieth Century; that is, onto the history of capital regarded as a *longue durée* that unfolds through a series of systemic cycles of accumulation.[9] The concept of the Long Twentieth Century provides the lens through which Ian Baucom rereads the cultural, geographical, and historiographical concept of the Black Atlantic in order to place the financial revolution and the slave trade in the same historical continuum as our present moment.[10] Baucom derives from Walter Benjamin and Frederic Jameson a philosophy of history based on the recurrence of forms and from Giovanni Arrighi an oscillatory history of capital. He also indirectly indicates another parallel *longue durée* in the history of visuality once it becomes bolted to the history of capital, as it occurs with the establishment of the slave trade.[11] It is this *longue durée* that I call the Long Photographic Century, to emphasize how photography (in the broad sense I explored in chapter 1 as a photochemical logic that includes pre-photographic forms such as the silhouette) offers the dominant mode of the visuality of capital — a generalization, in the visual sphere, of capital's hermeneutics of the surface. Photography is an image state that exchanges with a real it helps to visualize.

The theoretical pivot for the intersection between blackness, capital, and photography is the notion of "form." The form I have in mind is the commodity form, as Marx describes it in the opening chapter of *Capital*, volume 1. I read Marx's "form" as outlining a theory of (double) visuality, a theory of *seeing as*. Form is what expresses the *as*. My focus on blackness as a commodity form, therefore, attends to the way blackness continues to give appearance and visibility to commodity status. Importantly, just like the commodity form has become increasingly more speculative in finance capital, so has blackness moved from being the (seemingly natural) mark of the human commodity in New World slavery to being attached to material culture objects, to providing an aesthetic form within consumer culture, and finally to being the form of speculative entities produced by finance capital, what (with a Marxian and Benjaminian language) I describe as "phantasmagoria."

I begin this investigation on blackness as commodity form with a reflection on the concept, aesthetics, and semiotics of blackface, which I read as one of the most accomplished forms of reification of face value. I do so with an analysis of the Dick Gregory joke I used as an epigraph, then I remark on Spike Lee's film *Bamboozled* (2000), which can be regarded in itself as a palimpsest of various stages and expressions of blackness as commodity form. I conclude by looking at the work of artist Hank Willis Thomas, a perceptive interpreter of the diaphanous but pervasive imbrication of blackness in the aesthetics and desires of consumer culture. In Willis Thomas's work, blackness emerges as a visual language of social and consumer relations — a vehicle for the expression of capitalist desires — and as the "matter of expression" of the speculative logic of the Long Twentieth Century. At this chapter's conclusion, I return to the idea of blackness as phantasmagoria in Keith Obadike's *Blackness for Sale*, a work of cyberart that involves the eBay auction of the artist's blackness.

The objects discussed in this chapter have in common the ability to act as scenes of recognition (but sometimes also misrecognition, prevarication, exploitation, etc.) whereby a reified racial object or objectified racial subject is capable of pivoting around itself and turn the very principle of its reification into a critical vantage point onto the system that reifies it. The subject-made-object suddenly turns around and *sees*. Thus, not all the objects in this chapter are visual. On the contrary, sometimes they inhabit a place of avisuality and yet find a way to cut a figure, pierce the visual field, and fold its racial fold onto the outside; they manage to turn their *surface* into a *face* and claim their role as conditions of possibility of the visible itself.

Before beginning this analysis, I need to attend to the notion of face value as it emerges from the political economy of the racial sign.

SEEING DOUBLE

Lyndon Barrett proposes to look at blackness through the Marxian notion of value as a way of seeing double.[12] Other scholarship, from Shawn Michelle Smith to W. J. T. Mitchell's book *Seeing through Race*, and obviously Toni Morrison, as indicated in the introduction, recuperates the idea of race as a lens, a medium, something we see through. They do so by leveraging W.E.B. DuBois's notion of double consciousness as a visual theory of race. In DuBois's notion of second sight, the idea that in "seeing oneself being seen," the black subject occupies two places at the same time: she is simultaneously a viewed object and a viewing subject. Because of that doubleness, she also enjoys a unique vantage point onto the seer.[13] This idea of double vision informs my approach as well. Yet, for me it remains important to ground the idea of "seeing double" also in the structure of capital, as described by Marx, because of how foundationally the African slave's body has bolted visuality to the history of capital, turning blackness into a form of appearance of value. First, then, I want to attend to the relationship between form, value, and the double vision they afford.

A double vision characterizes the very opening of *Capital*'s first chapter, which begins with the rhetorical structure of the metaphor, the appearance of something as something else.[14] This Wittgensteinian "aspect seeing" is necessary to behold the specific yoking of the visible and the invisible, the material and the social, embodiment and representation, literal and figural, which come together in the notion of *form*. The first form we encounter in *Capital* is the commodity form, which becomes visible only in exchange: "Commodities . . . *appear as* commodities, or have the *form* of commodities, in so far as they possess a double form, i.e. a natural form and value form."[15] In other words, commodity is not a thing, but rather the *form* a thing assumes, a way of being, a manner of appearance, a principle of visibility, as well as the expression of congealed human labor and of an object's ability to exchange.

Two illustrious commodities mark the contours of Marx's notion of form. The first one is Marx's coat. I am not referring to the coat that constitutes a figure for the simple commodity Marx employs throughout *Capital*'s first chapter, a commodity that, unlike the wooden table enlisted to introduce the concept of commodity fetishism — the second commodity that bookmarks the notion of form — has not yet evolved all kinds of "grotesque ideas" in its head.[16] The coat I am talking about is Karl Marx's own overcoat, whose vicissitudes Peter Stallybrass has so eloquently illustrated.[17] Stallybrass found that Marx struggled to complete the research that would eventually lead to *Capital* because, at several junctures, he was forced to pawn his coat to sustain his impoverished family in London. Without it, he could not brave the London winter to go to the British Museum, nor could he be admitted to the museum's reading room without being suitably dressed. Stallybrass shows how the coat falls in and out of Marx's possession, how its form changes with each trip to and from the pawnshop, thus showing that possession itself is also only a form: it is a specific type of relationship between use and exchange, and also between the tangible and the intangible. Thrown into the sphere of exchange (at the pawnshop, for example) the contingent materiality of Marx's coat dissipates. Yet, once out of the pawnshop, the coat becomes tangible again and appears unchanged by its temporary transformation into cash. It can supposedly still warm Karl Marx's back. Marx's notion of form can be regarded as the unavoidable response to this process of constant metamorphosis of the "sublime" body of the coat.

The possibility to behold the appearance of something *as* something else comprised in the notion of *form* is necessary for Marx to explain the fact of exchange; that is, the fact that physically, qualitatively, and affectively different commodities become commensurable and relate to each other in some capacity. (Marx shows that within capital, equation — that is, exchange — is intrinsically violent. Commodity exchange entails reductions, abstractions, etherealizations and ultimately the spectralization of the sphere of the human, which, catachrestically, exchanges for nothing in return.)[18] Form is a pivot between dualities and different ontological orders — quality and quantity, use value and exchange value, contingency and system — but also across scale, between the micro and the macro level at which capital can be comprehended.[19] Form addresses also another riddle that *Capital* attempts to resolve: the failure of human labor to leave an indexical trace that would mark its product. Value, Marx states, is not visible in itself, but rather emerges only relationally through the value relation between two commodities in exchange. Value expresses human labor only through its reflection on another commodity.

In order to illustrate the relationship that connects the commodity form to value, Marx adopts the language of the medieval doctrine of the King's Two Bodies. He writes: "An individual A, for instance, cannot be 'your majesty' to another individual B, unless majesty in B's eyes assumes the physical shape of A, and moreover changes facial features, hair and many other things, with every new 'father of his people.'"[20] This passage accomplishes at least two things: it outlines the theory of embodiment Marx adopts in order to address the representational crisis of capital, and it dramatizes the double vision that Lyndon Barrett claims is necessary in order to behold the commodity form. Barrett's double vision is a type of seeing double, whereby one's embodiment acts as the mirror of another's value. Value cannot be found in the fibers, the substance, and the material of the commodity's natural body, but only in its sublime body as reflected on another (natural) body's surface. With modern-day slavery, whereby the commodity becomes human in the slave, this notion of form is brought to a dramatic point of crisis. Indeed, in the slave, the commodity form needs to perfect its structure of embodiment, in so far as the slave is the commodity with a biography, a composite construct where the human and the commodity coexist in an irresolvable tension.[21] So much so that, in nineteenth-century American legal discourse, as Stephen Best has shown, the slave is figured with two bodies: one biological, hence mortal, and one as "property," hence implicitly immortal. The theory of embodiment supporting the medieval doctrine of the King's Two Bodies underlies both Marx's notion of the commodity as well as the aesthetics of slave law.[22]

THE DANCING TABLE

Marx's account of commodity fetishism dramatizes the relationship between the two bodies of the commodity — its natural, phenomenological body and its body politic, the body that is socially constructed, like the king, like the Leviathan.[23] For Jacques Derrida, the specter of exchange haunts use value from the beginning of Marx's account and eventually forces him to act as a conjurer and call on stage the second notorious commodity — the Dancing Table — a wooden object animated by commodity fetishism in which Marx attempts to show the specters of abstracted human labor.[24] The scene of the Dancing Table offers a dramatization of the commodity's embodiment, which is obscured by the commodity fetish in the animation of the object and its determination to act as the ending point of the textual chain of value.[25] The table comes to life. It recognizes that it has a body and, rather than using it to reflect the value of another commodity, it uses it to dance and pretend its body is the custodian of its own value.[26]

For critical race discourse, this scene is very important because it stages what Fred Moten has called the "resistance of the object," registered in the slave narratives, as will be discussed momentarily.[27] There is another productive reading I want to mobilize. According to Bill Brown, the phenomenological experience of the table's sensuousness and tangibility gives rise to a tradition of misinterpretation of this passage that has become second nature in literary and cultural studies; that is, the investment in "understanding our desire for objects as more primary than understanding the structure through which they become commodities."[28] This tradition begins with Benjamin's account of our fascination with objects, our being drawn in by the material object world. In turn, Benjamin is able to expand on Marx's notion of fetishism because he misinterprets the fetish as a scene of seeing, connected to commodity display. If this tradition can be regarded as an attempt to restore to the commodity the traces of the human producers that fetishism has occulted and dissipated, through an attention to its sensorial and aesthetic properties, then it can also, at least in Benjamin, offer a way to think about the form of the commodity as a point of view; not only the manner of an appearance but also the locus of a gaze.[29] Benjamin, in fact, is responsible for identifying an important pivot the commodity can perform when it celebrates its becoming human in the prostitute. There, he claims, it can finally "look itself in the face."[30] This pivot for me is crucial; it is the movement that many of the objects I consider in this chapter perform in order to cut through their invisibility, to resist their being tucked away in the depth of the visual field. However, beyond Benjamin, the most compromised, legally sanctioned, and formalized human commodity is not the prostitute, but the slave. Hence it is to the slave narratives I want to turn in order to find a discussion of this pivot in the recurring scene of the Talking Book.

In *The Signifying Monkey*, Henry Louis Gates Jr. reads the trope of the Talking Book as a representation of the linguistic economy of slavery. In its first appearance in the slave narrative of Gronniosaw, the Talking Book is the book that the master reads, but, once approached by the slave, does not *talk* to him.[31] Of course, the book never talked, but as long as he is illiterate, the slave believes that it does; he mistakes the master's reading for the book's speech, and mistakes the book's silence toward him as the book's failure to see him. Gronniosaw, Gates argues, interprets this silence as a consequence of his blackness, a sign of absence of face and voice.[32] Recording the moment at which the slave's blackness obscures his human form in favor of the commodity form, the trope of the Talking Book registers the slave's inability to read as a failure of being seen. Eventually, the slave's acquisition of literacy — as testified by the very act of writing his own narrative — affords him a reflexive move, which is simultaneously linguistic, economic, and visual. The slave learns that the book had never spoken but was instead being read by the master, and also learns that he (the slave) can also read it and that his inability to read does not imply the book's failure to see him. Once the slave learns to see and read the commodity fetishism of which he is also part, he is also able to detect the signs of his repressed absence.[33] In short, the Talking Book performs the function of the Dancing Table until the slave can accomplish an act of exorcism and elevate himself to the status of seeing and speaking subject. This moment signals what Charles Mills would describe as the "non-Cartesian Sum" uttered by "property that does not remain silent but insists on speaking and contesting its status."[34] This is the pivotal moment in which the slave leverages the commodity fetish to represent "what is *missing* or absent"; that is, the recognition of his humanity. At this juncture, the commodity-become-human sees itself in the face.

I want to use this pivot as a methodological tool and explore the formalizing and superficializing function of blackness as commodity form. In turn, Marx says, the commodity form is only the "germ" of the money form, where this hermeneutics of the surface is further generalized. Money, in fact, is both the commodity that has become the universal equivalent and the medium for commodity circulation. Yet, as the reification of the very process of social mediation,[35] money becomes so naturalized that, in money, value seems indeed to be branded on the forehead. In money, value is understood and regarded as *face value*, as if a bill's or a coin's value naturally sprung from its (surface) denomination.[36] This hermeneutics of the surface is both the signature trait of modern-day racial slavery and of our hyper-speculative contemporary moment. Far from being incommensurable, the two belong to the same historical and epistemological map, *viz*, the Long Twentieth Century.

THE LONG TWENTIETH CENTURY

In *Specters of the Atlantic: Finance Capital, Slavery, and the Philosophy of History,* Ian Baucom claims that the money form of the social sphere was licensed and generalized by the transatlantic slave trade. Baucom argues that we have to regard the moment of finance capital of the British cycle of capital accumulation concomitant with the slave trade (1750–1825) not only as central to Black Atlantic history, but also to the "history of modern capital, ethics, and time consciousness," and continuous with our highly financial present.[37] In order to make this claim, Baucom models his philosophy of history on Benjamin's conception of the Baroque allegory as the literary anticipation of the logic of representation of the commodity form. Unlike Benjamin, however, Baucom is interested not in the common debasement of the thingly character of things that the allegory shares with the commodity, but rather in the financial phases of the oscillatory history of capital Giovanni Arrighi identifies in *The Long Twentieth Century: Money, Power, and the Origins of Our Times*; that is, those phases in which value is not accumulated in commodity production but rather in the quarters of high finance; the phases in which money seemingly breeds money, which Marx described with the abridged formula M-M.'

The phase of capital accumulation facilitated by the slave trade is characterized by the universalization of the money form of the social sphere, which Baucom sees "demonstrated, anticipated, and recollected"[38] in the events and discourses surrounding the 1781 *Zong* massacre when the slave ship's captain threw overboard 133 slaves, supposedly to save the ship and the cargo. The *Zong* massacre played a central role in abolitionist efforts and imagination because the ensuing trial was not conducted as a murder case, but rather as a property dispute to determine Captain Collingwood's compliance with the jettison clause in the insurance contract covering the *Zong* and its cargo. Baucom regards the *Zong* as exemplary of a new and larger speculative epistemology of "theoretical realism," whereby products of the imagination or of agreement — such as the value covered by the insurance contract — are considered real. In fact, what was never challenged at the *Zong* trials was not only the commodity status of the slaves, but also the fact that they indeed constituted an insurable commodity whose value was the product of an agreement that preceded the moment of exchange. Thus, the trials sanctioned the death of the less desirable slaves as the necessary condition for bringing into existence the imaginary form of value underwritten by the insurance contract. Ultimately, the death of the slaves hurried their conversion into money. The epistemological revolution underwriting the *Zong* trials is what puts the slave trade at the core of a historical continuum Baucom calls "The Long Twentieth Century."

There are several elements that concur in the formation of this epistemology of theoretical realism, but they all, in various ways and forms, indicate an extension of the logic of paper money to the social and cultural sphere — the "extension of not only commodity capitalism into the domain of the human, but the colonization of human subjectivity by finance capital."[39] This dominance of capital is characterized by and sustained within the system of credibility required by the substitution of paper money with bills of credit (a form of imagination of fictional things, a training in recognizing, reading, and believing character and the others' ability to do the same), and the accreditation of a "real" existence to the value agreed upon by an insurance contract. All of these innovations were also supported and normalized by other profound epistemological changes — for instance, the notion of the type, which appeared both in historicism and in the emerging form of the novel, but it is also a necessary concept for the practice of insurance, which is the business that trades in, invests in, and speculates on the typical and the average. In other words, the birth of values and the possibility to trade them in the growing eighteenth-century European financial markets is ontologically connected to what Bill Brown has called the "historical ontology of slavery"; that is, the collapsing of the distinction between personhood and thingness, and to the paradoxical form of physical and imaginative vision that could disregard the signs of personhood in the African's body and regard him or her, instead, as a form of economic return.[40] Ultimately, the slave occupied the body that mirrored a socially agreed value, thus bolting the history of visuality to the history of capital. In this milieu, the slave's blackness came to function not only, and quite intuitively, as a signifier of difference, but also as a means of exchange.[41]

Value, argued Marx, is an expression of social relations, which, however, is not directly visible in itself. The location of race onto the body achieved at the dawn of the Long Twentieth Century, instead, has given a form, a channel, and a mode of visibility to value. It has constituted a racial contract, as Charles Mills put it, as a form of political domination, which has become incarnated.[42] As a result, value has become embodied, sensorially and aesthetically tangible, and visible on the surface. Because of the way it yokes together the speculative and the carnal in the Long Twentieth Century, race produces a hermeneutics of *face value*. Value is facialized in the black body's epidermis.

A HELLUVA JOKE

I now return to the question posed earlier to guide me in this reflection on race as a form of appearance of capital and eventually on the visuality that this fact entails: the idea of blackness as commodity form, blackness as form of appearance of value. I want to examine the hermeneutics of face value at a site where it is both reified and put *en-abyme*; that is, turned into a tangible sensorial object but also into a regime of representation that reflexively comments on itself. I am thinking about the concept, the practice, and the aesthetics of blackface, which I want to first consider briefly through an analysis of the Dick Gregory joke used as epigraph to this chapter and then with a few remarks about Spike Lee's film *Bamboozled* (2000). Therefore, I begin with a pivoting object that directly calls into question the hermeneutics of face value in one of its most reified expressions. Building on scholars that have emphasized the "counterfeit" nature of minstrel performances, I approach blackface as a formation that is already aware that blackness is a form of appearance of value.[43]

In general terms, blackface can be regarded as the dramatization of the formality of blackness, of blackness *as* form. Simultaneously a channel and a mask, a medium for interracial contact and a message of racial hierarchy, blackface is a highly unstable object. Like the commodity and the slave, it has a dual nature and two bodies. One nature of this body is the product of a process of reification of the thingness of the slave, given a sensorial and aesthetic presence with burnt cork makeup, and the other is an extension of property relations in the cultural sphere. As mask, blackface is also a reflecting mirror where a complex web of social, material, and discursive relations becomes visible — for example, as Eric Lott has influentially argued — the dynamics of love and theft.[44] Furthermore, blackface is a second-degree racial signifier: with blackface makeup, obtained by applying burnt cork on the skin, the epidermal signifier — the phantasmatic index of racial identity — is in turn indexically and iconically signified. The first referent for blackface is not "race," but the epidermality of race. Blackface is an image *of* blackness *as* image of race.[45] In particular, blackface provides a type of social currency, elevating blackness to the function of the money commodity. Finally, blackface flaunts blackness as a signifier of exchange.

The "scene" that first prompted me to begin thinking about blackface as face value is a thought experiment that 1960s standup comedian and civil rights activist Dick Gregory posed as a joke in his first photo book, *From the Back of the Bus* (1962). I read this joke as a metapicture of blackface as face value — as the reification of the hermeneutics of the surface of the money form — a theoretical work that the joke achieves in the way it negotiates its location within and away from the tradition of minstrelsy and in the way it stages a hypothetical scenario of exchangeability between skin pigmentation and its twice-reified and twice-removed signifier; that is, burnt cork.

Dick Gregory came onto the scene in 1961 when he performed before an audience of white Southerners at the Playboy Club in Chicago. He took the stage and opened his routine: "Good evening, ladies and gentlemen. I understand there are a good many Southerners in the room tonight. I know the South very well. *I spent twenty years there one night . . .* "[46] This was the beginning of a brilliant career as an entertainer and later as a civil rights activist, which, among other things, led him to run for president in 1968 as a write-in candidate with the Peace and Freedom Party. His output is extensive — comprising not only live performances as stand-up comedian, lecturer, and activist — but also a number of comedy records, and books of jokes, history, and political analysis.[47] In all these instances, a staple of Gregory's comedy was the way in which he integrated his body into his work, first as part of his comedy routines and later as a tool of protest; for example, in his hunger strikes.[48] This is interesting not only theoretically insofar as it indicates Gregory's strategic employment of his body as a mirror of value, but also historically since Gregory is arguably the first black stand-up comedian who never wore — literally or metaphorically — the minstrel mask. Early on, he expressed his intention to be perceived apart and away from the minstrel tradition as the determination to come across not as a funny *colored man* (that is, a naturally amusing Negro) but rather as a colored *funny man* (that is, an entertainer whose skin happened to be black). He wanted his audience to read him as a provider of an entertainment value — which, in his case, coincided with social criticism — that did not naturally spur from his blackness, but rather from his skills and, in particular, his ability to behold a double vision. This is the pivot I am interested in — a pivot that Gregory employs in a number of jokes and statements but is most succinctly represented in the "burnt-cork" joke: *wouldn't it be a helluva joke if all this was really burnt cork and you people were being tolerant for nuthin'?*

This joke establishes a double "what-if" scenario. On the first part, it claims that it would indeed be ironic to realize that blackness is in fact a man-made signifier, a makeup, a coating that can be removed at will, or a pose, a performance, a game of "pretend," a discursive construction, a floating signifier.[49] Under this discovery, however, Gregory places another, deeper irony, which he communicates through its inverted mirror image: once realized that blackness is socially constructed, we would discover not that white people have been racist for no reason, but rather tolerant for nothing. Gregory's counterfactual is doubly ironic: white privilege, which within the fantasy scenario of the first part of the joke is made irrelevant, is still presented as a burden — the burden of being tolerant.⁵⁰ The joke contains also a double gesture of catachresis: first race's corporeality vanishes under the coating of blackface makeup — the body is disappeared and leaves in its wake a cloud of smoke like in a Méliès film — and then there is the discovery that white people's tolerance too exchanges for nothing in return. Furthermore, these two unequal exchanges exchange unequally among themselves as well: the waste of whites' supposed good feelings is incommensurable against the racist oppression skin pigmentation has historically authorized.

The joke is complicated on a phenomenological level as well. It appears on a two-page spread in Gregory's first photo book.⁵¹ The shifter Gregory employs — "this" — is visualized by a close-up of his face against a black background that comments on the social location of stand-up comedy within the abject space of the nightclub and on blackness as a form of representation of the illicit.⁵² Importantly, it also invites a sensorial engagement with Gregory's body — he is literally surrounded and almost dwarfed by blackness — immediately frustrated by the suggestion that blackness might not be a property of the body but only just a makeup. That there is no "there" there. By saying "this," Gregory is pointing to the blackness of his skin and, by extension, to his body as bearer of that blackness and of its supposed ontological truth. At the same time, the joke, just like the background, puts Gregory's body under erasure by summoning the specter of the minstrel mask as a second-degree signifier and a man-made sign. By evoking burnt cork, Gregory puts a mask over his face: a mask that is phenomenologically tangible, intimate, and carnal because it adheres to the skin. Yet, as soon as the first "what-if" has triggered a sensorial involvement in Gregory's corporeality, the second part of the joke lifts the mask onto what Ralph Ellison described as the "hole" behind it: the fear of the other side of the mask that the white minstrel entertainer experiences, the abyss that opens once one stands in the place of the object rather than the subject.⁵³ Gregory too reverses the chiasm between self and other. First, he channels an embodied response towards the tangibility of his skin color, asking one to see it instead as a disguise, a fabrication, a "what-if?" But then, as the audience is still trying to parse that out, he reroutes the gaze toward them. Now he is discussing an attitude, a type of conduct, and a propensity, *viz.*, tolerance. Thus blackness is both reified in the burnt cork makeup and spectralized in the phantasmatic mask Gregory is able to conjure. Now the minstrel mask hovers over his body, barely lifted, but still there. Gregory has willfully placed his body at the site of the phenomenological chiasm between self and other and then, with a conjuring trick, he has made its tangible corporeality vanish and has replaced it with a specter — at the very least, the possibility of an unmasking. Blackness is thus performatively dislocated from the body as its bearer and placed instead in the space between the visual object and the viewing gaze.

Gregory's joke conjures a scene reminiscent of the Dancing Table because his natural body is made to appear as a sublime body instead. Locating himself in the position of the table, he institutes an abnormal mirror, but twice so as a mirror that is capable of returning an image of the social relations fetishism would otherwise obscure. A conjurer and exorcist at once, Gregory ultimately stages blackness as phantasmagoria, the pre-cinematic device Marx evoked to describe the phantom-like objectivity of commodity fetishism. Instituted in the aftermath of the French Revolution, the phantasmagoria was comprised of a fully darkened room with a magic lantern placed behind a screen so that the screen and the apparatus would be concealed from view; the audience only saw floating images without anchorage in any specific place. This detachment of the visual from the material, this idea of images floating in space with no support and nowhere to land, is what Marx found useful to describe the sublime body of the commodity fetish and what Benjamin relied on to articulate his notion of exhibition value.[54] Otherwise called "ghost show" because it would project images of dead historical figures such as Danton, Robespierre, and others, the phantasmagoria was precariously perched between "science and superstition, Enlightenment and Terror," as Tom Gunning notes, "because it offered an experience in which the senses would contradict what was rationally known to be true."[55] Thus, the phantasmagoria offers a model to think about social materiality. On the one hand, it offers the sedimentation of social constructs onto material (animate and inanimate) bodies and, on the other, the idea that the social can produce effects of materiality. Ultimately, as is the case here, it can be used to characterize an increasingly simulacral ontology of the commodity blackness — the minstrel mask that Gregory manages to conjure with his joke.

In this joke, the question of blackness as commodity form is addressed in a remarkable semiotic complexity. Through this scenario of reversibility between black skin and burnt cork, Gregory substitutes a property of the body with makeup, the expectation of an indexical trace with an iconic effect of resemblance, a bodily script with a performance of identity, a face with a mask, finally suggesting that they might be each other's conditions of pos-

FIGURE 3.2. *Top:* J. S. G. Boggs, *Project: Pittsburgh* (1993). Back of a ten-dollar bill. *Bottom:* Back of an actual U.S. ten-dollar bill. *From Weschler, Lawrence.* Boggs. A Comedy of Values. Chicago: University of Chicago Press, 1999. © jsg boggs 2012. All rights strictly reserved. Studio of jsg boggs: jsgboggs@me.com.

sibility. Otherwise put, it is the act of substitution — seeing/handling one as the other — that carries the bite of Gregory's criticism because it calls attention to how these signifiers function as tokens of exchange and, therefore, to blackness as a vehicle of exchange itself. But what exactly is being exchanged?

Eric Lott proposes the term "counterfeit" as the most appropriate to describe the dialectic between avowal and disavowal in early minstrel acts — an idea that is also descriptive of the relationship between race and value understood as a problem of representation.[56] Unlike real money, counterfeit money is mimetic as well as simulacral. At face value, counterfeit money is indistinguishable from its authentic counterpart. What makes counterfeit money real is its ability to circulate, to perform as if it really was money. The work of Boggs — an artist who has been exploring the social materiality of money for a long time — can offer insights into the question of representation that face value attempts to resolve.[57] He does so by drawing currency of various denominations and from various countries and using his drawings as payment for various services and goods, such as a meal or a cab ride. Boggs never tries to have his money pass for real. On the contrary, when trying to use his drawings to pay for something, Boggs always makes explicit the value of the drawing in terms of the labor expended to produce it, but also the value that he expects will be attributed to it by the transaction, which he arbitrarily determines to be the denomination of the note; that is, its face value (figure 3.2).

Boggs's art is part craft and part performance, and the performative component demands that the Boggs note would be received at face value. When that happens, his drawing has become money. In its mimetic impulse, the Boggs note is a representation of a representation of value but it acquires monetary value when, by an act of will on the part of the recipient, it is exchanged as if it was indeed money. The bills he draws are just catalysts for a transaction he carefully documents that constitutes not only the money but also the actual art object, which is then sold, exhibited, and circulated in the art world. Boggs's art "momentarily slows the mindless frenzy of exchange, forcing us to mind it; and in so doing he forces the age-old monolithic stasis [that is, the money form] to budge and shudder."[58] In fact, the transaction whose traces (receipts, goods, etc.) in turn become a commodity exchanged in the art world is based on an informed agreement of the parties, all aware that they are exchanging a second-order representation of value.[59]

Here is where I find the comparison between Boggs and Gregory helpful: just as Boggs's transactions successfully raise the problem of the referentiality of money, foregrounding that our belief in its intrinsic value is indeed dependent on a social agreement, Gregory's burnt-cork joke challenges the fact that skin pigmentation, understood as the index of race, tends to remain the unchallenged starting point of the signifying chain. And just as Boggs successfully exposes the supplementarity of the sign — that there is no substance, no authenticity, no ontology behind the bill's denomination — Gregory criticizes how blackness continues to be perceived as ontologically grounded rather than the product of a historically specific hermeneutics of face value. The illusion of the transparency of the sign of value is what makes the pigmentation of the skin — just like the pigmentation of the bill — appear to carry value, while in reality it has no referent outside the regime of representation of which it is are a part.

Boggs has been in and out of jail in both Europe and the United States, and repeatedly considered in violation of U.S. law, which prosecutes whomever "makes or executes, in whole or in part, after the *similitude* of any U.S. currency, or makes *likeness* of such currency."[60] However, the more interesting "crime" I want to emphasize is not the production of a likeness of U.S. currency, but rather having made currency of a likeness. Boggs's deeper crime was not his act of mimesis, but rather the exposure of the simulacral and contractual nature of the supposed original and the fact that the work of resemblance can produce ontologizing effects. Gregory's joke achieves the same result, suggesting that it is the fact that blackness functions as currency that makes signifiers of blackness appear "authentically" black. It is the circulation of blackness as a sign of value — as a money form or money commodity — that induces the idea or expectation of its ontological thickness. Blackness, he ultimately suggests, is a vehicle, signifier, and product of exchange.

OPTIC BLACK

A television set occupies the frame. A handwritten note sits on top: "Feed the idiot box." This shot introduces the premiere of *Man Tan: The New Millennium Minstrel Show* in Spike Lee's film *Bamboozled* (2000). Hoping to be fired, television writer Pierre Delacroix, played by Damon Wayans, has scripted an updated minstrel show and is now awaiting the show's premiere. How will it look on TV?

Previously in the film, we have seen the taping of the series pilot — a plantation scene re-created in a TV studio through brightly dressed stereotypical characters — Aunt Jemima, Rastus, Nigger Jim, and more — a cartoonish set, and a cinematography that emphasizes the *mise-en-scene*'s vibrant colors. The TV broadcast begins with a similar visual aesthetic but this time the color palette is rendered through animated characters. As the premiere begins, we see a huge minstrel mouth opening to let out two computer-animated dancing puppets — caricatures of the show's two stars who, along with the production assistant, are watching the broadcast in dismay (figure 3.3).[61]

Then an abrupt aesthetic transition occurs: a cut to two commercials targeted at black audiences: one for an aphrodisiac drink named Da Bomb, and the other for a line of "ghetto" wear designed by Timmi Hillnigger. Both tits- and ass-style hip-hop music videos employ a rhetoric of 125 percent

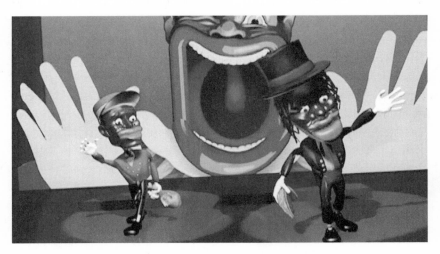

FIGURE 3.3. The *Millennium Minstrel Show* stars as animated puppets, *Bamboozled* (Directed by Spike Lee, 2000, 40 Acres & A Mule Filmworks/New Line Cinema), frame grab.

pure authenticity and of "keeping it real"; so real, Timmi Hillnigger claims in the commercial, "we give you the bullet holes." But now the colors are muted, the images are grainy, and look like low-definition video (figures 3.4 and 3.5). Why this shift?

Bamboozled has enjoyed tremendous critical success. It is a densely theoretical film which has generated a lot of theory in return — most particularly in relation to theories of reification, commodification, exploitation, abjection, racial grotesque, interracial passing, masquerade, questions of authenticity of black representations, stereotyping, and relationships between material culture and race.[62] While this rich scholarship informs my thinking, here the film is discussed only to explore a couple of points. The first is that the film's focus on blackface (which operates in a variety of diegetic, extradiegetic, stylistic, and theoretical ways) demands that we take seriously the film's surfaces. *Bamboozled* deploys blackface as a hermeneutics of the surface and a way to facialize the commodity form. Not only are so many faces and material surfaces black in the film, but, progressively, the film constructs blackness as a face. The second point is that the film's use of blackface offers a way to convey processes of reification of blackness as commodity form. Said otherwise, the function of blackness as that which brings to visibility commodity status — the form — is rendered materially, sensorially, and tangibly

FIGURE 3.4. Da Bomb commercial, *Bamboozled* (Directed by Spike Lee, 2000, 40 Acres & A Mule Filmworks/New Line Cinema), frame grab.

FIGURE 3.5. Timmi Hillnigger commercial, *Bamboozled* (Directed by Spike Lee, 2000, 40 Acres & A Mule Filmworks/New Line Cinema), frame grab.

FIGURE 3.6. The revenge of the Sambo artifacts, *Bamboozled* (Directed by Spike Lee, 2000, 40 Acres & A Mule Filmworks/New Line Cinema), frame grab.

throughout the film. Bill Brown identifies one of the film's great achievements in having recirculated in the same space blackface, stereotypes, and Sambo art, in order to show that their blackness expresses their shared commodity form. Because of the film's success in this expression, blackness appears as a signifier that sits equally on the surface of the body and of commodity culture; blackness is what allows these two realms to swiftly swap their skins.

Bluntly put, through the leverage of blackface, *Bamboozled* argues that the commodity form in contemporary material culture has a face, and that face is black. This is because material culture is still determined by the commodity relations of slavery. *Bamboozled* presents slavery not as a historical phenomenon — a historical event that occurred in the past and has attained its closure — but rather as a historical ontology; that is, an enduring systemic breakdown of the distinction between humans and things.[63] This breakdown is most evident in the racist memorabilia that populate the film because of how they materialize the stereotype, fixating "a demeaning and/or romanticizing racism with the fortitude of solid form."[64] These objects are second-degree stereotypes because their first referent is not the living breathing subject, but the stereotype itself, which they have managed to reify.[65]

To convey this pervasive ontological scandal, Spike Lee stages multiple scenarios of interchangeability between personhood and thingness; for example, by foregrounding the continuity between human movement, mechanical

FIGURE 3.7. The revenge of the Sambo artifacts, *Bamboozled* (Directed by Spike Lee, 2000, 40 Acres & A Mule Filmworks/New Line Cinema), frame grab.

movement, and animation. Manray — the show's talented main star — is an obvious transitional figure in this continuum, as his tap dancing is already capable of evoking proximity between the human and the automaton, especially in his final dance of death, when a barrage of bullets fired by the hip-hop militant group Mau Mau keeps him dancing at a maddening speed. And so is the Jolly Nigger Bank, the cast-iron piggy bank that Delacroix's assistant, Sloan, gives him so that he will remember "a time when black people were considered inferior." In the film's denouement, this object suddenly moves of its own will. Through this revenge of the racist artifacts that populate Pierre Delacroix's office, the film stages "the recollection of the ontological scandal perpetrated by slavery, as the reanimation of the reified black body" (figures 3.6 and 3.7).[66] This reenactment of the breakdown between person and thing, this return of the personhood that had been wiped from the slave in the form of animation of a mechanical object, for Brown, represents the American uncanny.

It is blackface's flickering effect that brings this reapparition to fruition. Not only are many faces metaphorically or literally black in the film, but blackness is also a vehicle of facialization. To gain a "face" — a recognizable site of personhood — even the racist collectibles have to "blacken up."[67] Lee renders this with camera angles and a lighting design that reconstitute, for artifacts already permeated by ontological instability, the personhood that had been robbed from the subjects after which they are supposedly modeled. Shot at a low angle or slightly to the side with an emphasis on their eyes, these artifacts, sitting silent and still in the depth of the visual field, suddenly become beholders of a gaze — an aesthetic strategy of reanimation that the film shares with David Levinthal's photographs of Sambo art, which also hang on the wall of Delacroix's office.[68]

Most of the film is spent coating everything in blackness, creating highly tactile images, and a progressively suffocating *mise-en-scène* in which the characters, and Delacroix in particular, are increasingly dwarfed by, and gradually indistinguishable from, items of material culture. Watching *Bamboozled*, Kara Keeling says, is like wading through a pool of shit. Everything is highly tactile and everything is pitch-black. More precisely, a performance of what W. T. Lhamon would call "optic black"— a pose, an attitude, a gesture that embraces blackness in order to flaunt a refusal to fit. Building on the image of "optic whiteness"— the metaphor of color capital that Ralph Ellison employs in the "Liberty Paint" episode in *Invisible Man* — the idea of "optic black" folds it inside out. It is less concerned with the denied black contribution to the production of whiteness, than with the shift in the location of blackness from the sphere of production to the sphere of exhibition. In optic black, blackness is not invisible, but rather hypervisible, and deliberately so. While Ellison indicts a cultural optics that spectralizes black labor for the production of a white color capital, the notion of optic black, instead, calls attention to the fact that blackness has become a visual signifier which is more valuable the more it is removed from the sphere of production. Blackness severs its connection to black labor, but once liberated from it, it acts instead as currency in the sphere of exchange. With optic black, blackness is on the surface and well on display. "[O]ptic blackness," Lhamon explains, "acknowledges and works through stereotypic effects, usually turning them *inside out*."[69] Optic black is performative and purposely exhibitionist.

"Optic black" describes the overall stance of the film and its ability to mobilize blackface as its own surface, its own projected outside and "in-your-face" blackness. But there are other forms of blackness that concern the surface of the film's images — besides the surfaces of people and things that populate it — in the way their interaction occurs through or produces blackness as an outcome. We see this in the scene in which Delacroix pitches his idea for the *New Millennium Minstrel Show* to his network producer, Dunwitty. At the opening of the scene, the two are sitting across from each other around a long conference table in Dunwitty's office, which is heavily decorated with large photographs of African American sports figures and a variety of pieces of African art (sculptures, masks, and so on). As Delacroix is describing his idea for a minstrel show, Dunwitty becomes increasingly excited. The scene is not shot in the customary shot/reverse-shot structure, but rather by alternating increasingly closer and more rapid profile shots of the two men. The long table standing in between them is progressively forgotten and, with each "call and response," the two men's faces are brought closer and closer to each other. Eventually, Dunwitty climaxes and makes explicit the mounting erotic tension the very idea of minstrelsy has triggered: "You know why I know that I like this? I am getting a boner." A minute later, Manray, one of the show's prospective stars, samples his tap dancing for Dunwitty on that same table. The shot composition with the camera positioned at a low angle from behind Dunwitty's head sitting at one end of the table implies that Manray is performing a lap dance over Dunwitty's erected phallus. Here the minstrel dynamics of love and theft are dramatized through postures and an editing and camera placement that brings the characters together, almost speaking in each other's face. We see them touching through the minstrel mask Delacroix's description has conjured up. Blackness is something in-between them, both the vehicle and the outcome of their erotic dance.

But in the sequence of the show's television premiere something else happens. A blackness that, up to this point, the film had primarily located on the surface of people and things, often as an added layer (the burnt cork makeup the performers are forced to wear, the black coating applied on top of the myriad racist household objects that increasingly populate the screen), changes location in the TV commercials. Blackness is no longer a saturation, but a graininess, obviously and deliberately digitally rendered.[70] Here blackness is a mood, a quality, and a *mise-en-scène*. The suggestion is that blackness pervades and, in fact, enables the language of the advertising image. The very transition between these various aesthetic regimes of the image shows how "the relationship between the projected black image and 'prefilmic blackness' [already and always] problematizes cinema's claims to function as an index of a prefilmic reality."[71] By emphasizing blackness as *mise-en-scène* of desire, *Bamboozled* puts the image at a remove from "the black" and, therefore, exposes a crisis of representation, but one that, Kara Keeling argues, was always already there: blacks never matched their media representations. Therefore, because of its digital aesthetics, the film can help us think through "digitization and film, representation and identity." In dividing these poles so (digitization and representation on one side, and film and identity on the other), Keeling underscores that blackness no longer sutures them together; blackness no longer folds one onto the other. At this point, the film is taking the question of blackface and surfaces directly to bear upon the role of the black body in stabilizing the ontology of the image. In this sense, the film stages a crisis in the photochemical imagination — a crisis it renders through its digital aesthetics and its optic black stance.

In its entirety, the sequence of the show's premiere stages a transition of blackness from the surface of the body to the surface of the commodity object to the grain of the advertising image. This sequence is also a transition between two ontological states of the commodity form of blackness — blackness as an object and blackness as aesthetics, blackness as a thing and blackness as a language (of desire). In the *New Millennium Minstrel Show*, "black" occupies the uncertain border zone between the human and the object: "black" is the animated puppet that, within the system of objects of the film, takes on the same ominous quality of the reanimated black memorabilia. Blackness supposedly abstracted from living bodies and turned into material signifier — burnt cork makeup — equally coats the faces of the entertainers, the puppets made to their likeness, and a host of mass-produced household objects whose function is to perpetuate nostalgically the social relations of slavery. With the TV commercials, instead, the filmic image presses against its surface, thus embracing the conceit of blackface as an aesthetic regime in which blackness functions as signifier of exchange. In the commercials, blackness is both the product and the medium of exchange.[72] It ushers in the aesthetic regime of what Michael Schudson has called "capitalist realism"; that is, the imagination/visualization of a way of experiencing things that supports the material and social relations of capitalism.[73] Advertising, Schudson has argued, is intrinsically self-referential: "it does not represent reality nor does it build a fully fictive world. It exists, instead, on its own plane of reality," one that allows it to fully absorb and thus render completely irrelevant, the question of truth value.[74] Thus, capitalist realism is fully self-contained and self-referential, and, just like the minstrel show, presents itself as mimetic, but it is instead entirely simulacral. Schudson conceptualizes advertising fundamentally as an interface for how (capitalist) social relations romance themselves, whereby the advertising image is the mere vehicle, the temporary embodiment necessary for this romance to take place. But it is also mere sur-face. It is the face that capitalism must provisionally, but also repeatedly, assume in order to interface itself, in order to lovingly caress its own skin. Thus, whereas in *The New Millennium Minstrel Show* blackness offers the face of reification that solidifies the commodified body into an object, in the case of the commercials blackness acts as the face of the signifying system that enables capitalist realism to say "I love you" to itself.

CAPITALIST ROMANCES

In *Bamboozled*'s commercials, the simulacral logic of passing, the frenzy of circulation, is a primary manner in which desire is expressed and articulated. The logic and the real or phantasmatic experience of commodity exchange is what capitalist realism takes as its amorous object. *Bamboozled* shows that this is the capitalist romance that renews itself in the advertising image and blackness is a crucial interface for this romance to take place.

The work of artist Hank Willis Thomas claims a similar place for blackness, as a signifier of the desire for/of capitalist exchange. Willis Thomas's primary medium is photography and his main aesthetic mode is that of creating works that are, at face value, indistinguishable from advertising images. His photographs are deliberately crafted to reproduce both the aesthetics and the intermediate ontological plane of capitalist realism, slipping in and around our consciousness just as advertising does, so that their commonplace appearance "gives them the kind of legitimacy accorded to things existing in the natural world."[75] This means that his works' ontological claim to the real is dependent both on their ability to camouflage as actual advertising, and on sharing advertising's cumulative effect — the insistence with which it clutters our visual landscape.[76] Yet, by engaging with the surface of the language of advertising — by taking advertising at its face value — Willis Thomas's works transform their self-referentiality into reflexivity: they do not just look like ads, or refer back to them, but they also manage to hold up a mirror to the property structure that underlies capitalism itself. This is a fundamentally Benjaminian move, if we recall Benjamin's characterization of the prostitute as the site in which the commodity celebrates its becoming human, in the attempt "to look itself in the face."[77]

As much as his work has been shown in galleries and museums, Willis Thomas's photographs have often been exhibited in public spaces, such as bus stops, billboards, and kiosks. When they appear in places that are common, shared, or unmarked, rather than institutionally designated, Willis Thomas's works seem to want to go, to some extent, unnoticed. They want to pass. But as they pass, they also call attention to what they pass *through* and *to*. With their quasi-metaphysical stillness they arrest viewers in their tracks just before being dispatched as most advertising is.[78]

Consider the pseudo MasterCard banner Willis Thomas created from a photograph taken at the funeral of his cousin Songha Willis, who was tragically shot in the back of the head outside Club Evolutions in Philadelphia on February 2, 2000 (figure 3.8). Built and publicly hung as a billboard outside the Birmingham Museum of Art in Alabama, this image's deceptive face, fully compliant with the aesthetics of other "priceless" MasterCard ads, encourages a distracted reception, while the superimposed text quietly, but sternly, demands that the viewer conjures up the horrible loss that lies beneath it and face advertising's cynical computation of value. This computation of value lays at the beginning of the Long Twentieth Century, the cycle of capital accumulation begun with the slave trade which — in augmented, self-reflexive, and increasingly speculative form — continues to this day. By camouflaging the work as a MasterCard ad, Willis Thomas's *Priceless* (2004) seeks to counteract this monetarization of human life by exhibiting, as its blind corner, the historical roots of the "speculative matter" of race.

The MasterCard "priceless" ads proceed as a series of computations that accumulate to finally climax in the mention of an item that is considered beyond the just reiterated logic of exchange and labeled "priceless." They are a mounting love, a vain promise of an orgasmic fullness that the advertising image is supposed to deliver. Ironically, even though purportedly detached from monetary value, it is this final image, and hence the visual itself, that is unintentionally posited as the ultimate token of exchange and surface for romance. Hank Willis Thomas's *Priceless*, instead, refuses to deliver such fulfillment and constructs its visual field in the opposite direction, as an implosion. It counteracts the ads' exhibitionism with a scene that withholds closure, resists romance, and ultimately stages the unexchangeable object as a nonvisualizable and nondisplayable blind corner. Thus, it turns the advertising visual field inside out, and it gestures toward the irrepresentable scene of exchange sitting at the heart of modern visuality, where the exchangeability of the slave gives rise to the money form of the social sphere. Consider this: the paper trail of the *Zong* trial, as well as its logbook, contains nothing that

FIGURE 3.8. Hank Willis Thomas, *Priceless,* 2004, Lambda photograph, 48× 60 in. HWT05.006. Courtesy of the artist and Jack Shainman Gallery, New York.

can bring the traded men, women, and children to visibility.[79] Only their movement can be beheld — their coerced transportation, the transactions they made possible, and their conversion into money. Hank Willis Thomas's *Priceless* presents the viewer with a similar impasse: it demands a gaze that is willing to be arrested by the recognition of its own failure to restore what has not left a computable trace. Thus, it functions as a metapicture of the Long Twentieth Century's abstractive logic of exchange.

Like Dick Gregory, Willis Thomas too can be regarded as both a conjurer and an exorcist, performing acts of aesthetic and ontological camouflage, which begin with the name of the series of works that brought him to the attention of the art world. The series is called B®ANDED — a name that announces the intended exploration of the intimate relationship between commodity form and race through an effect of *différance.* The name suggests how subtle displacements of the signifier can open up the possibility to explore the work of race as a work of writing, the inscription of a visual order onto the body — a branding — as well as a work of resemblance, the institution of a system of visual equivalences whereby presence is always deferred.[80] Itself branded with the recognizable mark of intellectual property, the series title further evokes the commodity logic lodged within artistic expression. Moreover, the title announces the desire to work from within a given regime of representation by manipulating its surface — its face value, in fact — by problematizing the connection it establishes between face and value: here, made to flicker, with the use of the symbol ®.

I read the B®ANDED series, built predominantly around the dialectic between advertising logos and the visual and material culture of the archives of slavery, in relation to his later UNBRANDED series, in which Willis Thomas digitally removed the captions from print advertisements featuring African American models or directed at black consumers published between 1968 (the year Martin Luther King Jr. was assassinated) and 2008. While the first series focuses on effects of corporealization that the black shares with the commodity, the latter engages more directly with the ontology of the advertising image and its desire to circulate. Stripping these images of their advertising text reveals the underlying work and trajectories of desires. The goal is to show how blackness functions as a language through which capitalist realism enables material relations to be rendered and resolved as visual relations. Considered together, the two series are built on the realization that the visuality of the black body is always already flickering between the human form and the commodity form. With works that pass as, mimic, and share the social ontology of the advertising image, Willis Thomas succeeds in unfolding this flickering by slowing down the rapidity with which the advertising image exchanges. Laboring on resemblances, his acts of camouflage foreground the "iconic" properties of the sign; that is, its exchange value or face value, so that resemblances are not posited as effects of ontological affinities, but rather as their cause.

In the B®ANDED series, the work of resemblance occurs between advertising images and imagery of slavery, segregation, and lynching, thus suggesting an ontological affinity between the two. The key to understand it is in the relationship between location (how can the historically seen object become a viewing subject?) and matter of expression, and, as I use this formalist notion, my intention is to place emphasis on "matter" — that is, on a materialist understanding of artistic expression — but also on a question that postblack art continuously poses: what is the "matter" of race?[81] By plunging the archives of slavery in order to recirculate its early mass-culture artifacts, Hank Willis Thomas creates implosive visual fields that take us back to the matter of race, specifically to the financial revolution as the moment when race acquired what Charles Mills describes as a socially material substance.[82] Willis Thomas's art argues that the matter of race is fundamentally speculative.

The artist makes this point by unearthing not only the archives of Black Atlantic history, but also their system of representation. In *Absolut Power* (2003) he reproduces the *Description of A Slave Ship* (1789) in the shape of an Absolut vodka bottle (figure 3.9). With this gesture he reactivates, from the heart of the commodity object, the logic of computation that presided the *Description*, prepared by the London Committee for the Abolition of the Slave Trade, which combined the real measurements of the slave ship *Brookes* with the customary utilization of its space for cargo in a typical transatlantic voyage. The result, as Marcus Wood has shown, is a visualization of the logic of finance capital in cartographic form, according to the conventions of naval architecture.[83] Yet, despite featuring schematically drawn bodies that are nothing more than placeholders for a projected profit, the *Description* garnered widespread support for the abolitionist cause, because it was read naturalistically, as a portrayal of the actual stacking of slaves on board. Despite the fact that the aesthetic formality of this picture, as Wood calls it, performs the same work of abstraction that finance capital obtains on the living, breathing humans subjected to its logic, its viewership demanded that the miniscule silhouettes be read under the sign of the human. The *Description*, then, is itself caught in the paradox of racial visibility that Willis explores: it carries the expectation that the signs of blackness would be transparent renderings of black bodies and lives, whereas their visuality is the expression of another logic of signification that I take from Michael Kaplan's idea of iconomics.[84]

"Iconomics" is the rhetoric of financial speculation as it is expressed by the stock market index, which measures the status of the system by providing a "picture" of the investors' feelings about it. The market index, claims Kaplan, is an indexical icon. Thus, as a social imaginary, iconomics is a system of simulation whose only referent is the speculation that market participants make about what every other participant speculates. The *Description*, in other words, is an early example of the semiotic and visual short circuit of iconomics — obviously a Long Twentieth Century phenomenon — that, Willis Thomas's work shows, is coextensive with the way race is still looked at. The compulsive naturalistic readings of (culturally determined) signs

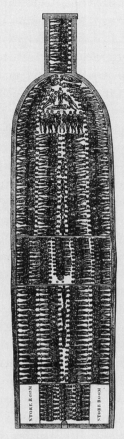

ABSOLUT POWER.

Figure 3.9. Hank Willis Thomas, *Absolut Power*, 2003.
Inkjet print on canvas, 60 × 40 in. HWT05.002. Courtesy of
the artist and Jack Shainman Gallery, New York.

of race, in a twisted logic, is a way to affectively breathe human life into speculative entities, even though race and blackness themselves are nothing other than "figures" of a specific social contract, forms of appearance of (a socially constructed) value. To prevent this type of representational reading, *Absolut Power* provides a flickering effect between the slave ship and the vodka bottle in order to establish a reversible relationship between inside and outside, container and contained, then and now. The ship is both the vessel and the content of commodity exchange; the liquor bottle is both the commodity exchanged for slaves and the means of transportation to their commercial destination.

To be sure, the icon of the slave ship has been extensively reused and repurposed; just consider, as an example, the cover of Bob Marley's album *Survival* (1979). But the specificity of Willis Thomas's deployment relies on locating this icon within the contemporary logic of the advertising image so that the sociohistorical, but also epistemological, roots of its hyperbolic rhetoric are laid bare. Just like the credit system, disrobed in *Priceless*, was built on the abstraction of black humanity, so too the visualization of the slave ship, as figuration of this perverse ontological failure, is brought back to its rhetorical and socioeconomic conditions: it figures absolute power; in fact, the absolute of power, and ontologically so.

Willis Thomas's work engages with the surface of advertising through a compounding of indexicality: through superimposition and layering — branding; by creating flickering images, which, as it is the case in *Absolut Power*, have the visuality of an X-ray image, simultaneously from the inside and out; and by disrobing existing ads. We also see this indexicality in *Scarred Chest* (figure 3.10).

In the UNBRANDED series, instead, advertising images are defaced. The images reach a new stillness while also appearing unprotected and uncovered. They exist in tension with the idea of the brand. Whereas the advertising image is evanescent and unanchored, the brand functions instead as a center of corporeal density, a site of stabilization of the frenzy of circulation, but also a form of embodiment that competes with the embodiment of race. As Rosemary Coombe states, the brand is a "second skin" that products develop in order to interface their consumers. She notes how with the rise of mass consumption, trademarks and logos offered a promise of bodily contact for the unmarked and disembodied bourgeois subject that sought to experience corporeality through consumption.[85] Through its own prosthetic body, the brand could safely offer a little taste of the Other.[86] More deeply, if the slave is an embodied commodity, a commodity in corporeal form, the brand is the result of anthropomorphization of the commodity. Branding functions in opposite ways in these two cases: while a mark of ownership reduces the slave into thingness, for the commodity branding is a site of personification. Finally, because it is the locus of consumer attachment, the brand is a visual object and an emotion, and as Sara Ahmed explains, emotions are forms through which social interactions shape bodies by producing their surfaces.[87]

Willis Thomas's *Branded Head* literalizes the role of racial embodiment in the commodity romance (figure 3.11). The Nike "swoosh" "branded" (in scare quotes, the meaning of which is discussed in chapter 4) on the model's head conveys also the physical intimacy between blackness and commodity status as it refers back to the practice of branding slaves and popular abolitionist images such as *The Scourged Back* (figure 3.12), as well as the opening image to this chapter.

By repurposing that image, Willis Thomas shows blackness and commodity culture as two orders of inscription onto the body, as *impressions* of a sociomaterial arrangement, not intrinsic properties of the object. Thus the brand is a surface, but also a pivot, the site of a nonreciprocal chiasm between personhood and thingness. As a site of personification, branding performs the outlining of a *face*. The brand, in other words, facializes the commodity and, with a Benjaminian move, it can also be conceived as a vantage point, as a place where capitalist realism can see itself in the face.

I save for the next chapter a more in-depth consideration of how *Branded Head* engages with the ontology of the photographic image because that discussion offers a way to discuss the notion of the Long Photographic Century as the passage of the image through race and capital. Here instead, I am more interested in what Hank Willis Thomas's work can tell us about blackness as commodity form, as principle of visibility of commodity status. As discussed in relation to the branded forehead of the dark-skinned slave in *Emancipated Slaves*, the subject's race appears constructed by the branding of the brand just as strongly as by the blackness of the skin. In *Branded Head* it is the commodity form that takes the semblance of the index: it brands, it acquires its own corporeality, and, acting like a second skin, it becomes face value.

In Willis Thomas's work the "brand" is also a meeting point between the panoptic and disciplinary dimensions of plantation life, and (its updated ver-

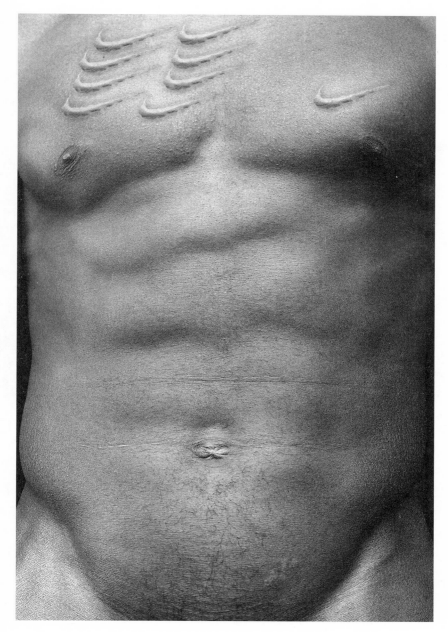

FIGURE 3.10. Hank Willis Thomas, *Scarred Chest, Edition 1 of 3, with 1 AP*, 2003. Lambda photograph, 60 × 40 in., 61 × 40 ¼ in. HWT05.008. Courtesy of the artist and Jack Shainman Gallery, New York.

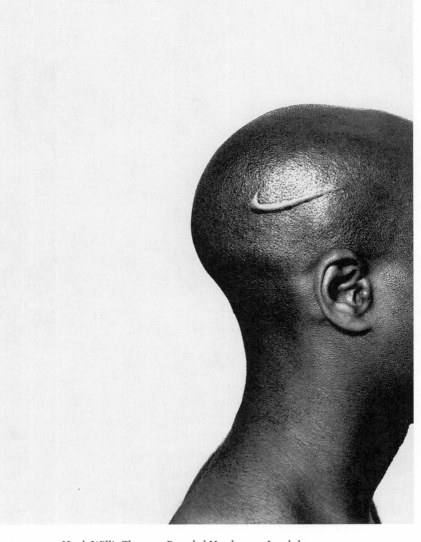

FIGURE 3.11. Hank Willis Thomas, *Branded Head*, 2003. Lambda photograph, 40 × 30 in. HWT05.001. Courtesy of the artist and Jack Shainman Gallery, New York.

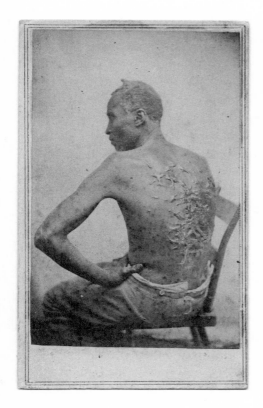

FIGURE 3.12. McPherson
& Oliver (attributed).
The Scourged Back, 1863.
International Center of
Photography, Purchase, with
funds provided by the ICP
Acquisitions Committee, 2003.

sion) the contemporary role of blackness in consumer culture. So when Willis
Thomas mimics, or signifies on, highly recognizable commercial logos such
as Nike, Timberland, or the NBA, he explodes them into scenes of subjection,
hybridity, and racial violence. For instance, in *Jordan and Johnnie Walker in
Timberland circa 1923* (2004) the NBA silhouette hangs from the Timberland
tree while the Johnnie Walker logo, with its back at the lynching, walks away
from the scene. Other times, Willis Thomas reanimates the logo, bringing it
back to its supposed naturalistic origin as the sign of the corporeality of the
Other. In *Shooting Stars*, which addresses the issue of black-on-black crime,
one NBA-branded Michael Jordan silhouette holding a gun chases another
whose profile has been supplemented by a racially explicit hairdo.

While the *B®ANDED* series focuses on effects of corporealization that the
black shares with the commodity, Willis Thomas's *UNBRANDED* series engages
more directly with the place of blackness within the ontology of the advertising image and its desire to circulate. For this series, Willis Thomas collected

a number of print advertisements from 1968 to 2008 that featured African American models or were directed at black consumers, and he digitally removed their caption. Thus, the UNBRANDED series further superficializes a language that is already entirely focused on its outer appearance and has no referent outside of its own economy of desire. Without captions anchoring them to a specific sales pitch, the images float and freely exchange, speaking only to each other rather than to the consumer product to which they were originally connected. Thus, what comes to the surface is the logic and lure of exchange for which *Priceless* provides the metapicture.

Inoculated within this self-referential and highly mobile field, the black body is aesthetically absorbed within the narcissistic thinness of the advertising tableau, thus bringing to the surface the centrality of blackness in consumer culture's trajectories of desire.[88] Black bodies appear sometimes simply as items within a color palette and other times as part of a wish fulfillment, which always serve as vital ingredients to the reproduction and reaffirmation of a color capital that remains optic white.

For instance, the peacock chair that in the late '60s had become part of the image of black militancy in the famous Huey P. Newton portrait is repurposed by the language of advertising in a way that diffuses the specter of African American takeover and uncovers instead dynamics of desire (figure 3.13). Willis Thomas's excription, in turn, reanimates the titillation that lays hidden within the shock effect of the image of an armed black man. Retitled as *Are You the Right Kind of Woman for It?*, the peacock chair is now the fulcrum of an erotic fantasy staged as a playful and yet daring reversal of a scenario of colonial domination.[89] Clad in colonial attire, shiny black boots, cigar in mouth, an African American model sits in the chair with two white women at his side and a tropical-fruit basket at his feet. The décor echoes the mildly exotic color palette of the fruit in the women's outfits, their sandals, and the flowers they wear in their hair, thus establishing a visual equivalence between the color*ed* man and the color*ful* women. Almost touching each other's hands over the man's crotch, the two women submit to the part of the "(not quite) virgin land" the black colonizer will conquer and possess. As much as unbranding the advertisement foregrounds its disembodied evanescence, the image of the black man with a (literal and metaphorical) gun is not fully etherealized and continues to linger in the erotic associations it has already stirred up.

Willis Thomas's work shows how it has become increasingly difficult to

FIGURE 3.13. Hank Willis Thomas, *Are you the Right Woman for it?*, 1974/2007. LightJet print, 39 × 43 inches. HWT07.003. Courtesy of the artist and Jack Shainman Gallery, New York.

talk about the body, and the black body in particular, in nonfigural terms, in ways that do not make it exchangeable. *Priceless*, for instance, frames the survivors' grief while the mourned body is off-sight, off-frame, and in the coffin. And yet it is still surrounded by the traces of the transactions that that type of body initiates (and is always at the center of), which the work conjures in the viewer equally through the text and through the face of the image, its likeness to other comparable images. But what happens when there is no face to speak of? No face to the body and no face to the object? What happens to the commodity blackness when it can no longer be inter-faced?

Keith Obadike's *Blackness for Sale* is acquiring an important place within contemporary literature on cyberart (figure 3.14).[90] Like *Priceless*, Obadike has created a similar pivot by leveraging the phantasmagoric substance of blackness rather than its carnal phenomenology. He has figured out a way to foreground transactions that blackness can license by camouflaging as a legitimate commercial exchange, an eBay auction of the artist's blackness. In his product description, Obadike draws a very definite distribution of

Keith Obadike's Blackness
Item #1176601036

Black Americana

Fine Art

	Currently	**$152.50**	First bid	**$10.00**
	Quantity	**1**	# of bids	12 (bid history) (with emails)
	Time left	**6 days, 0 hours +**	Location	**Conceptual Landscape**
			Country	**USA/Hartford**
	Started	Aug-8-01 16:08:53 PDT	✉ (mail this auction to a friend)
Bid!	Ends	Aug-18-01 16:08:53 PDT	☐ (request a gift alert)

Bid!

Seller (Rating)   **Obadike**
                  (view comments in seller's Feedback Profile) (view seller's other auctions) (ask seller a question)

High bid   **itsfuntobid**

Watch this item

Payment   Money Order/Cashiers Checks, COD (collect on delivery), Personal Checks
Shipping   Buyer pays actual shipping charges, Will ship to United States and the following regions: Canada

Update item   **Seller:** If this item has received no bids, you may revise it.
                  Seller revised this item before first bid.

Seller assumes all responsibility for listing this item. You should contact the seller to resolve any questions before bidding. Auction currency is U.S. dollars ($) unless otherwise noted.

Description

This heirloom has been in the possession of the seller for twenty-eight years. Mr. Obadike's Blackness has been used primarily in the United States and its functionality outside of the US cannot be guaranteed. Buyer will receive a certificate of authenticity. Benefits and Warnings Benefits: 1. This Blackness may be used for creating black art. 2. This Blackness may be used for writing critical essays or scholarship about other blacks. 3. This Blackness may be used for making jokes about black people and/or laughing at black humor comfortably. (Option#3 may overlap with option#2) 4. This Blackness may be used for accessing some affirmative action benefits. (Limited time offer. May already be prohibited in some areas.) 5. This Blackness may be used for dating a black person without fear of public scrutiny. 6. This Blackness may be used for gaining access to exclusive, "high risk" neighborhoods. 7. This Blackness may be used for securing the right to use the terms 'sista', 'brotha', or 'nigga' in reference to black people. (Be sure to have certificate of authenticity on hand when using option 7). 8. This Blackness may be used for instilling fear. 9. This Blackness may be used to augment the blackness of those already black, especially for purposes of playing 'blacker-than-thou'. 10. This Blackness may be used by blacks as a spare (in case your original Blackness is whupped off you.) Warnings: 1. The Seller does not recommend that this Blackness be used during legal proceedings of any sort. 2. The Seller does not recommend that this Blackness be used while seeking employment. 3. The Seller does not recommend that this Blackness be used in the process of making or selling 'serious' art. 4. The Seller does not recommend that this Blackness be used while shopping or writing a personal check. 5. The Seller does not recommend that this Blackness be used while making intellectual

FIGURE 3.14. Obadike's *Blackness for Sale.* Screen grab.

the sensible, among other things, that the "blackness" he is selling can be used to create black art, but not serious art; it can be used to say the N-word without repercussions, but it is not recommended while seeking justice or employment. It offers "cool," but not fairness. Following the marketplace's rules of engagement allows Obadike to describe the commodity blackness in its contemporary form; that is, as a phantasmatic entity — valued for what it enables, both discursively and socially. Just like damali ayo's *rent-a-negro .com*, a website where it is seemingly possible to rent a well-mannered African American woman, Obadike exposes a number of factors that determine the variable value of blackness and offers to sell not what blackness is, but rather what it does. In both these works, blackness does not preexist the act of exchange; rather, it exists as the manufactured product of a transaction that the works themselves initiate. Consequently, the works expose that racial identity is not lodged in a preexisting essence, but it is rather reconfigured as a number of possible subject positions in response to the art itself.[91] By being openly set forth in the form of a commodity, it offers the best vantage point on the capitalist system as a whole. Blackness, then, emerges as a structuring principle and a language of social relations.

For Jennifer González, "Obadike's project reminds us of the purely phantasmatic nature of this commodity relation to race that takes place in the public sphere of the Internet."[92] That is, a sublime blackness triggers the transaction. Obadike withholds the face (there is nothing to see; no image accompanies his auction except for the text of the auction itself), yet he conjures it up. Its success shows the ability for the specter of value to summon its missing or deferred body — just like Toni Morrison's Maggie, just like the NAACP lynching shadow. Beyond that, *Blackness for Sale* brings to the surface another important sense in which the index speaks to the value of blackness — a value that has become independent from its visual presence. "Many people," claims Obadike, "understand blackness as something that lives in the realm of vision and because there was no photo on the auction page it gave room for some to fantasize about how they would occupy this space."[93] Thus, his goal was to test the value of blackness in a commercial context shared with cookie jars and darkies posters, but by withholding any image and just allowing consumers to fantasize as to what blackness would mean to them. That is, *Blackness for Sale* conjures up scenarios of seduction, but also of social injustice, putting the prospective buyer in the position of having to *flesh out* each of the described transactions. Consider, for instance, the following listed benefits: "5. This Blackness may be used for dating a black person without fear of public scrutiny. 6. This Blackness may be used for gaining access to exclusive, "high risk" neighborhoods." And, among the warnings: "4. The Seller does not recommend that this Blackness be used while shopping or writing a personal check." Throughout this product description, blackness functions within the context of what I earlier defined as "iconomics" — as a performance of the market index. Even though it does not unfold through visual means, Obadike's artwork functions pictorially, as an indexical icon, because it provides a picture of a system that, having to face its own desires, is caught in the act of looking at itself in the face.

As Harry Elam argues, the increased visibility of blackness in contemporary visual and material culture paradoxically attests to a new and dematerialized way in which it functions as an agent of abstraction. Blackness seems to circulate on its own quite apart from black bodies and, consequently, from the history of black people as well. Blackness, he argues, has acquired the status of currency: "blackness functions as something that you can apply, put on, wear, that you use to assuage social anxiety and perceived threat: the desire to be included without the necessity of including black folk."[94] The problem, Elam specifies, is that "it remains exceedingly attractive and possible in this post-black, postsoul age of black cultural traffic to love black cool and not love black people."[95] The fact that blackness can be made "detachable" from black bodies — where it was made to adhere by what had been constructed as its natural, ontological, visuality — can be regarded as an indication of a new phase of development of the commodity form, what I described as *blackness as phantasmagoria*; that is, the stage in which an increasingly simulacral status of the visual develops its own, independent, social materiality. From a space of avisuality nested within the heart of commercial exchange, the space that Hank Willis Thomas's work wears on its sleeve, *Blackness for Sale* illustrates this phantasmagoria by showing how blackness has transitioned from being a bodily index to a market index, from being the signifier of a corporeal property to being the signifier of a speculative ontology, the money form that haunts the social sphere.

FOUR
THE LONG PHOTOGRAPHIC CENTURY

Two look-alike estranged half brothers reconnect at their father's funeral. One, powerful and wealthy (Vincent), is suspected of having killed his father. To escape the criminal investigation, he stages his own death by car accident and engineers a way for his working-class brother, Clay, to occupy the car. The accident, however, is only partially successful and Clay survives, though he is disfigured and suffers from amnesia. A tabula rasa inside and out, he is sutured back together physically by the appropriately named plastic surgeon Renée Descartes, who reconstructs his image by studying photographs and footage of Vincent, and psychologically by psychiatrist Dr. Max Shinoda. Through this process he is made to take on the identity of Vincent.

This is the premise of Scott McGehee and David Siegel's 1993 film *Suture*, a film about a case of mistaken identity between two characters who are diegetically treated as if visually identical, but are played by a white and by a black actor: Michael Harris (Vincent) and Dennis Haysbert (Clay). Shot in black and white, the film presents a relentlessly polarized visual scheme to offer the spectator a visual difference between the two characters that, however, the film's diegesis disavows: nobody in the film appears to realize that the two half brothers look nothing alike. Furthermore, as only the spectators can see, the "suturing" process undertaken to restore Vincent's image and identity is actually taking place on the body and in the memory of Clay. In turn, Clay exists only in representations of his brother.

The film, as Kaplana Sheshadri-Crooks observes, stages the écart between seeing and saying of Magritte's La Trahison des images —"this is not a pipe"— because it demands that the spectator imagines a visual equivalence between the two actors that the image does not provide.[1] It also obviously disrupts the suturing process as understood within Lacanian-inflected film theory as a film's ability to stitch the spectator to its placeholder in the text. The diegesis is color-blind, but the images are not. Thus "race" appears in this film as a series of visual codes polarized as black and white, which, in Saussurian fashion, create a system of equivalences and differences without positive terms. Building also on high-contrast black-and-white cinematography, the film uses racial embodiment to create a visual grid in which bodies do not matter, only their color does. At the same time, the discrepancy between a color-blind diegesis and color-coded images calls attention to the film's own photographic skin as raced.

My reading of Suture begins with the observation that if the film can use the epidermal signifier merely as a signifier of "difference" this is because this coding has been fully naturalized. By visualizing difference so, through black skin, the film relies on the surface of the body as its most effective location. But why is that so? What kind of visual culture, scopic regimes, logics of seeing, and archival structures are needed for that to be the case? What are the epistemological, but also disciplinary, formations that sustain this mapping of the visual field? On what ground do these two visually distinct bodies exchange as identical? And, ultimately, what can this film's use of "black" and "white" teach us about what we think images are?

The need to begin to answer these and similar questions is what initially prompted me to seek a framework large enough and specific enough to comprise a history of deployment of "black" and "white" as visual forms — a framework Suture relies on and so effectively recapitulates. In chapter 3 I argued that this framework becomes available once we see how blackness gets bolted to the history of capital, which I have labeled the Long Photographic Century. I have also described the way the photochemical imagination is the product of the passage of the image through race and capital as the ability for both race and photography to function as the "money of the real," not only as systems of equivalences but also systems of surfaces that reify the mediation they are supposed to provide. In this chapter I focus more directly on the visuality of this phenomenon. The objects analyzed here show how the image state of photography offered the dominant mode of the visuality of capital, a generalization, in the visual sphere, of capital's hermeneutics of the surface. They also indicate that this hermeneutics overrides the digital divide. Whereas in chapter 3 I was mostly concerned with the way in which capital generalizes a hermeneutics of the surface rehearsed (applied, extended, perfected) in the understanding of the black body during the Long Twentieth Century, this chapter focuses more strongly on objects that recapitulate the history of visuality produced by the bolting of race to capital. They do so sometimes by entering in relation with the money form of the visual sphere and other times by concentrating more specifically on the relationship between photographic visuality and the hermeneutics and phenomenology of the black body.

As has already been suggested, the photochemical imagination can be seen to express two main impulses: on the one hand, the experience of photographic connection as a form of racial embodiment and, on the other, the possibility for the photographic image to exchange on its surface. In *Suture* these two poles are formally rendered by the film's attention to Clay's flesh, and by the film's attempt to render Dennis Haysbert's body as if its blackness was wholly detached from it; that is, as a silhouette.

To reflect on the black surface this film attempts to project, I turn to silhouette artist Kara Walker, arguably the most controversial African American artist alive. The target of several attacks by fellow artists, scholars, and the general public for the obscenity of her imagery and the alleged reviving of deep-seated racial stereotypes, Kara Walker's work seems at the same time to be an indispensable talking point in a good amount of scholarship on race and visual culture.[2] For many scholars, Kara Walker has succeeded where no other contemporary artist has in initiating a conversation about the resilience of the historical ontology of slavery and its still-privileged position at the core of the American uncanny.[3] I agree with this assessment and yet also take a slightly different approach. For me, a great part of the radical impetus, but also the difficulty in the reception of her work, stems from the reflection on the ontology of the image that her use of the archaic pre-photographic form of the silhouette in a post-cinematic moment affords. In turn, her ontological inquiry is only possible if considered against the backdrop of the *longue durée* in the history of visuality described by the Long Photographic Century. Her silhouettes synthetize a history of the photochemical imagination we are still coming to terms with — one that recognizes how the stabilization of a specific relationship between surface and depth has occurred through the mediation of the black body.

Suture and Kara Walker's silhouettes work on the surface in similar ways, primarily by detaching it from the (expected) body behind it. Thus they invite what Stephen Best and Sharon Marcus recently called "surface readings," where the surface stands on its own as that which is openly given to the senses and it is no longer what we look *through*, but rather what we look *at*.[4] They do so by deploying the possibility for blackness to perform as the money of the real, to live on its surface. Not only do they traffic in blackness, but their blackness is all surface. This does not imply that bodies are no longer important or have no stakes in the matter. But, in putting the visual signification of race at a remove from the bodies it is supposed to differentiate and administer, they succeed in showing how the language of black and white remains seemingly intact, even when it is supported by nothing behind it. Said otherwise, they employ blackness and whiteness as simultaneously flickering and floating signifiers — flickering like duck-rabbit optical illusions, so that they bring to the fore that seeing is always seeing *as*; and "floating" in the way in which they render the surface intransitive, distant, detached.

Finally, the Long Photographic Century is also what connects the NAACP lynching photograph and the digital scar/brand in Hank Willis Thomas's *Branded Head*. Both display a case of layering — a shadow superimposed in the printing process to an existing photographic picture in the former and a carnal growth digitally overlaid on top of the photograph of a model's head in the latter. I see them as bookmarking in some respects the long passage of the image through race and capital across the digital divide. And as they do that, they also map it both vertically and horizontally: on the horizontal axis, just like *Suture*, they provide a system of equivalences, a map of the logic of commodity exchange whereby they offer substitute and equivalent signs for race (for instance, the blackness of the shadow in the first case and the branding of the brand, in the second). On the vertical axis, the layered structure of the image replicates, while it also complicates, the racialized structure of the photographic body. Even though the images are fleshed out, the interplay between these layers never yields a clearly identifiable skin.

RACIAL GESTALT

Kalpana Seshadri-Crooks reads *Suture* alongside Toni Morrison's "Recitatif" as texts that achieve similar effects of "symbolic passing." She regards *Suture* as the unwritable text *par excellence* and "Recitatif" as the unfilmable text. I too see these two texts as closely, possibly chiasmatically, related. Both build upon the desire for a visually present black body to deliver unfettered access to a sociological world behind it. Both display the desire for race to represent difference. However, one withholds sight of the body and makes its black/white designation undecidable, while the other withholds "reality" to the black body we see. Leveraging a body that is *Intractably* present (Intractable because of the "reality" of the profilmic, not because it connects to the "historical" world of the diegesis where the character's racial difference is instead unacknowledged), and yet representationally absent, the film explores the possibility for the black body to unhinge seeing from saying. Ultimately, in *Suture* the body's hypervisibility faces its vanishing in the fictional world.

Suture is an essay film conversant with classical film theory, but also firmly located within a neo-noir cinematic style.[5] Alongside the expressionistic reliance on the *mise-en-scène* to convey interior states, the erudite citation of psychoanalytic discourse and some of its visual tropes (oneiric *mise-en-scène*, surrealist dream sequences reminiscent of the Dalì-Hitchcock collaboration in *Spellbound*, for example), the high-contrast cinematography entertains a direct dialogue with the racialized aesthetics of film noir — emphasized by scholars such as Manthia Diawara, Eric Lott, and Dan Flory, among others — a visual style that translates the "racial unconscious" of the genre in elements of the cinematography and the *mise-en-scène* as a chromatic play of darkness and light, blackness and whiteness. Thus, at the generic level, race already inhabits the film.[6] This fact, however, is not clearly acknowledged by the film. On the contrary, the film appears to want to live on its surface. From the beginning, it is visually polarized. The film opens proleptically, anticipating a decisive event that will occur later in the narrative: Vincent breaks into his own mansion now occupied by Clay in order to finally kill him. Formally, the sequence establishes a crucial visual and chromatic symmetry sustained for the remainder of the film: a close-up of a hand picking up a rifle is matched to the close-up of another hand carrying a gun, with both props commanding the camera movement in proper Hitchcockian fashion; a white man dressed in black is crosscut to a black man clad in white pajama pants and undershirt, shot against an optic white background. This rhyming editing structure finally leads to a perfectly vertical and emphatically polarized two-shot which concludes with an explosion and a quick fade to black (figure 4.1).

Flattened against a mottled background, the actor's bodies are employed as pure chromatic poles to visualize a split identity. The image creates instability between foreground and background, thus challenging what Brian Price summarizes as "the priority of line (or drawing) over color, and the enforced integration of figure and ground in realist production, and in Western optics more generally."[7] Both bodies lose their thickness, their fleshed out presence.

Psychologist Max Shinoda's voice-over superimposed to this sequence presents the concept of identity as a stable core, an uninterrupted connection with one's past, a form of permanence guaranteed by the presence of self-schemata; that is, structures of knowledge that have the ability to assure continuity between the present, the past, and the future. He says:

> "How is it that we know who we are?" . . . However confused we might be
> about any other particulars of our existence, we always know that it is us,
> that we are now who we have always been. We never wake up and wonder,
> "Who am I?" Because the knowledge of who we are is mediated by what
> we, doctors of the mind, call our self-schemata: the richest and most stable
> and most complex structures we have. These are the structures that connect
> to our past and allow us to imagine our future. To lose these connections
> would be a sign of pathology, a pathology called amnesia . . .

Gesturing to the film's function as an archive of photographic visuality, the voice-over presents identity in historicist term: a stable core, an uninterrupted connection with one's past. It argues that identity is a form of permanence guaranteed by the presence of schemata; that is, structures of knowledge that have the ability to assure continuity between the present, the past, and the future. Identity is conceptualized as stability and as dependent on a historical continuum. As the film unfolds, however, we realize that what is being

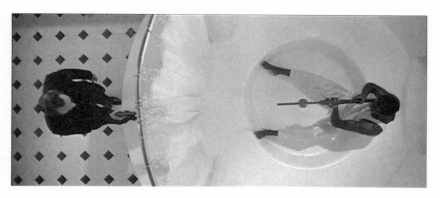

FIGURE 4.1. Racial gestalt, *Suture* (Directed by Scott McGehee,
David Siegel, 1993, Kino Korsakoff), frame grab.

discussed and threatened is not merely the core of the person, but also the
concept of the identical, and its complementary pole, the idea of difference.
Suture undertakes a characteristically modernist agenda — to wreck a crisis
in the unity of the subject by attacking identity through the notion of the
identical.

The opening voice-over also indicates how *Suture* speaks, among other
things, of history and historiography through a unique use of the epidermal
signifier of race. Unintentionally, then, the film embodies the Long Photographic Century; that is, it sutures together the structure of embodiment and
forms of appearance of value of the Long Twentieth Century on and over its
photographic body and the body of a black actor. It does so by employing a
split model of subjectivity in which exterior appearances are read as surface
signs of an interior essence, which is in turn the result of a suturing process
between the technologies of vision of photography and cinema, and the
nineteenth-century eugenic project of the social sciences responsible for the
characteristic codification of racial difference as a visual fact.[8]

Suture's filmmakers claimed to have been driven by the desire to explore
questions of identity (understood as subjectivity) and difference and to have
chosen for this reason to use "color-blind casting," a disclaimer that is necessary only when color is so conspicuously at stake.[9] What we are forced
to appreciate, though, is that the film utilizes the epidermal signifier as a
self-evident signifier of difference. Clay's blackness, above and beyond the
audience's knowledge that he is the wrong man, demands that they respond to

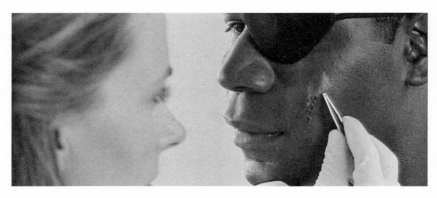

FIGURE 4.2. Physiognomic thinking, *Suture* (Directed by Scott McGehee, David Siegel, 1993, Kino Korsakoff), frame grab.

the film's images from a position of color blindness. The film thus unsutures its spectator, who is constantly forced to imagine a visual identity between the two characters that the film does not provide. The effect of this discrepancy between the visual and the diegetic, between the face of the image and what might lie behind it, is particularly evident in the scene where surgeon Descartes removes stitches from Clay's face while he confesses to her his fear of having indeed killed his father. In trying to assure the person whom she believes to be Vincent of his innocence in his father's death, Descartes voices the language and the epistemology of indexicality of physiognomic thinking, thus mapping onto Clay's body the indexes of an interior essence. "Vincent . . . you have far too elegant a nose to have shot someone. You have what they call a Greco-Roman nose: sleek, with a small prominence at the bridging point. Physiognomists were sure that people with Greco-Roman noses were inclined towards music, literature, and the arts. Definitely not deviant behavior like killing people," she tells him as the camera is fixed on their close-up and her action commands the viewer's haptic engagement with Clay's flesh (figure 4.2). She continues, "You have a crisp, angular jaw: a sign of patience and refinement. And your fine straight hair — almost always a sign of good mental temperament, not to mention digestion. And your mouth: thin, smooth lips, slightly open. Lips that are sign of an affectionate, kind-hearted and generous person."

In appealing to physiognomy and its underlying assumption of a correspondence between appearance, character traits, and moral values, she argues that exteriority (contradicted by the image) adequately reflects interiority, and that classical beauty is a certain index of moral good. Ironically, as she attributes Clay's moral traits to the person whom she thinks is (and the body she describes as) Vincent, she is also folding the physiognomic mapping of the visual field inside out: we see (even though she obviously does not) that the actor embodying Clay does not have the nose or forehead that prompted her reading. The character, however, does possess the moral traits that she has attributed to the nose and the forehead of the actor embodying Vincent. This sequence therefore effectively detaches bodily racial signifiers from their reference to a moral universe behind them, whereby they operate instead as pure signifiers of value. Furthermore, not only are spectators expected to somehow imagine a supra-racial visual identity between Vincent and Clay, but, because of the relentless chromatic polarization of the image in a stark black-and-white cinematography and the sustained dichotomic *mise-en-scène*, color blindness is also a position that the image emphatically contradicts.

It is in this effort to construct a (racially) zero-degree (mental) image that the film resonates with a properly modernist inquiry into signification; that, as Seshadri-Crooks argues, it stages the *écart* of Magritte's painting: this is not a pipe. Just like, in Foucault's reading, *La Trahison des images* refutes resemblance in favor of similitude — that is, it rejects the presupposition of a referent and champions instead a chain of similarities in the simulacrum — this sequence exposes the simulacral nature of the epidermal signifier. *Suture* is both dependent on, and critical of, a racialized map of the visual, which it engages through a visual conceit that simultaneously mobilizes resemblance and dissemblance. "In the domain of film," writes Marcie Frank, "the problem of looking alike is often presented as the problem of being alike, for film techniques can create resemblances where none exists."[10] Her claim refers to David Cronenberg's *Dead Ringers* (1988), but it is relevant here to appreciate the wedge that *Suture* places in between the body as bearer of race and its color as mere signifier of difference. By casting actors who do not look alike as characters who do, the film embraces dissemblance as a way to expose the simulacral roots of resemblance.

Furthermore, the way in which the film flattens the image into a polarized visual grid is reminiscent of other modernist artistic experimentations with the possibility of opening a wedge between the surface chromatic coding of race and race as a lived in the body and as performative identity. Because of its abstract quality and modernist potential, during the Harlem Renaissance the silhouette became a privileged form of expression of the new Negro. I am thinking specifically about two prominent artists during the Harlem

Renaissance who employed silhouettes in order to experiment with ways to signify the African American body while bypassing its epidermality and its confinement within overdetermined ethnographic representations. For instance, even though he had been schooled in the tradition of the ethnographic portraits of Winold Reiss, Aaron Douglas's silhouettes are not modeled after ethnographically defined bodies but after art styles: the posture is inspired by Egyptian art, the slit eyes by African masks, and their graphic qualities by art deco. In addition, Douglas's distinctive use of rays of light to create multiple planes in the image is stylistically reminiscent of cubism but performs a rather different function — that of elevating the image to a metaphysical space where various historical temporalities and geographical and social spaces freely coexist. Douglas's use of silhouettes allows him to figure African Americans without portraying them, and therefore express African American contributions to the making of Western modernity as cultural and historical forces.[11]

Richard Bruce Nugent's lexicon in *Drawings for Mulattoes* also gestures toward the primitivist inclinations of modernism insofar as he models his rendering of physiognomic traits not after the scientific paradigm but rather after African masks (figure 4.3). But, importantly, he effects an ironic reversal of the chromatic codes of racial identity — the African mask on the left is white and the Caucasian profile on the right is black — and of their imagined settings: palm trees for the Caucasian side, and icons of urban modernity on the African side. This reversed mapping of color onto race creates a perceptually shifting relationship between foreground and background, thus making the viewer aware of how blackness and whiteness alternate as the conditions of visibility of the figures. It is the *gestalt* of the image that indexes race, not any one of the featured bodies. Nugent's *Drawings* are addressed to mulattoes, the paradigmatic problem citizens, the potentially passing subjects that challenge and disrupt the split model of subjectivity presupposed and reproduced in photographic representation.[12] Yet, rather than celebrating lighter skin tones á la Archibald Motley, Nugent provides a chromatically polarized rendition of the visually ambiguous racial identity of the mulatto.[13] He peels apart, so to speak, what is mingled together in the genetic makeup in order to reclaim blackness and whiteness as symbolic constructs and two coexisting but also performative polarities.[14] But even then we are forced to wonder: what makes the blackness of one profile *the* signifier of racial blackness? How do we eventually see it? What processes, assumptions, interpretive grids, do we have to mobilize in order to attribute

DRAWING FOR MULATTOES—Number 2
By Richard Bruce

FIGURE 4.3. Bruce Nugent, *Drawing for Mulattoes #2*.
From *Ebony and Topaz*, 1928.

a definite racial identity to any one of the formal elements of this work? Nugent's drawings too produce — visually, this time — the same situation of racial unknowing Morrison created in "Recitatif." Blackness and whiteness are here both flickering and floating signifiers.

These examples point to the expressive potentials of a modernist process of color reduction that *Suture* employs as well. In *Suture* too the "blackness" of the character's skin appears in its metaphorical iconicity — as a signifier of exchange rather than an index of racial identity. And yet, can we watch this film as a pure chromatic exercise? Or is not this film in fact exhibiting the naturalization of the Long Twentieth Century process of systematization and universalization of the value of appearances — the process that has turned blackness into a form of appearance of value? The discrepancy between the visual equivalence between the two characters demanded by the diegesis and the spectatorial experience of their visual difference continues to rehearse the "perplexity" of value and the hidden violence of commodity exchange.[15] At the visual level, Vincent's and Clay's bodies do not exchange on equal footing. As we are increasingly given access to Clay's past life through a series of dream sequences and scattered flashbacks, we can appreciate that, refusing to address "race" on the surface of the image, the diegesis marks the difference between the two characters in terms of class.[16]

At the end of the film, just when Clay, who has regained his memory and has realized he is not Vincent, resolves to take full possession of his brother's identity (his house, his clothes, artistic tastes, and position in society), Vincent comes back to kill him. This sequence, which is an extended replay of the proleptic opening discussed earlier, concludes with Clay shooting Vincent in the face, making him unrecognizable in order to complete the suturing process that allows him to assume his brother's identity. This narrative closure, which is criticized in voice-over by Dr. Shinoda, cannot counteract the fact that, at the level of cinematic suture, the film has been offering the viewer an "impossible" stand-in or placeholder, thus threatening the entire suturing process.

IMAGINING THE TABLES TURNED

The fundamental inequality of the characters' visual exchange is best appreciated by focusing on another structuring principle of the film: *Suture* is constructed around the form of the counterfactual, those "if-then statements or contrary-to-fact speculations that constitute both a necessary feature of all literary and legal hermeneutics and a common component of historical and philosophical inquiry."[17] As Stephen Best argues, the counterfactual form seeks causal links by producing a mirrorlike imaginary and inverted equivalent of the actual world. It is a thought experiment that depends on the ability to imagine the tables turned. Because it is so linked to the imagination, the counterfactual is also subjected to the limitations of sympathy, which at times fails to envision an inverted equivalent of the existing world. Importantly, the counterfactual underlies both the doctrine of separate-but-equal and the ideology of color blindness. Specifically, "[c]ounterfactualism provided the doctrine of equal protection with its logical correlate, with that "fuzzy logic" that enabled the courts to imagine a separate-but-equal (alternative and parallel) universe."[18] Counterfactuals, however, represent merely a hypothetical position of equality, because they can only be achieved by ignoring the effect of historical contingencies. I am specifically interested in the fact that the system of sympathy triggered by the counterfactual obeys to (and shares the same limitations of) the principle of exchange characteristic of the commodity form. But so does the visuality of passing.

Plessy vs. Ferguson offers a well-mined case study to understand the shortcomings of counterfactualism and passing. A light-skinned man, Plessy was recruited to challenge the constitutionality of the 1890 Louisiana state Act to Promote the Comfort of Passengers. His attorney, Albion Tourgée, argued that Plessy was being denied the claim to whiteness that his appearance entitled him to enjoy.[19] Amy Robinson has already shown how the logic of passing mirrors of the logic of commodification: "Passing requires a culture in which exchange functions as the primary distributive mechanism." She explains further, "*[o]nly* in the context of a culture of exchange can the commodity rehearse the social logic of passing."[20] In this intricate conjunction between counterfactual imagination and the economy of the visible, produced by both racial passing and commodity exchange, "black" and "white" again function as money of the real.

Tourgée's briefs are located at the initial stages of the discussion of the doctrine of separate-but-equal, but also at the beginning of Jim Crow rule — a legally sanctioned visual and sensorial regime of segregation on the base of color.[21] Tourgée appealed to the court's sympathy but unfortunately, as Amy Robinson shows, his notion of formal equality was tainted by his reliance on visual distributive mechanisms. Consider this argument he makes: "Suppose a member of this court . . . should wake tomorrow with a black skin and curly hair — the two obvious and controlling indications of race — and in traveling through that portion of the country where the "Jim Crow Car" abounds, should be ordered into it by the conductor. It is easy to imagine what would be the result, the indignation, the protests, the assertion of pure Caucasian ancestry."[22] Without challenging the idea of whiteness as precious asset and property, Tourgée argued that separation entails inequality and marks the black race with inferiority.[23] Supreme Court Justice Brown replied that feelings of inferiority are personal and they are not to be regulated by the courts. Thus, "testing the plaintiff's social imaginary, his vision of an alternative present — and finding it wanting — the *Plessy* court confirmed why the current present is the *only* present possible."[24]

I mention this to reiterate the formal equality but intrinsic violence of the logic of commodity exchange especially in the way it extends to the visual sphere and to the bodies that are managed through it. Significantly, in *Suture*, Clay successfully completes Plessy's pass. Only Dr. Shinoda knows that he is not Vincent and describes Clay's pass with the customary language of illegitimate appropriation, claiming, in voice-over, that he is the wrong man, living a wrong life. Furthermore, the film withholds visual equivalence between the characters so that the blackness of Clay's skin is "impressed," so to speak, with the mark of misappropriation. Even though Clay fills Vincent's placeholder and takes possession of his life and resources, actor Dennis Haysbert as Clay does not equally exchange for actor Michael Harris as Vincent. A tension remains between notions of identity understood in relation to the "identical" and identity understood as the sameness that underwrites exchange. The film performs an exchange without mimesis, thus showing how likeness is not a property of the object but rather the necessary vehicle and channel of exchange. Contradicting Tourgée's argument that segregation is an impossible social project because passing subjects demonstrate the difficulty to read racial identity from the body's surface, in *Suture* segregation fails because the characters are color-blind and cannot see difference. Yet, the spectator is put in the position of desiring to see this difference affirmed and hoping that the characters would avow her visual apprehension. Ultimately, by emphasizing its unequal exchange, *Suture* mocks the formal equality of a counterfactual logic and its inability to fully bear upon a racialized distribution of the sensible.

There is no "what-if" that can be imagined or summoned which would deny the photographic evidence of Dennis Haysbert's body as black. The Intractability of the black body goes beyond the burden of analogy of the photographic image — what led Christian Metz to claim that every film shot is already a statement, an assertion (this is a cat . . . this is a pipe . . .) — or the rule of resemblance, whereby, as Foucault says, likeness leads to (the illusion of) reference. The Intractable for blackness doesn't simply mean "this is . . . " but, after Fanon, it means "look!': "look at this!" Hence *Suture* does not so much test the dynamics of disavowal connected to the fetish nature of the imaginary signifier (I know it, but nevertheless . . .)[25] in the sense that we see a black man but we are supposed to imagine a white one, that we see what nobody else sees, that we are made aware that the diegetic world is of a different ontological order as the filmic utterance. This is the type of disavowal that spectators had already experienced with, let's say, Louis Buñuel's *That Obscure Object of Desire* (1977) or in its inverted form with David Cronenberg's *Dead Ringers* (1988). Instead, the disavowal this film requires concerns the willingness to recognize or not a certain presence — the presence of race in the image — by asking the viewer to determine where the truth of the image lies, whether in the seen or in the said, in its depth or its surface. It demands that the viewer ponders whether, and in what circumstances, might the image wear its truth on its sleeve.

LIFE TO THOSE SHADOWS

Kara Walker's silhouettes pose very similar questions. In most of Walker's installations everybody is black.[26] This blackness, however, is not the portrayal of a figure's phenotype, but rather the reified version of their evacuated index. This blackness is the ontological mark of highly unstable images, of an image state that shares photography's indexical and iconic grid but not photography's ability to put us always on the same side of what we see. Furthermore, their blackness functions both as a conjuring tool, because of their capacity to summon a past that is still contemporaneous, and as a receptacle of viewers' affective responses and investments. Walker has created forms that maximize what the viewer brings to them. They seemingly prod their own existence from a state of individual and collective slumber.[27] Thus, Walker has opened a provocative drift in the history of pre- to post-cinematic representations: the question of where her figures come from is just as, if not more, uncomfortable than the question of what they show. The slippage between their origin and their iconography addresses recurring ontological questions within the history and theory of film and visual culture — namely those regarding the "substance" of cinematic shadows and the dialectic between presence and absence within the imaginary signifier — recasting them as inseparable from the racialization of the visual. As John P. Bowles, for instance, argues: "The debate surrounding her art demonstrates the difficulty we have with work that implicates viewers in the perpetuation of whiteness's claim to privilege."[28] The way in which her silhouettes explosively mingle the indexical and the iconic order of signification intervenes in our understanding of the two most influential paradigms for the image: the shadow and the mirror. Furthermore despite — and possibly because of — its stillness, her work provides an extended and uncompromising version of the cinematic screen as the meeting point of projection and reflection. Finally, it shows how the phenomenology of the photographic surface supports itself on the phenomenology of the black body and, therefore, once again how processes of racialization are integral to the very ontology of the photographic image.

With the title "Life to Those Shadows" — a title borrowed from Noel Burch's work on early cinema[29] — I want to describe the ability for Kara Walker's silhouettes to keep in productive tension several strands that compose the Long Photographic Century — for instance that between image and liveness, mimesis and mimicry, mirror and shadow. The life Walker breathes into these forms — a life partly borrowed from the viewer — allows them to recapitulate the Long Photographic Century, to function as "time machines" through different states of the image — photography, cinema, and digital imaging.

Kara Walker's installations are arranged in continuous scenes that reproduce the 360-degree space of pre-cinematic spectacles such as the panorama and the diorama and confront the spectator unflinchingly, with an absolute presence (figure 4.4). From a distance, they expound a composed elegance. Upon closer scrutiny, they reveal not only decisive racial characterizations, but also a commingling of bodies engaged in "unspeakable acts."[30] Her bodies are "living": they defecate, copulate, suck, ejaculate. They are ecstatic and grotesque, often extending beyond their own boundaries and the boundaries of decency. Part of the controversy her work has triggered is fueled by a representational reading of her silhouettes an approach that their ontological status and their ability to act as archival tools within the Long Photographic

FIGURE 4.4. Kara Walker, *Slavery! Slavery! Presenting a* GRAND *and* LIFELIKE *Panoramic Journey into Picturesque Southern Slavery or "Life at 'Ol' Virginny's Hole' (sketches from Plantation Life)" See the Peculiar Institution as never before! All cut from black paper by the able hand of Kara Elizabeth Walker, an Emancipated Negress and leader in her Cause*, 1997. Cut paper on wall, 11 × 85 feet. Installation view: *Kara Walker: My Complement, My Enemy, My Oppressor, My Love*. Hammer Museum, Los Angeles, 2008. Photo: Joshua White. © Kara Walker/Courtesy of Sikkema Jenkins & Co., New York.

Century radically criticize. It is her medium of choice — life-size black cut-paper figures glued onto the gallery walls — rather than her iconography that I believe is responsible for a more profound discomfort her work produces in viewers and critics. To put it differently, her silhouettes are more radical for what they *are* than what they *show*. Against what some of her critics argue, she did not bring those images to life; rather, they were always already there.[31]

I approach Kara Walker as a visual theorist of the Long Photographic Century who makes an important intervention in at least three areas. The first is the ontological question: What are her silhouettes? And how do they relate to other technologies and genres of the Long Photographic Century? Even though the silhouette is a pre-photographic figurative form, I want to think about what it means to use it in a post-cinematic context, understood after Steven Shaviro as a media regime of digitality in which "intensive affective flows," mirrored by and intertwined with "intensive financial flows," are expressive (that is, both symptomatic and productive) of a certain "surfeit of affect,"[32] but also, from an institutional standpoint, as a time where digitalization has further challenged the institutional role of cinema. Second, the substance of her silhouettes, their materiality, their ontological thickness and their phenomenological properties intervene in the question of embodiment evoked in her work through the relationship between two different traditions of representation — bourgeois portraiture and the physiognomic sciences. Third, Walker's silhouettes pose a question about support, which circles back to the ontological question: Where do these figures come from and where are they now? Against their seemingly clear location, firmly glued onto the gallery wall, Walker's silhouettes are fundamentally phantasmagoric: they refuse to land, secure a support and, in doing so, they draw a geography of race relations whereby Otherness is always kept in front and at a distance. Furthermore, Walker's silhouettes invite the (unwilling) viewer's racial commingling by evoking a permeable and unstable photographic membrane, as well as the scene of exchange instituted by the use of the black screen in early cinema.

One of the most pressing questions among interpreters of Walker's work has been how to describe the ontological status of her figures and, therefore, how to cope with their ambiguous indexicality, which in her work assumes novel and important connotations. Indexicality extends from a temporal and existential order of signification (that is, index as the present sign of a past state of affairs; index as the "having-been-there" of the object, index as trace) to a spatial one, which involves both presence and contiguity. In Walker's work, indexicality entails a spatial theory of relations of identity and difference. Simply put: what are we looking at? Silhouettes or shadows? We know they are cut paper, but why then do they feel tethered to some body? This spatial paradox is further complicated by tensions existing along other axes as well; namely, the temporal, the existential, the mimetic. Are her figures dead or alive? Fixed or mobile? Are they inventions or citations? Copies or originals? Reflections or projections? Hence, in Walker's work, indexicality becomes primarily a question of *self* and *other*.

What about Walker's work shocks viewers — besides the visualization of a deep complicity, what Sharpe has called a "monstrous intimacy," in the social relations of slavery, or the multiple violations of the body across race, gender, and age — is the fact that we recognize these figures all too well: at first iconographically and then because they inhabit several representational modes, spaces, and traditions at once. It is the violent collision of the silhouettes' pristine and abstract forms with the carnality evoked by these bodies' behaviors and their compulsive penetrations that manifests the double legacy of Walker's figures — the use of the silhouette within the genre of portraiture and its use by institutions and disciplines for social control.

Walker's silhouettes, Ann Wagner argues, speak an economic language of substitution and erasure insofar as each figure enlists the viewer's complicity in investing the black hole of the body's departure with the sense of the metaphysical presence of a portrait.[33] Within the bourgeois context of portraiture, in fact, the blackness of the silhouette was not racially coded, but rather functioned fetishistically — that is, as Homi Bhabha has influentially argued, also stereotypically — because the sign of a bodily absence was transfigured into a mark of personhood through the affective investment of the viewer.[34] Just like the mythical young woman in Pliny's account had imbued the reified trace of her dead lover with a sense of presence, the blackness of the bourgeois silhouette was filled by sentimental memory and nostalgia. The blackness of the silhouette functioned as both a signifier of emptiness, insofar as it indexed the absence of the body, and of fullness, projected by the lover's desire to see that same blackness as a trace of the body that had cast it — a present sign of a past presence. Within bourgeois portraiture the silhouette was animated by the desire to transform a hole into the possibility of wholeness.

The blackness of the silhouette, however, has a very different valence in the context of the social sciences and specifically physiognomy. Joann Caspar Lavater praised the silhouette's "modesty" and its "'weakness"; that is, its lack of texture and detail, because it made it the most suitable form of representation for physiognomic analysis. It provided an abstract map of the body onto which it was possible to seemingly read, but in reality project, an imagined relationship between its inside and its outside, its outward characteristics and its interior essence. The veracity of the silhouette for Lavater relied in its indexicality while its legibility was provided by its iconicity. The silhouette, he wrote, is "the emptiest but simultaneously . . . the truest and most faithful image that one can give of a person . . . because it is an immediate imprint of nature."[35] Thus, within the paradigm of the social sciences, the blackness of the silhouette can be seen to indicate the writing of nature in two ways: as that which provides the body with a shadow, from which the silhouette is then derived as its reified, durable, and transportable version, and as that which provides race with its epidermal signifier, the blackness of the skin. As a meeting point between mimesis and contiguity, in the context of physiognomic analysis, the blackness of the silhouette becomes a racially overdetermined index through mimicry of the chromatic attributes of certain bodies' skin, and as a signifier of the Other of the body: its indirect presence under the form of the shadow. Another crucial transition between an indexical to an iconic order of signification occurs here: because black is the sign of the silhouette's likeness to the body it indexes, it becomes the "face" of the index as well. Black becomes *the* signifier of likeness, of resemblance as a visual regime: not just an iconic sign, but also a signifier for the iconic. Not just exchangeable, but the signifier of exchange.[36]

This double legacy accounts for the silhouette's overdetermination in relation to the substance it indexes as well: the silhouette is simultaneously carnal and categorical. Carnal because in the social sciences the silhouette is used to map those bodies that do not have access to the disembodied notion of personhood underlying bourgeois subjectivity. Categorical because of its function as a criterion of classification of a subject's position within the Great Chain of Being. The silhouette of the social sciences, in other words, is burdened with the "spectral" presence of the white male normative body, while being filled with the carnality of the racial Other.

This dialectical blackness of the silhouette allows Walker to show not only the imbrication of the paradigm of bourgeois portraiture and that of the social sciences, but also to show them as the recto and verso of the same figure. We see this in the *Untitled* work of figure 4.5. It is a paper cutout where on the left-hand side we can see the profile of a European genteel man, and on the right-hand side a female "primitive" standing back to back with him.[37] With this work, Walker depicts the bourgeois portrait as both materially inseparable and visually indistinguishable from the "shadow archive" of race science. She shows how the silhouette of the social sciences exists in a relationship of contiguity with bourgeois portraiture — indeed as its condition of possibility — as the literal version of what Allan Sekula has metaphorically described as the shadow archive of bourgeois photography; that is, the police records and the eugenist's files. But while Sekula's metaphorical shadow indicates a hidden counterpart, an adversary and yet complementary — enabling —

FIGURE 4.5. Kara Walker, *Untitled*, 1995. Cut paper on paper, 38 × 24 ¼ in., framed. © Kara Walker/Courtesy of Sikkema Jenkins & Co., New York.

position, Walker's archive evokes that and more. In her work the shadow is what sticks to the body as its inalienable Other. Thus, she provides an effective visual counterpart to Homi Bhabha's claim that, in the colonial framework, the representative figure of the Manichean delirium of black and white is the Enlightenment man tethered to the shadow of the colonized man.[38] The self-representation of the colonial man, argues Bhabha, depends upon a staged division between body and soul that underlies the artifice of identity. The native occupies the carnal pole while the Westerner occupies the spiritual one. The tethered shadow of the colonized man offers "the 'Otherness' of the Self inscribed in the perverse palimpsest of colonial identity."[39] At the same time, Walker shows how both traditions of silhouette use meet in the same blackness: the white normative body is always haunted by the remnants of the Other's flesh, precisely because its abstraction is made possible by racial overembodiment.

Walker's work emphasizes the shadow's inalienable contiguity with the body to which it belongs. Each of her figures, in other words, scandalously reveal its own archival position within the history of visuality, hence behaving not only as a visual object but also as scene of constant reversibility between an indexical and an iconic order of signification, as well as a theater of desire suspended between a fullness and a lack. It is in this sense that she recapitulates, by combining them, the two foundational paradigms for the ontology of the image within the visual arts: the shadow and the mirror. We can read in her work the Plinian tradition which understands images indexically — in contiguity with the real, as its cast shadows — and the Platonic tradition conceiving of images iconically, as purely apparent beings, linked to the real by their mirrorlike resemblance. Or, as discussed in chapter 1, we find the understanding of the image as the other of the same or, conversely, as the same in a state of double.[40] What are Walker's figures, then? Are they shadows or reflections? Are they Others or Doubles? And whose other, whose double? Their ambiguous indexical status (was/is a body there? And exactly where?) indicates how Walker's work relentlessly pursues a condition of both/and, which is also an in-betweenness, effectively engaging also the cinema screen, in an expanded and unflinching manner, as the meeting/arresting point between projection and reflection. This condition of both/and, and in-betweenness is present not only because her installations give the impression of a cyclical temporality that has been provisionally suspended, but also because the unclear location of her figures extends the ontological question regarding their substance and origin to the substance and location of their support. Thus, they offer an *entrée* to thinking about race as an epistemology and a phenomenology that *secures* a support.

It is therefore crucial to appreciate the way in which her work engages with the cinematic screen. First, her scenes extend the cinematic screen by freezing it. In her installations, narrative temporality unfolds horizontally within a fully comprehensive and unbroken space, frozen in a perpetually unfolding and continuous image. This layout, shared not only with pre-cinematic de-vices such as the panorama and diorama but with landscape and historical painting as well,[41] presents itself as an alternative archive, a different indexing of history as a layered contemporaneity, as repetition and accumulation. "Too active to seem moribund, and too recognizable to be dismissed as safely part of the past," Ann Wagner contends, Walker's silhouettes, "cross-breed past with present."[42] They function metahistorically as haunting incarnations of racial templates. Not only do her figures act in the present — indexing a past that refuses to pass — but they also confront us directly, thus extending the cinematic screen durationally as well: they are uncompromisingly present and unapologetically in our presence.

Walker's metahistorical analysis — the use of archaic forms within a post-cinematic moment — offers provocative insights into the question of presence that have become urgent again after the digital turn: not only the presence *of* the image, or the presence of the world *in* the image, but also our presence *to* the image. Walker's work intervenes in this conversation by emphasizing that part of the affective investment in indexicality is due to how it secures the observer's location *vis-à-vis* the object of the gaze. In David Rodowick's terms, Walker's silhouettes extend the ontological perplexity that photogra-phy manifests along the temporal axis to the spatial axis as well: her figures double the paradox of temporal perception of photography with the paradox of spatial recognition of optical illusions such as the duck-rabbit figure.[43] Not only do they ask how things absent in time can be present in space, but also how can such different things both be there in the same space. How can her figure be so fleshed out and yet so abstract? So fleshy, and yet so iconic? And, more radically: how can they be both "us" and "Other"?

In order to expose the affective charge that indexicality bears as a spatial theory of representation, Walker creates images before which the viewer cannot claim to know his or her location. Images such as the *Untitled* gauche of figure 4.6 confound because they are unanchored: they seem to exist on both sides of an implied photographic surface. The diegetic source of light in this lynching scene is located behind the bodies. The figures on the left side of the image are white because they are rendered as "hollow-cuts"— silhouettes in which the profile is removed from a white paper, which is then glued on top of a black paper. They are rendered as a void, as if they had been cut out from the thick darkness of the night. On the right side, instead, the moonlight partly blocked and partly filtering through the holes of a charred body indicates that it is present and positioned directly before the viewer. In this case, the silhouette effect is produced by overexposure, by how the body blocks the light thus placing us, at least for this half of the image, in an uncomfortable proximity with it. While the bodies on the left-hand side have vacated their place and have left a void in their wake, the body on the right-hand side is still there, in our presence, in a diegetic space we can imagine as continuing uninterrupted into our viewing space. What this shows is that if the photochemical imagination demands a support, a writing pad onto which light leaves its trace, then it also implicitly determines an unambiguous location for the viewer in relation to the image. It produces and relishes on what Metz described in relation to the cinema screen as the "segregation of the spaces," an idea that in his work expresses the unfulfilled desire of the viewer to join the screen image, and the way in which the physical absence of the objects on screen affects a supplementary "turn of the screw" bolting desire to lack.[44] Walker's work, however, shatters the sense of safety that separation might offer — the knowledge, the wish, the hope that there would be a clearly marked line between "us" and "them." Walker reverses the direction of this desire: the segregation of the space is no longer the trigger but rather the hoped-for fulfillment of this desire. Absence is never entirely such and thus the viewer's location, mastery, and knowledge of what is there and what is not is never fully secured.

The ambiguity and reversibility of Walker's figures and her experiments with both sides of the photographic surface establish a dialogue also with scholarship that highlights the permeability of the early cinema screen and its connection with other phenomenological discourses on the body *as* screen, and specifically the three phenomenologies of the inside coming together in 1895 — cinema, X-ray photography, and psychoanalysis — identified by Akira Lippit and already discussed in chapter 1. The black screen of early cinema is one of the sites of thematization of this permeability.[45] The black screen, argues Trond Lundemo, is a technique of suspension of the indexical

FIGURE 4.6. Kara Walker, *Untitled*, 1998. Gouache on paper, 58 × 101 in., 147.3 × 256.5 cm. © Kara Walker/Courtesy of Sikkema Jenkins & Co., New York.

basis of photographic images in order to introduce an alternative to optical models of vision.[46] Its function might be to conceal montage, or to elicit astonishment, or to open onto an abyss of deep space behind the surface of the image, or to punctuate a narrative change. Sometimes, as in *The Big Swallow* (Williamson, 1901), it marks an exchange between the inside and the outside of the body.[47] Most certainly, as Stephen Best has pointed out in his analysis of *What Happened in the Tunnel* (1903), it functions as a scene of exchange and a locus of reversibility bearing racial implications because of how the screen blackness is equated to the blackness of the substituted diegetic body.[48] Considered in the context of the *Plessy vs. Ferguson* Supreme Court decision handed down six years earlier, the film can also be seen as testing the limitations and the repercussions of the counterfactual imagination underling the separate-but-equal doctrine. In all cases, the blackness of the screen is a space of suspension, penetration, and possible reversals.

Similarly to the permeable black screen of early cinema, Walker's figures act as portals towards a phantasmatic indexical source — the body that would supposedly produce them — as well as towards their "insides." We slide in and out through these bodies, aware that while their blackness is a present sign of the body's absence, it is also the sign of an overdetermined carnality. Like X-ray photographs, their blackness provides a view of the body simultaneously from the inside and out, from the space it has vacated and

FIGURE 4.7. Kara Walker, *Darkytown Rebellion*, 2001. Cut paper and projection on wall, 15 × 33 feet, Installation view: *Kara Walker: My Complement, My Enemy, My Oppressor, My Love.* Walker Art Center, Minneapolis, 2007. Photo: Dave Sweeny. © Kara Walker/Courtesy of Sikkema Jenkins & Co., New York.

from its phenotype.[49] Hence, the discomfort her installations provoke might not derive solely from the actions that these figures are engaged in, but, at least for certain viewers, from the realization of inhabiting a wholly and inescapably racialized space and the experience of being haptically drawn toward inhabiting a raced body. Even the flatness of Walker's figures is highly unstable, hard to pin to the gallery wall. "Casting their own shadows into a [*sic*] incalculable mise-en-abyme behind them," observes Darby English, "these figures can seem to either threaten further advance into viewers' space or retreat from their very points of appearance."[50] With this movement they expand the cinema screen toward its inside, toward its impossible depth, as well as toward the space of the viewer. This effect is amplified in her installations combining paper cutouts with projected light, where the viewers' bodies are directly implicated by their cast shadow onto the work (figure 4.7). These installations heighten the theater of gazes — viewers looking at the work and looking at each other looking — by engineering a way to project onto the work

FIGURE 4.8. Kara Walker, *Testimony: Narrative of a Negress Burdened by Good Intentions,* 2004. Still. 16mm film and video transferred to DVD, black and white, silent; 8:49 min. Edition 1/5. Collection Walker Art Center, Minnea. © Kara Walker/Courtesy of Sikkema Jenkins & Co., New York.

a (however fleeting) trace of those very looks. That trace, the viewer's cast shadow onto the gallery wall, once again calls into question the substance and the liveness of her figures by equalizing them with the viewer's projection.

This sense of double movement is further heightened in Walker's stop-motion puppetry videos (figure 4.8). Here, the question of presence assumes other connotations: not only the foregrounding of the artist's presence by letting her hand appear within the frame while maneuvering her cutouts within a deep space, but also its relationship to cinematic movement and duration; specifically, the fact that the moving image is created by a succession of discrete durational wholes so that, animation offers "a lingering look at an *extended* arrest of movement."[51] Furthermore, the puppets are so flat, so flimsy, and their movements so awkward that they appear as shadows severed from their bodies, running amok, possibly, as Robert Storr suggests, to further underline their status as product of a hysterical white imagination spooked by its own shadow, "by the shadow it conjured out of the presence in its midst of what it mistook for its God-given antithesis."[52] Lest we forget these shadows' displaced connections to living bodies, in a now-expected twist these ghostlike creatures reclaim their carnality and ejaculate toward the viewer and against the screen. The thickness and life of the flesh that Walker's figures initially appeared to have fully abstracted return as bodily fluid traveling through space, connecting, once again, not only the space of the work with the space of the viewer, but the (wet) skin with the (wet) screen.

The fact that, throughout Walker's work, blackness is the meeting point between the screen and the skin suggests that the structural asymmetry between the inside and outside of the body in the last instance reflects the structural asymmetry of race in the field of vision. Background and foreground, positive and negative, mass and space, inside and outside, fullness and void, presence and absence: Kara Walker's work makes the relationship between these poles depend on the interaction between blackness and whiteness as conditions of legibility of images. Yet, unequal ones. Blackness, in fact, is always susceptible of being a signifier of surface as well as of depth — the surface of some-*body* and yet also the marker of a void. By highlighting the phenotype as a screen of projection and reflection, Walker identifies the epidermality of race as a hermeneutics of the surface that predates and supports those developed in the late nineteenth century. If, as Storr asks, "in the Eurocentric tradition blackness has historically been the shadow that whiteness casts, what is the shadow of blackness? . . . a black hole at the core of Western culture?"[53] Or, as David Marriott phrases it: "what is it that haunts: the phenomenal resemblance to an uncanny unlikeness, or the sudden dissemblance in the reflected image, as if one's own specular image had become ghosted in return?"[54] Ultimately, the Long Photographic Century that Kara Walker's silhouettes unfold pivots around the black body as the visual object *par excellence*, where the shadow meets its substance — the black body as the ontological ground of the visual, as the stand-in for a continuing photochemical imagination.

TOUCHING BLACKNESS. AGAIN.

The question of presence — what are we in the presence of? What counts as present? What do we see when we see blackness and what do we touch when we see it? — is crucial to Hank Willis Thomas's work as well, and it characterizes one of the ways in which the NAACP photograph and *Branded Head* can be seen to bookmark the Long Photographic Century, the former from a photochemical standpoint and the latter from a digital one. Yet, they also question the tenability of the idea of a digital divide, given that in both images race makes "photography" perform as the money of the real. In both images race both triggers and mediates an economy of exchange that institutes several equivalent signifiers: it is because of the overwhelmingly racist nature of the practice of lynching that we connect the hanging shadow to an African American body; it is because of slavery's practice of branding the slaves that we can see the Nike "swoosh" in competition with the epidermal signifier of race as another inscription of a visual order onto the body. Thus, these two images prompt larger questions as well: if one of the forms the digital divide has taken is the idea of the severing of the photochemical ties with the profilmic object, then how does blackness fare when it moves across it? What happens to the racial index in digital environments? Or, to bring these questions to bear upon the specific object I want to discuss, what is the ontological thickness of *Branded Head*'s digital scar? The hypothesis I want to pursue is that this digital scar shares some of the social ontology that characterizes race as well, and a materiality that is socially produced and culturally read.[55]

Branded Head (figure 3.11) stands in relation to the NAACP photograph like *Scarred Chest* (figure 3.10) stands in relation to the *Scourged Back* (figure 3.12).

All four images offer a map of the Long Photographic Century by raising a "what-if" question — that is, by introducing the possibility, even though not the actuality, of a counterfactual. In all four it is the visual and ontological instability of what is overlaid on top of the image that raises this question. What if the lynching shadow was projected by a body that is in fact just off-frame, in the same diegetic space as the crowd? What if the Nike "swoosh" was actually tattooed/marked/branded onto the model's flesh? What if the whipping marks were on the surface of the image rather than the surface of the body? All these scenarios share a heightened sense of tactility of the image but also confound the expectation or the confidence in our ability to unequivocally locate race. Through layers that have an uncertain and undecided ontological status, they manage to figure the in-betweenness of race.[56]

The haptic properties of these images are crucial for the argument they make. Because black skin already renders the visible by providing a paradigmatic relationship between visuality and embodiment, the sight of blackness is both pretext and guarantee for a certain effect and affect of corporeality.[57] If, as suggested in my discussion of *Camera Lucida*, blackness works as a hinge between seeing and touching, there is a chance that, at least in these works, blackness might function also as a hinge between a photochemical and a digital imagination. When the image passes through the digital, it "exudes a fantasy of immateriality," whereas the photochemical state is nurtured by the fantasy of the trace. In turn, as mentioned in chapter 1, "what makes it possible to leave traces and to read them is the material continuity, physicality and sensuousness of the world."[58] That is, our feelings about this materiality determine whether the visual, as Laura Marks suggests, acts or not as a connecting tissue.[59] My sense is that Hank Willis Thomas's work builds a site for an encounter between the photochemical and the digital over the body of the black.[60]

Because of the way we ultimately tether it to the body, race proves Brian Massumi's claim that the analog retains experiential priority over the digital, that the analog is always "*a fold ahead*."[61] Race is in the inter-face, and the in-betweenness we recognize *as* a *face* is always analog. The line we draw between the photochemical and the digital is in part the effect of the different haptic engagements triggered by these images. *Branded Head* and even more *Scarred Chest* exist in dialogue with the *Scourged Back*. Yet, compared to that image they raise troubling questions about their materiality. Where is, and what counts as, flesh? And how is it "branded"? The very concept of branding presupposes an embodied support for the brand. Thus, these digital inscriptions lend materiality to the body on which they are applied, which comparatively function as their photochemical support — the more *fleshed out* of the two image states. At the same time, we have to admit this is true only on the plane of face value, a plane that Hank Willis Thomas's work embraces as its critically strategic location. As already discussed, Willis Thomas's works are deliberately constructed to pass as advertisements: they inhabit advertisements' locations — they have been exhibited on billboards, at bus stops, and so on — and they look like it. At the same time, they pass through advertising in the sense that they seemingly occupy, at least momentarily, its same ontological plane. As they do so, regardless of their mode of production, they exist in a state of resemblance, which, as Foucault's reading of Magritte reminds us, is the product of socioculturally constructed grids of discourses and practices.

Alternatively, if we focus on the skin of the image, we can read Willis

Thomas's digital layering as an incision, a material and poetic cut that divides the visual field, disrupting the surface integrity of the black body as black.[62] These works could then be regarded as a critique of a certain photochemical imagination — the way in which photography has supposedly recorded, but also provided substance and currency, to the seeming self-evidence of race. So, on the one hand, the visual integrity of the black body is squarely located within — in fact, it has historically facilitated — a photochemical imagination: the fantasy of the continuous sensuousness of the world just like skin pigmentation is supposedly in continuity with a person's genetic makeup. Yet, on the other hand, Willis Thomas's digital layering calls attention to how the body's surface is constantly formed and redrawn in social interactions. It does not preexist them; rather, it is haptically constituted with each encounter. The digital does not allow any secure surface, at least not in the way in which the black body presents it.

Put bluntly, the black body authorizes the photographic image to act as the surrogate of touch. Here, then, the black body does not so much act as an object of photographic representation, but rather as a stand-in for a lingering photochemical imagination across the digital divide, as a resilient repository of a definite, Intractable, system of signification and a quasi-carnal affective link with the reality that it photographically connects. It thus acts as the phantasmatic locus where the photographic becomes flesh, where it breathes and bleeds. Ultimately, *Branded Head*'s digital scar is fleshed out because it sits on top of a black body, the body that has ultimately fleshed out and stabilized the image state of photography itself.

It would be tempting to claim that the digitality of Willis Thomas's layering expresses race as a social construct — or, even more radically, if we follow Baucom's argument, as the visual epistemology and the visual culture of the current hyperfinancial phase of capitalism — as a speculation. Within this perspective, the photochemical would most strongly express the carnality of race, insofar as the affects associated with it — at least those discussed in Barthes's *Camera Lucida* — depend on the idea of a material continuum connecting the photograph to its object and its viewer. The digital, on the other hand, would be the image state that represents capital's logic of computation. As attractive as this reading might be, I suggest instead that it is the interaction between the digital and the photochemical imaginations that carries the value of the ontological/epistemological argument Willis Thomas undertakes. Consider how Willis Thomas's *Absolut* (figure 4.9)

FIGURE 4.9. Hank Willis Thomas, *Absolut Reality*, 2007. LightJet Print,
66 ¾ × 51 in., framed. HWT07.044.001. Courtesy of the artist and Jack
Shainman Gallery, New York.

mobilizes the digital in order to insert an icon of consumer culture in the body of the image.

Rendered as an organic entity — the man's blood having temporarily and accidentally outlined a consumer icon — the vodka bottle detaches the photographic surface from the visual field behind it. Wet and bloody, the texture of the photograph inoculates the bottle within the Intractable grain of the forensic image, thus offering a counter-scene to Willis Thomas's UNBRANDED series where, instead, the black body was inoculated within the color palette of capitalist realism. Here, the sign of capitalist realism is made to bleed and is therefore weighted down to a much thicker ontological plane — that of the corporeality of race and death. What oozes out of this body is what in *Branded Head* was conspicuously sitting on top. In this image Willis Thomas folds the photographic field onto the outside like a shirt cuff, effectively relocating the black body within: now the photograph possesses a permeable and traversable surface that, like an X-ray image, turns the object and the vantage point of the viewer inside out. The photograph no longer has a clear surface, an obvious skin. Our gaze has no clear stopping point. We are forced to see the inside, the outside, the skin, the blood, and the consumer icon together at all times.

Like Barthes, Willis Thomas too treats photography as an embodied space of habitation: it is a space of confinement for the black body, to be sure, when photography flattens its surface against the body's epidermis redoubling its branding function. But, by rendering the photographic as a field instead of a surface, an affect instead of a sign function, he allows that same body to cut through and reverse the racialized mapping of the visual field. The black body in Willis Thomas's work, enfolded and unfolded so, no longer delivers under the pretense of an umbilical cord the carnal connection that grounds the truth value of images; instead, it provides a socially material connecting tissue for the social bond that we establish and renew with each and every image. The digital brand, scar, and growth, is the reflexive site where we discover that what we are haptically drawn toward is not a natural but rather a socially material object. An object — the black body as black — which both renders and fleshes out the expectations, fears and desires of a continuing photochemical imagination.

CONCLUSION
IN THE SHADOW

I began this book by evoking Toni Morrison's image of the fishbowl and W. J. T. Mitchell's recent argument that race is a medium, which seems to finally bring to the mainstream of visual culture studies the mandate that Morrison launched so long ago. Yet, this book has offered a way to reach another question that lies underneath the ability for race to act as a medium; namely, the idea that race has perfected a theory of the ontology of the image with which we still wrestle. It is hard to let go of certain images due to the comfort they bring with their fullness and the trustworthiness they inspire with their seemingly incontrovertible indexicality. The photochemically fixated black body is one such image, both cause and product of a visual fold whereby truth, value, and meaning can be secured by, and be read on, the surface. Because of this fold, the black body has and continues to fuel a photochemical imagination that lingers even in our prevalently digital environment.

Put more bluntly, *seen through race*, the affects surrounding the photo-chemical imagination, which in recent film and new media theory have coalesced again around the question of indexicality, suggest that under the umbrella of semiotics, broadly conceived, two conflations might have occurred. First, a conflation of phenomenology with ontology; that is, the confusion of an experience of visible blackness with an image ontology that understands it as a perfectly intelligible and trustworthy sign. Second, a conflation of hermeneutics with ontology, that is, a type of reading of the surface as always securing a path toward its inside, its value, its meaning, which then becomes the template for what images are understood to be.

I have addressed this by attending to a series of objects (a series of "pipes") tucked in the depth of the visual field. These objects have challenged their status by pivoting on themselves, returning the gaze, cutting a figure. They have done so in a variety of ways — through deferral, by excision, magnifica-tion, germination; by overlaying; by repeating with a difference; by instituting a wedge between identity and the identical; by scrambling and reconfiguring the relationship between surface and depth; by forcing a gap and inhabiting the space in between the surface and depth; and ultimately by nourishing the gap between visible and visual. As much as the blackness of the black body is the result of a fixation and an outward fold, the objects discussed manage to interrupt the racial fold and reverse its direction and, in the process, turn the visual field inside out.

Thus, the ontological question I posed and I believe race continues to pose but, because of these slippages, has not yet been frankly addressed, is not one about the ontology of blackness, in the way, for instance Fred Moten tackles it in "The Case of Blackness," or David Marriott discusses it in *Haunted Life*.[1] My discussion has not been about the possibility, in Fanon's eloquent formulation, for the black man to have an ontological resistance in the eyes of the white man.[2] Rather, the ontological issue focused on in these pages is about blackness in the field of vision and the suturing between the visible and the visual, the seeable and the sayable that the black body is capable of performing, the anxieties the black body is able to assuage about what images are and what they refer to, where they might lead or land, and the intelligible surface that it is seemingly able to secure.

But what, then, is a racial image?

Commonsensically, we understand racial images to be those that deliver a racial content, ultimately, a body. When the body is secured, "racial images" perform an ontologizing function: they are understood to be as accurate as mirror reflections and yet as tethered, contiguous, and, therefore, trustworthy as shadows. Thus racial images are those that can be trusted at face value. The complication, though, is that the mirror is the mode through which the white, Western subject encounters the Other, as a mirror image, but one that reflects back something that is skewed, frightening, opaque, and thus needs to be disavowed. As Marriott's reading of Fanon shows, the face-to face encounter between the black and the white produces blackness as a specter. The native too, Fanon explains, encounters her own other as a mirror, but quickly realizes that what is reflected back is neither here nor there; the black *imago* exists only in-between, like a ghost show, a phantasmagoria. Throughout this book, I pursued the possibility of a way out of the "black representational space," as suggested in the introduction, whereby this moment of phantasmagoric visuality can be productively mobilized to turn these visual relations inside out, and blackness can be unhinged from the body and the image, but still claim its "ontological resistance."

Toni Morrison explains the delicate balance that needs to be reached. Her reading of canonical American literature is not concerned with racial representations but with the "tremors" that pervade the literary utterance in the attempt to sometimes accommodate, and sometimes deny, the Africanist presence. She writes: "In matters of race, silence and evasion have historically ruled literary discourse. Evasion has fostered another, substitute language in which the issues are encoded, foreclosing open debate . . . To notice is to recognize an already discredited difference. To enforce its invisibility through silence is to allow the black body a *shadowless* participation in the dominant cultural body."[3] Morrison's image is poignant: to ignore the formative role of race in literary whiteness is like robbing the black body of its shadow. The shadow here operates as a figure for the ontological resistance of blackness that needs to be sought, as well as makes available yet another reading of the NAACP photograph which literalizes this move by overlaying a shadow on top of the crowd.

The ontological complexity of the lynching shadow in the NAACP photograph has guided my readings throughout. Its formal properties inspired my attempt to read race formally and to look for ways in which it articulates the visual by both corporealizing and monetizing it. They have illustrated how race has given both a fleshed-out presence and a readable surface to the visual. They have shown how the visual has wrapped itself around a specific type of body and claimed it as its point of stability and its paradigmatic sign. Yet, whereas in the photochemical imagination, blackness seems to sit on top of an image, just like Antonio Beato's fly, posing as the image's corporeal interface and ontological augmentation, seen instead from the shadow, blackness appears as cast onto a contingent environment, onto a surface it helps to create, but it can just as easily redraw and dissipate.

The very story of this photograph registers several passages of the image. This photograph has never existed for me as an item of material culture. Rather, I casually encountered it in the NAACP files at the Library of Congress in the form of a microfilm, which I printed out and then scanned at home so that I could store it and eventually project it on a classroom screen. The poor quality of all these reproductions encouraged a formal reading of the image and slowly showed that the reverse fold of the shadow is not only the mirror, but also the silhouette where the shadow's existential contingency and ephemerality is undone. Rather than tethered and formally unstable, the silhouette is detachable, portable, yet fixed and reified. Furthermore, this poor quality heightened counterfactual elements of this image, the "what-if" that animates it; that is, the possibility that the shadow might indeed be coming from its diegetic space. In encouraging visual ambiguity, this shadow increased the possibility of working as an unstable and flickering image, one that, like Ligon's *Self-Portrait*, makes its viewer aware that seeing is always seeing *as*. The counterfactual this image potentially raises, furthermore, is one that extends across the digital divide. Even though the process of overlaying this shadow occurs by photochemical means, the very fact that it is a doctored image gestures ahead toward sentiments associated with the artefactuality of the digital image and the anxiety about its truth value that the question of indexicality is supposed to address.

As discussed in chapter 1, its artefactuality has a bearing on the evidentiary value of this image but, as I addressed in relation to Willis Thomas's *Branded Head*, it does not significantly impact its haptic properties. The impulse to flesh out the shadow remains, but, once it is so explicitly racialized, the implications are profound and complicated: When a black body fleshes out an image, the latter acquires an "excess flesh," which the NAACP shadow instead evacuates and excises.[4] The superimposed shadow phantasmagorizes the body, so that it is neither here nor there.

Once I received the high-resolution file, which was acquired to reproduce in this book, the picture showed other dimensions. Not only the formal fact that the shadow doesn't even fully overlay across the photograph, a sure giveaway sign of the fact that it is indeed superimposed, but I discovered people in it, rather than a blurry and anonymous crowd, a textural counterpoint to the smoothness of the shadow's blackness. Now I can see through this picture into the diegetic world it makes available. I can see the faces, and in what direction they are looking. The image is haunted even more. The chasm between the visual and the social field that the lynching scene opens so dramatically is accentuated here by the doctored nature of this image. This could be any crowd, not necessarily the crowd of a spectacle lynching, yet the clarity of the image now makes the visibility of at least some of the people a factual possibility. Yet, if the body doesn't come from the diegetic space, where does it come from? How to describe the space of its superimposition? Is this shadow in the space of the crowd or the space of the viewer or, alternatively, on the sleeve of the image?

As a paradigm, the shadow has the ability to bring to the fore the idea that race most prominently inhabits the *state* and not the content of the image. Seen as a mirror, the racial image is epistemologically oriented — it is a tool for knowing — and, therefore, it is understood representationally. Seen as a shadow, it is racially agnostic and representationally weak, but it always implies attachment, proximity, and contingency. The shadow is an indication of the body's extension into its surroundings and, therefore, calls attention to the spaces and modes of interaction between bodies. It is a figuration of the body's skin, understood not as the racially charged epidermis, but rather phenomenologically as a flexible, porous, and constantly redefined boundary between self and other, impression and expression, inside and outside. Thus, it is a reminder that the boundaries of bodies are never securely given, but are instead always negotiated in the interactions they entertain with other bodies. Even though indexical, the shadow is more a shifter than a trace, more a deferral than a referral, more of an affect than a sign function. More broadly, the shadow affords a spectral ontology and can be leveraged to think about states of the image that are precarious, fleeting, tethered, and oblique. The shadow recognizes that in front of images we seek ways to stabilize them, semiotically, rhetorically, ontologically, and ethically. The shadow realizes our fixation with fixation, but, for its part, it refuses to comply.

NOTES

INTRODUCTION

1. Toni Morrison, *Playing in the Dark: Whiteness and the Literary Imagination* (New York: Vintage Books, 1992), 17.

2. I emphasize the idea of "repetition with difference" after Homi Bhabha, "Of Mimicry and Man: The Ambivalence of Colonial Discourse," in *The Location of Culture* (New York: Routledge, 1994).

3. W. J. T. Mitchell, *Seeing through Race* (Cambridge, MA: Harvard University Press, 2012).

4. I am especially referring here to two recent publications: Nicholas Mirzoeff, *The Right to Look: A Counterhistory of Visuality* (Durham, NC: Duke University Press, 2011), and the already mentioned Mitchell, *Seeing through Race*.

5. In this sense, I share Mitchell's position that we are not in a post-racial society but rather in a moment in which race is put under erasure. He too discusses race as an ontology but not as an image ontology the way I endeavor here. See Scott Loren and

Jörg Metelmann. "What's the Matter: Race as Res," *Journal of Visual Culture* 10, no. 3 (2011): 397–405; and Mitchell's response "Playing the Race Card with Lacan," *Journal of Visual Culture* 10, no. 3 (2011): 405–9.

6. Here I understand visuality in general terms as the quality of being visual, not in the way Nicholas Mirzoeff does in *The Right to Look* where visuality ultimately indicates a political formation administered through visual means and is connected to the peculiarly Western process of visualizing history, hence "both a medium for the transmission and dissemination of authority, and a means for the mediation of those subject to that authority." Mirzoeff, *The Right to Look*, xv.

7. An important terminological clarification is in order: I use the term "black body" when I want to emphasize the outcome of a historical and epistemological process of suturing race onto the body (in Charles Mills's terminology, the outcome of the embodiment of race as form of political domination), whereas I use the term "raced body" when I intend to call attention to the act of framing such body as the bearer of the self-evident sign of race. Charles W. Mills, *From Class to Race: Essays in White Marxism and Black Radicalism* (Lanham, MD: Rowman & Littlefield, 2003), 168–69.

8. In turn, this is not an attempt to suggest that "black" and "white" in their visual sense should have an ontology, but rather that these two notions operate (rhetorically, semiotically, affectively, and so on) *as if* they did. When the ontological question is posed in relation to the "lived experience" of blackness, as Fred Moten does in "The Case of Blackness," the stakes and repercussions are quite different. There the challenge is to figure out under what practical and theoretical circumstances the black can hold, as Fanon explains, an "ontological resistance in the eyes of the white man." I return to this issue in the conclusion. See Fred Moten, "The Case of Blackness," *Criticism* 50, no. 2 (2008); Frantz Fanon, *Black Skin, White Masks*, trans. Richard Philcox (New York: Grove Press, 2008 [1952]), 90.

9. In "Surface Reading: An Introduction," *Representations* 108 (2009) Stephen Best and Sharon Marcus discuss the notion of surface reading in relation to the long hegemonic practice of symptomatic reading. Their intervention is important in keeping distinct the idea of reading the surface in search for a meaningful depth behind it and the idea of reading the surface as such. I briefly come back to this issue in chapter 4.

10. With the terms "troubled" and "troubling" I evoke the premise for Nicole Fleetwood's book *Troubling Vision*: "*seeing black is always a problem in a visual field that structures the troubling presence of blackness.*" Emphasis in original. Nicole R. Fleetwood, *Troubling Vision. Performance, Visuality, and Blackness* (Chicago: University of Chicago Press, 2011), 3. Her book shares a lot of concerns that are similar to mine, but not the focus on the ontological question.

11. I am referring here to what in the late '80s and early '90s Cultural Studies was described as the "burden of representation." See the seminal essay by Kobena Mercer

and Isaac Julien, "De Margin and De Center," *Screen* 29, no. 4 (1988). For a summary of the question of representation at that time see chapter five on "Stereotype, Realism, and the Struggle over Representation," in Ella Shohat and Stam Robert, *Unthinking Eurocentrism: Multiculturalism and the Media* (London and New York: Routledge, 1994).

12. Darby English, *How to See a Work of Art in Total Darkness* (Cambridge, MA: MIT Press, 2007). This expectation ultimately relies on the understanding of black art as a form of self-portraiture, which, as Kobena Mercer recalls, "in its received sense is a structurally impossible genre for the black artist to occupy," especially when, in Fanon's words, the colonized is "constantly struggling against his own image." Kobena Mercer, "Busy in the Ruins of a Wretched Phantasia," in *Frantz Fanon: Critical Perspectives*, ed. Anthony Alessandrini (London and New York: Routledge, 1999), 203. Fanon, *Black Skin, White Masks*, 170.

13. We can see the phenomenological lineage beginning with Fanon's *Black Skin, White Masks*. It continues through commentators such as Charles Johnson, "A Phenomenology of the Black Body," *Michigan Quarterly Review* 32, no. 4 (1993); Gayle Salamon, "'The Place Where Life Hides Away': Merleau-Ponty, Fanon, and the Location of Bodily Being," *differences* 17, no. 2 (2006); Teresa De Lauretis, "Difference Embodied: Reflections on *Black Skin, White Masks*," *Parallax* 8, no. 2 (2002); Sara Ahmed, *Strange Encounters: Embodied Others and Post-Coloniality* (London and New York: Routledge, 2000); Sara Ahmed, *The Cultural Politics of Emotions* (New York: Routledge, 2004). More generally, my phenomenological approach to the visual is informed by Vivian Sobchack, *The Address of the Eye: A Phenomenology of Film Experience* (Princeton, NJ: Princeton University Press, 1992); Vivian Sobchack, *Carnal Thoughts: Embodiment and Moving Image Culture* (Berkeley and Los Angeles: University of California Press, 2004); Laura U. Marks, *The Skin of the Film: Intercultural Cinema, Embodiment, and the Senses* (Durham, NC: Duke University Press, 2000); Jennifer M. Barker, *The Tactile Eye: Touch and the Cinematic Experience* (Berkeley and Los Angeles: University of California Press, 2009).

14. See Anne Anlin Cheng, *Second Skin: Josephine Baker and the Modern Surface* (Oxford: Oxford University Press, 2011), where she traces how, in the Modern Primitivism that coalesced into Josephine Baker, the skin of the Other meets the modernist ideal of the pure surface.

15. Frantz Fanon, *Black Skin, White Masks*, 91. The insistence on evisceration comes from David Marriott, *Haunted Life: Visual Culture and Black Modernity* (New Brunswick, NJ: Rutgers University Press, 2007), see especially chapter 1.

16. Johnson, "Phenomenology of the Black Body," 606.

17. Here, I understand the fold mostly after the phenomenological readings of Fanon mentioned above, in particular Johnson's essay on the "Phenomenology of the Black Body," not in relation to the exciting and mostly Deleuzian scholarship on the fold, for example Brian Massumi, *Parables for the Virtual: Movement, Affect, Sensation*

(Durham, NC: Duke University Press, 2002); Anna Munster, *Materializing New Media: Embodiment in Information Aesthetics* (Hanover, NH: Dartmouth College Press, 2006); Timothy Murray, *Digital Baroque: New Media Art and Cinematic Folds* (Minneapolis: University of Minnesota Press, 2008); Laura U. Marks, *Enfoldment and Infinity: An Islamic Genealogy of New Media Art* (Cambridge, MA: MIT Press, 2010). My sense of the fold is also different from Nyong'o, *The Amalgamation Waltz: Race, Performance, and the Ruses of Memory* (Minneapolis: University of Minnesota Press, 2009).

18. Toni Morrison, *Playing in the Dark: Whiteness and the Literary Imagination* (New York: Vintage Books, 1992), 12–13.

19. Morrison describes the "Africanist" presence in American literature as a "dark and abiding presence that moves the hearts and texts of American literature with fear and longing," and a "haunting, a darkness from which our early literature seemed unable to extricate itself." Morrison, *Playing in the Dark*, 33.

20. Morrison, *Playing in the Dark*, xi.

21. Emphasis in original. Elizabeth Abel, "Black Writing, White Reading: Race and the Politics of Feminist Interpretation," *Critical Inquiry* 19, no. 3 (1993), 477. My question, however, would not be "how" but, "why." What authorizes the conflation between a black woman's biological body and her textual body so that the black text is held up as the mirror of the black woman's body? Why this conflation and what is really being embodied in each case?

22. Abel, "Black Writing, White Reading," 471.

23. Abel, "Black Writing, White Reading," 472.

24. Trudier Harris, "Watchers Watching Watchers: Positioning Characters and Readers in Baldwin's 'Sonny Blues' and Morrison's 'Recitatif,'" in *James Baldwin and Toni Morrison: Comparative Critical and Theoretical Essays*, ed. Lovalerie King and Lynn Orilla Scott (New York: Palgrave Macmillan, 2006), 111.

25. Henry Louis Gates lists, among the critical fallacies that have severely limited the analysis of black literature, the "anthropology," the "perfectibility" and the "sociology" fallacies. "Because of the curious valorization of the social and polemical functions of black literature, the structure of the black text has been *repressed* and treated as if it were *transparent*. The black literary work of art has stood at the center of a triangle of relations . . . , but as the very thing *not* to be explained, as if it were invisible, or literal, or a one-dimensional document." Emphasis in original. Henry Louis Gates Jr., "Criticism in the Jungle," in *Black Literature and Literary Theory*, ed. Henry Louis Gates Jr. and Sunday Ogbonna Anozie (New York: Methuen, 1984), 5–6.

26. Lee Edelman, "The Part for the (W)hole: Baldwin, Homophobia, and the Fantasmatics of 'Race,'" in *Homographesis* (New York: Routledge, 1994). Edelman leverages the idea of synecdoche Homi Bhabha explores in his analysis of the colonial scene of the retrieval of the English Bible, discussed in "Signs Taken for Wonders,"

in *Race, Writing, and Difference*, ed. Henry Louis Gates Jr., (Chicago: University of Chicago Press, 1985).

27. Emphasis added. Homi Bhabha, "Interrogating Identity: Frantz Fanon and the Postcolonial Prerogative," in *The Location of Culture* (New York: Routledge, 1994), 64.

28. Audre Lorde, "Eye to Eye: Black Women, Hatred, and Anger," in *Sister Outsider* (New York: Ten Speed Press, 2007), 147.

29. "The white woman's refusal to touch the black child does not simply *stand for* the expulsion of blackness from white social space, but actually re-forms that social space through re-forming the apartness of the white body" (emphasis in original). Ahmed, *Strange Encounters*, 51.

30. The concept of avisuality comes from Akira Mizuta Lippit, *Atomic Light (Shadow Optics)* (Minneapolis: University of Minnesota Press, 2005). For a discussion of "Recitatif" that is compatible with this notion see also Kalpana Seshadri-Crooks, "What's in a Name? Love and Knowledge Beyond Identity in 'Recitatif,'" in *Desiring Whiteness: A Lacanian Analysis of Race* (London: Routledge, 2000).

31. Fanon, *Black Skin, White Masks*, 89.

32. In this context, I find it hard to separate effect from affect. My notion of *effect* comes from Roland Barthes's concept of the "reality effect," which he describes as a direct collusion of a referent and a signifier (at the expense of an evacuation of the signified from the sign). Roland Barthes, "The Reality Effect," in *The Rustle of Language* (New York: Hill & Wang, 1986), 148. At the same time, and extending some reflections Vivian Sobchack makes in an insightful essay on Barthes, the reality effect can be seen also as an *affect* of referentiality. Vivian Sobchack, "The Insistent Fringe: Moving Images and Historical Consciousness," *History and Theory* 36, no. 4 (1997). Influential is also Massumi's idea of the indexicality of the affective fact as outlined in "The Future Birth of the Affective Fact: The Political Ontology of Threat," in *The Affect Theory Reader*, ed. Melissa Gregg and Gregory J. Seigworth (Durham, NC: Duke University Press, 2010).

33. Nicholas Mirzoeff, "The Shadow and the Substance: Race, Photography, and the Index," in *Only Skin Deep: Changing Visions of the American Self*, ed. Coco Fusco and Brian Wallis (New York: International Center of Photography, 2003), 126.

34. Fanon, *Black Skin, White Masks*; Bhabha, "Interrogating Identity"; see also Bhabha, "Remembering Fanon: Self, Psyche, and the Colonial Condition," in *Rethinking Fanon the Continuing Dialogue*, ed. Nigel Gibson (New York: Humanity Books, 1999).

35. English, *How to See*, 37. This is a rather shared reading of the passage, see Marriott, *Haunted Life*; Mercer, "Busy in the Ruins"; Kara Keeling, "In the Interval: Frantz Fanon and the 'Problems' of Visual Representation," *Qui Parle* 13, no. 2 (2003).

36. Fatimah Tobing Rony, *The Third Eye: Race, Cinema, and Ethnographic Spectacle* (Durham, NC: Duke University Press, 1996), 6.

37. Michel Foucault, *The Order of Things: An Archaeology of the Human Sciences* (New York: Random House, 1970), 9.

38. Michel Foucault, *This Is Not a Pipe*, trans. James Harkness (Berkeley and Los Angeles: University of California Press, 1983), 19.

39. W. J. T. Mitchell, *Picture Theory: Essays on Verbal and Visual Representation* (Chicago: University of Chicago Press, 1994).

40. Foucault, *This Is Not a Pipe*, 20.

41. Mitchell, *Picture Theory*, 66.

42. Foucault, *This Is Not a Pipe*, 44.

43. Foucault, *This Is Not a Pipe*, 44.

44. Foucault's initial reading of the function of Magritte's pipe points out that it could be understood as a "calligram." Foucault, *This Is Not a Pipe*, 19–31.

45. English, *How to See*, 204. See also Huey Copeland, "Glenn Ligon and Other Runaway Subjects," *Representations* 113, no. 1 (2011); Glenn Ligon et al., *Glenn Ligon: Some Changes* (Toronto: Power Plant, 2005); Simon Morley, *Writing on the Wall: Word and Image in Modern Art* (Berkeley and Los Angeles: University of California Press, 2003).

46. English, *How to See*, 212.

47. I develop this idea in chapter 1.

48. Emphasis added. English writes, "A mindset that regards a surface (or appearance) as an end, after all, threatens to reduce the contingencies of an art situation to the sheer materiality of works and their viewers. Ostensibly merely aesthetic, such an 'image' also captures the two-dimensionality governing much of our thinking about culture, and by extension the very model of social relations against which Ligon's work is critically directed. This is why we might regard the most basic formal operation in Ligon's work not as representational but as abstractive." Darby English, "Glenn Ligon: Committed to Difficulty," in *Glenn Ligon: Some Changes*, 38.

49. Curiously, Ligon makes a similar point in an interview with Stephen Andrews. While discussing his Richard Pryor jokes paintings, he claims that "a nigger is a nigger is a nigger. Pardon me, Gertrude." Stephen Andrews, "Glenn Ligon: In Conversation," in *Glenn Ligon: Some Changes*, 185.

50. In *Troubling Vision*, Fleetwood discusses the possibility for black images to act non-iconically, especially in chapter 1 on African American photographer Charles "Teenie" Harris.

51. The idea of photography as an image state comes from Raymond Bellour, "Concerning 'the Photographic,'" in *Still Moving: Between Cinema and Photography*, ed. Karen Beckman and Jean Ma (Durham, NC: Duke University Press, 2008); Raymond Bellour, "The Double Helix," in *Electronic Culture: Technology and Visual Representation*, ed. Timothy Druckrey (New York: Aperture, 1996). A compatible non-medium specific way to think across both moving and still images, photochemical and digital images can be found for example in Kara Keeling's Deleuzian notion

of the "cinematic." See Kara Keeling, *The Witch's Flight: The Cinematic, the Black Femme, and the Image of Common Sense* (Durham, NC: Duke University Press, 2007).

52. This notion comes from Jacques Rancière, *The Politics of Aesthetics: The Distribution of the Sensible*, trans. Gabriel Rockhill (New York: Continuum, 2004).

53. This visual conceit whereby invisibility has visibility at its heart is developed by Fred Moten, *In the Break: The Aesthetics of the Black Radical Tradition* (Minneapolis: University of Minnesota Press, 2003), and Lippit, *Atomic Light*.

54. Even though Afrofuturism is an established artistic, theoretical, and historiographical framework, here I employ the term in a loose sense, especially given Mutu's rejection of the label. The website afrofuturism.net has an extensive bibliography of critical and literary works that are counted under this umbrella, but two foundational texts are Alondra Nelson, "Afrofuturism: A Special Issue of Social Text," *Social Text* 20, no. 2 (2002); and Kodwo Eshun, "Further Considerations of Afrofuturism," *CR: The New Centennial Review* 3, no. 2 (2003).

55. Karl Marx, *Capital: Volume 1: A Critique of Political Economy*, trans. Ben Fowkes (New York: Penguin Classics, 1990), 167.

56. In my essay "Reification, Reanimation, and the Money of the Real," *World Picture Journal* 7 (2012) (available at http://www.worldpicturejournal.com/WP_7/Raengo.html), I focus specifically on this pivotal move as both theoretical and stylistic in Ken Jacobs's *Capitalism: Slavery* (2006), a digital animation of a stereoscopic card picturing slaves at work in a cotton field, and Nick Hooker's 2008 digital video for Grace Jones's song "Corporate Cannibal."

ONE **THE PHOTOCHEMICAL IMAGINATION**

1. Jacqueline Goldsby explores the authorial claims on lynching photographs usually by professionals and most often with the complicity of law enforcement, such as in the case of the photographs of Jesse Washington's 1916 lynching in Waco, Texas, which were taken from the town's courthouse. Jacqueline Goldsby, *A Spectacular Secret: Lynching in American Life and Literature* (Chicago: University of Chicago Press, 2006), 133. See also Patricia Bernstein, *The First Waco Horror: The Lynching of Jesse Washington and the Rise of the NAACP* (College Station: Texas A&M University Press, 2005); Sam Perry, "Competing Image Vernaculars in the Anti-Lynching Movement of the 1930s" (PhD diss., Georgia State University, 2011).

2. Robert L. Zangrando, *The NAACP Crusade against Lynching, 1909–1950* (Philadelphia: Temple University Press, 1980).

3. Scholars refer to the visuality of lynching in terms of tableau to emphasize its *mise-en-scéne*, its theatricality, the pageantry of racial supremacy that needs to perform itself over and over again to maintain its social footing. See for instance,

Robyn Wiegman, *American Anatomies: Theorizing Race and Gender* (Durham, NC: Duke University Press, 1995); Dora Apel, *Imagery of Lynching: Black Men, White Women, and the Mob* (New Brunswick, NJ: Rutgers University Press, 2004). Tableau also refers to what James Snead would describe as "metaphysical stasis," the exhibition of the black (singular) and his/her social position as an unchanging essence. See James Snead, *White Screens, Black Images: Hollywood from the Dark Side* (New York and London: Routledge, 1994). See also Toni Morrison's retooling of Snead's categories in *Playing in the Dark: Whiteness and the Literary Imagination* (New York: Vintage Books, 1992), 67–68.

4. Nicholas Mirzoeff, "The Shadow and the Substance: Race, Photography, and the Index," in *Only Skin Deep: Changing Visions of the American Self*, ed. Coco Fusco and Brian Wallis (New York: International Center of Photography, 2003).

5. The idea of lynching as a cultural logic comes from Goldsby, *A Spectacular Secret*.

6. I borrow the term "artefact" from Akira Lippit, *Atomic Light (Shadow Optics)* (Minneapolis: University of Minnesota Press, 2005), 53.

7. Morrison, *Playing in the Dark*, 17.

8. Charles W. Mills, *The Racial Contract* (Ithaca, NY: Cornell University Press, 1997); W. J. T. Mitchell, *Picture Theory: Essays on Verbal and Visual Representation* (Chicago: University of Chicago Press, 1994); Martin Heidegger, "The Age of the World Picture," in *Off the Beaten Track* (New York: Cambridge University Press, 2002); Nicholas Mirzoeff, "On Visuality," *Journal of Visual Culture* 5, no. 1 (2006); W. J. T. Mitchell, *Seeing through Race* (Cambridge, MA: Harvard University Press, 2012).

9. This ethical dilemma is described by Dora Apel, "On Looking: Lynching Photographs and Legacies of Lynching after 9/11," *American Quarterly* 55, no. 3 (2003).

10. Robyn Wiegman describes this suturing process when she claims that the disciplinary function of lynching was exerted through a "panoptic mode of surveillance and its materialization of violence in public displays of torture and castration [so that] the black subject is disciplined in two powerful ways: by the threat of always *being seen* and by the spectacular *scene*" (emphasis added). Wiegman, *American Anatomies*, 13.

11. Discussed in Abdul R. JanMohamed, *The Death-Bound-Subject: Richard Wright's Archaeology of Death* (Durham, NC: Duke University Press, 2005).

12. "While we might attribute to the slave system many of the features of the society of spectacle," writes Wiegman, "for instance, from the dynamic of the auction block to brandings, whippings, and other rituals of public torture, the panoptic can be located in such phenomenon as the organizing layout of the plantation, the ideological elision between slavery and dark skin, and the legalization of miscegenation as an abstracted property relation. The disciplinary power of race, in short, must be read as implicated in both specular and panoptic regimes." Wiegman, *American Anatomies*, 39.

13. Emphasis added. Wiegman, *American Anatomies*, 81.

14. See also James Allen, *Without Sanctuary: Lynching Photography in America* (Santa Fe, NM: Twin Palms Publishers, 2000).

15. Apel, "On Looking"; Apel, *Imagery of Lynching*; Dora Apel and Shawn Michelle Smith, *Lynching Photographs* (Berkeley and Los Angeles: University of California Press, 2008); Wiegman, *American Anatomies*.

16. I am inspired here by literature employing Giorgio Agamben's concept of bare life to discuss the specific disenfranchisement of the African American population becoming once again visible with Katrina — what Henry Giroux calls "the biopolitics of disposability"; that is, the idea that Katrina has created yet another state of exception within which blacks are made present before the law but not represented by the law; blacks are bearers of obligations but not of rights. Giorgio Agamben, *Homo Sacer: Sovereign Power and Bare Life* (Stanford, CA: Stanford University Press, 1998); Henry Giroux, "Violence, Katrina, and the Biopolitics of Disposability," *Theory, Culture & Society* 24, no. 7–8 (2007); Nicholas Mirzoeff, "The Sea and the Land: Biopower and Visuality from Slavery to Katrina," *Culture, Theory and Critique* 50, no. 2 (2009). See also Jared Sexton, "People-of-Color-Blindness: Notes on the Afterlife of Slavery," *Social Text* 28, no. 2 (2010).

17. Charles W. Mills, "Non-Cartesian Sums: Philosophy and the African-American Experience," in *Blackness Visible Essays on Philosophy and Race* (Ithaca, NY: Cornell University Press, 1998), 6.

18. Leigh Raiford, "The Consumption of Lynching Images," in *Only Skin Deep: Changing Visions of the American Self*, ed. Coco Fusco and Brian Wallis (New York: International Center of Photography, 2003), 270.

19. Mirzoeff, "The Shadow and the Substance," 123, emphasis added.

20. Raiford, "The Consumption of Lynching Images," 267.

21. See essays by Coco Fusco, Nicholas Mirzoeff, and Jennifer Gonzales in *Only Skin Deep: Changing Visions of the American Self*, ed. Coco Fusco and Brian Wallis (New York: International Center of Photography, 2003).

22. Emphasis added. Coco Fusco, "Racial Time, Racial Marks, Racial Metaphors," in *Only Skin Deep*, 16.

23. See also Beth Coleman, "Race as Technology," *Camera Obscura* 24, no. 1 (2009).

24. Emphasis in the original. Stanley Cavell, *The World Viewed: Reflections on the Ontology of Film* (Cambridge, MA: Harvard University Press, 1979), 24; David Rodowick, *The Virtual Life of Film* (Cambridge, MA: Harvard University Press, 2007), 55.

25. My idea of the regime of image-ness is derived in part from Jacques Rancière, *The Future of the Image*, trans. Gregory Elliott (New York: Verso, 2007).

26. Emphasis added. Frantz Fanon, *Black Skin, White Masks*, 89. See also Stuart Hall, "The After-Life of Frantz Fanon: Why Fanon? Why Now? Why *Black Skins, White*

Masks?," in *The Fact of Blackness*, ed. Alan Read (Seattle: Bay Press, 1996); Teresa De Lauretis, "Difference Embodied: Reflections on *Black Skin, White Masks*," *Parallax* 8, no. 2 (2002). I am partly relying on Greg Hainge's suggestion that photographic fixation is analogous to the process of constitution of normative bodies. Greg Hainge, "Unfixing the Photographic Image: Photography, Indexicality, Fidelity and Normativity," *Continuum: Journal of Media & Cultural Studies* 22, no. 5 (2011).

27. I have a strong desire to read this image in relation to the frontispiece of Thomas Hobbes's *Leviathan* as similarly offering a representation of the formation of the social contract. But with important differences: whereas in the *Leviathan* the observer is aligned with the look of the citizens, in the NAACP photograph we are unable to see what they are looking at. Instead, we are aligned with the shadow of the body that catalyzes the reenactment of their covenant and, what's more, we look at the citizens "through" it. Whereas in the frontispiece of the *Leviathan* we are delivered a representation of the moment of contractual agreement in the body of the sovereign, in the NAACP photograph instead we are denied the representation of the outcome of the contractual moment. Rather, we are given its empty shell, the sheer structure of its circularity. Lacking a representation of its successful achievement, the covenant is suspended while its necessary conditions are laid bare. In chapter 2 I return to this in relation to Fred Wilson's installation *Cabinet Making 1820–1960* and describe it as the "critical use of the missing body."

28. Shawn Michelle Smith, *Photography on the Color Line: W.E.B. Du Bois, Race, and Visual Culture* (Durham, NC: Duke University Press, 2004), 127.

29. Shawn Michelle Smith, "The Evidence of Lynching Photographs," in *Lynching Photographs*, ed. Dora Apel and Shawn Michelle Smith (Berkeley and Los Angeles: University of California Press, 2008), 23. See also Dray, *At the Hands of Persons Unknown*.

30. Homi Bhabha, "Remembering Fanon: Self, Psyche, and the Colonial Condition," in *Rethinking Fanon: The Continuing Dialogue*, ed. Nigel Gibson (New York: Humanity Books, 1999), 186. I discuss this again in chapter 4 in relation to Kara Walker's work.

31. Mary Ann Doane, "Indexicality: Trace and Sign: Introduction," *differences* 18, no. 1 (2007), 2.

32. Charles S. Peirce, *The Essential Peirce: Selected Philosophical Writings*, ed. Nathan Houser and Christian J.W. Kloesel (Bloomington: Indiana University Press, 1992), 226. Quoted in Mary Ann Doane, "The Indexical and the Concept of Medium Specificity," *differences* 18, no. 1 (2007): 133.

33. Doane, "The Indexical," 136.

34. Rosalind Krauss, "Notes on the Index: Seventies Art in America," *October* 3 (1977).

35. Krauss's goal, claims Doane, was to detach the index from realism: "While realism claims to build a mimetic copy, an illusion of an inhabitable world, the index only purports to point, to connect, to touch, to make language and representation

adhere to the world as tangent — to reference a real without realism." Doane, "Indexicality," 3–4.

36. Krauss, "Notes on the Index," 69.

37. Doane, "The Indexical," 142. Doane is commenting on Georges Didi-Huberman, "The Index of the Absent Wound (Monograph on a Stain)," *October* 29 (Summer 1984). See also Dudley Andrew's discussion of the Turin Shroud in, "The Economies of Adapation," in *True to the Spirit: Film Adaptation and the Question of Fidelity*, ed. Colin MacCabe, Kathleen Murray, and Rick Warner (Oxford and New York: Oxford University Press, 2011).

38. Here I am inspired by Bruno Latour's discussion of the controversy between Hobbes and Boyle partly surrounding the indexicality implied in the idea of the writing of Nature that underpins the empirical method. See Bruno Latour, *We Have Never Been Modern* (Cambridge, MA: Harvard University Press, 1993).

39. Deixis in the cinema links to what Metz calls "the actualization" of the image: the fact that the image of a revolver always means "Here is a revolver!" See Christian Metz, *Film Language: A Semiotics of the Cinema*, trans. Michael Taylor (New York: Oxford University Press, 1974), 67.

40. Tom Gunning has made a strong case for the way in which photographic iconicity has traditionally supplied the truth-value to the index understood as trace. See Tom Gunning, "Moving Away from the Index: Cinema and the Impression of Reality," *differences* 18, no. 1 (2007).

41. This distinction is made by Giovanna Fossati, *From Grain to Pixel: The Archival Life of Film in Transition* (Amsterdam: Amsterdam University Press, 2009). See also Francesco Casetti, "Sutured Reality: Film, from Photographic to Digital," *October* no. 138 (2011).

42. See also Tom Gunning's essay "What's the Point of an Index? Or, Faking Photographs," *Nordicom Review* 25, no. 1–2 (September 2004).

43. Brian Massumi, "The Future Birth of the Affective Fact: The Political Ontology of Threat," in *The Affect Theory Reader*, ed. Melissa Gregg and Gregory J. Seigworth (Durham, NC: Duke University Press, 2010); Hainge, "Unfixing the Photographic Image."

44. Vivian Sobchack, *Carnal Thoughts: Embodiment and Moving Image Culture* (Berkeley and Los Angeles: University of California Press, 2004), 142.

45. A gesture toward this idea is made by Frank Kessler, "What You Get Is What You See: Digital Images and the Claim on the Real," in *Digital Material: Tracing New Media in Everyday Life and Technology*, ed. Marianne van den Boomen et al. (Amsterdam: Amsterdam University Press, 2009). See also Fossati, *From Grain to Pixel*; Antony Bryant and Griselda Pollock, *Digital and Other Virtualities: Renegotiating the Image* (London and New York: I. B. Tauris, 2010). Bryant and Pollock recognize that the proliferation of modes of virtuality reproposes the question of indexicality at the very

least on an ethical level. They also frame one of the relationships between indexicality and virtuality as one from truth to trust, thus suggesting how the index might be also explained as what I have been calling a reality a(e)ffect.

46. This is a reason why "passing" threatens so profoundly the visual epistemology of race, not to mention the confidence in photography's ability to deliver the truth on its own surface. See P. Gabrielle. Foreman, "Who's Your Mama? 'White' Mulatta Genealogies, Early Photography, and Anti-Passing Narratives of Slavery and Freedom," *American Literary History* 14, no. 3 (2002). See also Drew Ayers's insightful discussion of the survival of this epistemological structure in DNA portraits in "Humans without Bodies: DNA Portraiture and Biocybernetic Reproduction," *Configurations*, 19 no. 2 (2011).

47. Here Geimer refers to the fact that the photograph is of Egyptian monuments which Bazin uses as an example of the mummy complex that inspired the plastic arts to strive to preserve life through a representation of life. See Peter Geimer, "Image as Trace: Speculations About an Undead Paradigm," *differences* 18, no. 1 (2007); André Bazin, *What Is Cinema?*, trans. Hugh Gray, vol. 1 (Berkeley and Los Angeles: University of California Press, 1967). See also Dudley Andrew and Herve Joubert-Laurencin, *Opening Bazin: Postwar Film Theory and Its Afterlife* (New York: Oxford University Press, 2011).

48. Roland Barthes, *Camera Lucida: Reflections on Photography* (New York: Hill & Wang, 1981), 80. I capitalize Intractable to refer explicitly to Barthes's use of the term.

49. Geimer, "Image as Trace," 15.

50. For a compelling exploration of photographs as material culture objects see the anthology by Elizabeth Edwards and Janice Hart, eds., *Photographs Objects Histories: On the Materiality of Images*, Material Cultures (London and New York: Routledge, 2004); and, in particular, Bacthen's essay "Ere the Substance Face."

51. Smith, "Lynching Photographs," 20.

52. I use the term "inter-skin" rather than inter-face to underline the haptic properties of this contact. As Elena del Rio puts it, when the image "becomes translated into a bodily response, body and image no longer function as discrete units, but as surfaces in contact, engaged in a constant activity of reciprocal re-alignment and inflection." Elena Del Rio, "The Body as Foundation of the Screen: Allegories of Technology in Atom Egoyan's *Speaking Parts*," *Camera Obscura* 37–38 (1996): 101.

53. Moreover, as Kessler argues, this impulse conflates the necessary distinction between *profilmic* and *afilmic*; that is, what was in fact before the camera and not what exists in the world independently from it. See Kessler, "What you See is What you Get," 192.

54. Jonathan Auerbach, *Body Shots: Early Cinema Incarnations* (Berkeley and Los Angeles: University of California Press, 2007); Brian Massumi, *Parables for the Virtual: Movement, Affect, Sensation* (Durham, NC: Duke University Press, 2002); Allan Sekula, "The Body and the Archive," *October* 39 (1986); Sobchack, *Carnal Thoughts*.

55. Akira Mizuta Lippit, *Atomic Light*.

56. Lippit, *Atomic Light*, 52. Emphasis in original.

57. Lippit, *Atomic Light*, 77.

58. A few exemplary titles: Jean-Michel Rabaté, *Writing the Image after Roland Barthes* (Philadelphia: University of Pennsylvania Press, 1997); Nancy M. Shawcross, *Roland Barthes on Photography: The Critical Tradition in Perspective* (Gainesville: University Press of Florida, 1997); Geoffrey Batchen, ed., *Photography Degree Zero: Reflections on Roland Barthes's Camera Lucida* (Cambridge, MA: MIT Press, 2009).

59. Mary Ann Doane, *The Emergence of Cinematic Time: Modernity, Contingency, the Archive* (Cambridge, MA: Harvard University Press, 2002); Laura Mulvey, *Death 24x a Second: Stillness and the Moving Image.* (Chicago: University of Chicago Press, 2006); Siegfried Zielinski, *Deep Time of the Media: Toward an Archaeology of Hearing and Seeing by Technical Means*, trans. Gloria Custance (Cambridge, MA: MIT Press, 2006); Damian Sutton, *Photography, Cinema, Memory: The Crystal Image of Time* (Minneapolis: University of Minnesota Press, 2009).

60. There is quite a bit of history of expanding the "photographic" beyond photography. In "Notes on the Index," Rosalind Krauss mapped 1970s art arguing that the photographic offered a functional model for abstraction every time a conventional sign was turned into a trace — or conceived, received, and felt as such; Susan Sontag claimed that contemporary arts are "logical extensions of the model established by photography," and "all art aspires to the condition of photography." See Susan Sontag, *On Photography* (New York: Farrar, Straus and Giroux, 1977), 149. Also quoted in Raymond Bellour, "Concerning 'the Photographic,'" in *Still Moving between Cinema and Photography*, ed. Karen Beckman and Jean Ma (Durham, NC: Duke University Press, 2008), 269.

61. Raymond Bellour, "The Double Helix," in *Electronic Culture: Technology and Visual Representation*, ed. Timothy Druckrey (Aperture, 1996), 175. Emphasis in original.

62. Emphasis added. Bellour, "Concerning 'the Photographic,'" 253.

63. Sybille Krämer, "Was Eigentlich Ist Eine Spur" (paper presented at Spurenlesen: Zur Genealogie von Kulturtechniken, Humboldt-Universität, Berlin, February 10–12, 2005); quoted in Geimer, "Image as Trace," 16. In *Touch: Sensuous Theory and Multisensory Media* (Minneapolis: University of Minnesota Press, 2002), Laura U. Marks expresses her dissatisfaction with the idea that a loss of indexicality would necessarily imply a loss of materiality.

64. I am drawing on Mitchell's influential distinction between picture and image in Mitchell, *Picture Theory*.

65. Victor Stoichita, *A Short History of the Shadow* (London: Reaktion Books, 1997), 170.

66. This myth has been influentially evoked in relation to the "desire" of images by W. J. T. Mitchell, *What Do Pictures Want? The Lives and Loves of Images* (Chicago: University of Chicago Press, 2005), 66–67.

67. Stoichita, *A Short History of the Shadow*, 12.

68. Stoichita, *A Short History of the Shadow*, 24.

69. Stoichita, *A Short History of the Shadow*, 27. Emphasis in original.

70. Stoichita refers to Piaget's studies of phases of children's discoveries of the shadow, in his *A Short History of the Shadow*, 29–31.

71. This idea of the shadow and the ghost in the machine is found most notably in Ralph Ellison's *Invisible Man* (New York: Random House, 1982 [1947]), but also in Joel Dinerstein, *Swinging the Machine: Modernity, Technology, and African American Culture between the World Wars* (Amherst: University of Massachusetts Press, 2003). A few more samples, influenced in part by Michael Rogin, *Blackface, White Noise: Jewish Immigrants in the Hollywood Melting Pot* (Berkeley and Los Angeles: University of California Press, 1996): Elizabeth Abel, "Shadows," *Representations* 84 (2004); Alice Maurice, "What the Shadow Knows: Race, Image, and Meaning in *Shadows* (1922)," *Cinema Journal* 47, no. 3 (2007). The shadow features also in Robert Storr, "Spooked," in *Kara Walker: My Complement, My Enemy, My Oppressor, My Love*, ed. Philippe Vergne (Minneapolis: Walker Art Center, 2007).

72. William Henry Fox Talbot characterized his invention as the "art of fixing a shadow." See William Henry Fox Talbot, "A Brief Historical Sketch of the Invention of the Art," in *Classic Essays on Photography*, ed. Alan Trachtenberg (New Haven, CT: Leete's Island Books, 1980); see also Mirzoeff, "The Shadow and the Substance," 114.

73. Here I am paraphrasing Vivian Sobchack's influential essay, "What My Fingers Knew." Specifically, I refer to the way Sobchack describes her tactile experience of the shots of Jane Campion's *The Piano* in which Baines touches Ada's flesh through the hole in her stocking: "precisely *whose* flesh I felt was ambiguous and vague. . . . That is, I had a carnal interest and investment in being *both* "here" *and* "there," in being able *both* to sense *and* to be sensible, to be *both* the subject *and* the object of tactile desire." Vivian Sobchack, "What My Fingers Knew: The Cinesthetic Subject, or Vision in the Flesh," in *Carnal Thoughts Embodiment and Moving Image Culture* (Berkeley and Los Angeles: University of California Press, 2004), 66. Emphasis in original.

74. "Ghostly membrane" is Carol Mavor's expression in "Black and Blue: The Shadows of *Camera Lucida*," in *Photography Degree Zero: Reflections on Camera Lucida*, ed. Geoffrey Batchen (Cambridge, MA: MIT Press, 2009), 215.

75. Quoted in De Lauretis. As she summarizes, "the body-ego is a permeable boundary — an open border, so to speak — and a site of incessant material negotiations between the external world, on one side, and on the other side, the internal world of the psyche, the drives, the unconscious, and the ego's mechanisms of defense — repression, disavowal, projection, and so forth." De Lauretis, "Difference Embodied," 57.

76. Gayle Salamon, "'The Place Where Life Hides Away': Merleau-Ponty, Fanon, and the Location of Bodily Being," *differences* 17, no. 2 (2006): 101. Or in Homi Bhabha's words, "The contour of difference is agonistic, shifting, splitting, rather like Freud's description of the system of consciousness which occupies a position in space lying on the border-line between outside and inside, a surface of protection, reception and projection." Homi Bhabha, "Signs Taken for Wonders," in *Race, Writing, and Difference*, ed. Gates Henry Louis Jr. (Chicago: University of Chicago Press, 1985), 156.

77. Salamon, "Where Life Hides," 109.

78. Charles Johnson, "A Phenomenology of the Black Body," *Michigan Quarterly Review* 32, no. 4 (1993), 606.

79. Fanon, *Black Skins, White Masks*, 91.

80. bell hooks, "Eating the Other," in *Black Looks: Race and Representation* (Cambridge, MA: South End Press, 1992).

81. This idea of skin is strongly inspired by Jennifer Barker, *The Tactile Eye: Touch and the Cinematic Experience* (Berkeley and Los Angeles: University of California Press, 2009).

82. Barthes, *Camera Lucida*, 81 (emphasis added).

83. Kenneth S. Calhoon, "Personal Effects: Rilke, Barthes, and the Matter of Photography," *MLN* 113, no. 3 (1998), 613.

84. Notable exceptions, within a vast literature on *Camera Lucida* are: Mavor, "Black and Blue"; Margaret Olin, "Touching Photographs: Roland Barthes's 'Mistaken' Identification"; and Shawn Michelle Smith, "Race and Reproduction in *Camera Lucida*," all in *Photography Degree Zero: Reflections on Camera Lucida*, ed. Geoffrey Batchen (Cambridge, MA: MIT Press, 2009).

85. Moten focuses on Barthes's comments on the photographs of Emmett Till and foregrounds the "sonic substance" of these photographs in the alleged whistle (or the "bye baby") that Emmett directed at a white woman and in his mother's moaning (black mo'nin' he calls it) which is restaged, represented, reheard in Mrs. Bradley's reopening of the casket and in the body's photograph. Interestingly for my concern, Moten recalls Barthes's wondering what the parents of Emmett Till would have thought of the universalist pretension of the Family of Man exhibition, which constructed a composite image of humanity by insisting on photographs of deaths and births. In invoking Mrs. Bradley in a critique of the naturalistic and universalizing photography of the bare fact of death Barthes also "fails to recognize her own metaphotographic contribution to that critique," and proves instead his inability to see these photographs as showing an unnatural death, "the *death's* difficulty, the suffering of the mother, the threat of high mortality rate and the seemingly absolute closure of his future." Emphasis in original. Fred Moten, *In the Break: The Aesthetics of the Black Radical Tradition* (Minneapolis: University of Minnesota Press, 2003), 209.

86. Olin, "Touching Photographs," 78.

87. Smith, "Race and Reproduction," 245. The structure of sympathy that Hartman finds governing abolitionists' descriptions of scenes of torture — that is, a condemnation of the practice dependent upon the possibility of imagining oneself in the other person's shoes — is at work here as well, with the effect of turning the self-affirmative claim to social visibility of Van Der Zee's sitters and photographic art into, in fact, a "scene of subjection." Saidaya V. Hartman, *Scenes of Subjection: Terror, Slavery, and Self-Making in Nineteenth-Century America* (New York: Oxford University Press, 1997).

88. Mavor, "Black and Blue," 227, 215.

89. Barthes, *Camera Lucida*, 34. Smith, "Race and Reproduction," 246. We witness, in Barthes's description of the mask of blackness, a reenactment of the transformation of the subject into an object legally sanctioned by the slave system.

90. The way Barthes titles this image further indicates this slippage. The original title for the photograph is not "born a slave," but "born in slavery": *William Casby, born in slavery, Algiers, Louisiana, March 24, 1963.* For the concept of the "historical ontology of slavery" see Bill Brown, "Reification, Reanimation, and the American Uncanny," *Critical Inquiry* 32 (2006).

91. Barthes, *Camera Lucida*, 34.

92. Barthes, *Camera Lucida*, 109.

93. Barthes, *Camera Lucida*, 106.

94. Barthes, *Camera Lucida*, 110. Emphasis in original.

95. Barthes, *Camera Lucida*, 80. Emphasis in original.

96. Roland Barthes, "The Photographic Message," in *Image-Music-Text* (New York: Hill & Wang, 1977), 17.

97. Susan Sontag, *Regarding the Pain of Others* (New York: Picador, 2003).

98. Mavor, "Black and Blue," 214.

99. As Sobchack explains, the term "cinesthetic" is meant to comprise the way in which the cinematic experience triggers and relies on both synaesthesia (or intersensoriality) and coenaesthesia (the perception of a person's whole sensorial being). At stake is the possibility to explain how meaning emerges from the conjunction of the spectator's bodies and cinematic representation. Sobchack, "What My Fingers Knew," 67.

100. Sobchack, "What My Fingers Knew," 79, 76. Emphasis in original. About the film experience she writes, "my body's intentional trajectory, seeking a sensible object to fulfill this sensual solicitation, will *reverse its direction* to locate its partially frustrated sensual grasp on something more literally accessible . . . *my own subjectively felt lived body*" (emphasis in original).

101. To be sure, Vivian Sobchack argues that only the cinema can provide this reversibility and that unlike the cinema, the photograph cannot be inhabited; it cannot "entertain, in the abstraction of its visible space, its single and static *point* of view, the presence of a lived and living body — so it does not really invite the spectator *into* the scene so much as it invites contemplation *of* the scene" (emphasis in original).

Sobchack, *Carnal Thoughts*, 144. However, I argue that this description applies only to the photograph's *studium* and that Barthes was committed to demonstrating just the opposite: the essence of photography for him lies in the way in which it appeals to his living body. The photograph's *punctum* not only registers a bodily response and a process of habitation, but it also restores movement to the stillness of the photograph, life to its corpsing effect. The *punctum* emerges not only from the temporal dimension of our own gaze on the photograph, but it exists — and changes — in our memory of it. Barthes writes, "In this glum desert, suddenly a specific photograph reaches me: it animates me, and I animate it." Barthes, *Camera Lucida*, 20.

102. A great discussion of how race is sensorially constructed is found in Mark M. Smith, *How Race Is Made: Slavery, Segregation, and the Senses* (Chapel Hill: University of North Carolina Press, 2006) where he attends to the subtle processes of segregation within one's sensorium. Consider how in slavery and in the Jim Crow South, the prohibition to look and touch for blacks coexisted with black women nursing white babies.

TWO ON THE SLEEVE OF THE VISUAL

1. See Nicole Fleetwood's discussion of blackness and the iconic image in *Troubling Vision: Performance, Visuality, and Blackness* (Chicago: University of Chicago Press, 2011).

2. See Jennifer M. Barker, *The Tactile Eye: Touch and the Cinematic Experience* (Berkeley and Los Angeles: University of California Press, 2009); Gayle Salamon, "'The Place Where Life Hides Away': Merleau-Ponty, Fanon, and the Location of Bodily Being," *differences* 17, no. 2 (2006).

3. Sara Ahmed, *The Cultural Politics of Emotions* (New York: Routledge, 2004), 1.

4. In Richard Shiff's description, "catachresis . . . applies a figurative sense as a literal one, while retaining the look or feel of figurality." Richard Shiff, "Cezanne's Physicality: The Politics of Touch," in *The Language of Art History*, ed. Salim Kemal and Ivan Gaskell (Cambridge: Cambridge University Press, 1991), quoted in Vivian Sobchack, *Carnal Thoughts: Embodiment and Moving Image Culture* (Berkeley and Los Angeles: University of California Press, 2004), 82.

5. Michel Foucault, *This Is Not a Pipe*, trans. James Harkness (Berkeley and Los Angeles: University of California Press, 1983). W. J. Thomas Mitchell, *Picture Theory: Essays on Verbal and Visual Representation* (Chicago: University of Chicago Press, 1994).

6. Paul Ricoeur, *The Rule of Metaphor* (Toronto: University of Toronto Press, 1977 [1975]).

7. For Seshadri-Crooks, Maggie represents an ending point as well. For her, "Recitatif" offers the opportunity to explore the function of terms such as "black" and

"white" as names. She asks, "When the signifier 'black' or 'white' points to a specific body, what have we discovered about it?" "[A]re 'black' and 'white' descriptions, or are they names? Are names descriptions? That is, of course, the more fundamental question." Kalpana Seshadri-Crooks, "What's in a Name? Love and Knowledge Beyond Identity in 'Recitatif,'" in *Desiring Whiteness: A Lacanian Analysis of Race* (Durham, NC: Duke University Press, 2000), 133.

8. For Quintilian, *abusio* describes "the practice of adapting the nearest possible term to describe something for which no actual term exists." Quoted in Lee Edelman, *Transmemberment of Song: Hart Crane's Anatomies of Rhetoric and Desire* (Stanford, CA: Stanford University Press, 1987), 10.

9. Indeed, for Pierre Fontanier, catachresis is determined by the "same relations" as are rhetorical figures proper: "correspondence, connection or *resemblance* between ideas; and they operate in the same way: as metonymy, synecdoche, or metaphor." Emphasis added. Pierre Fontanier, *Les Figures Du Discours* (Paris: Flammarion, 1977), quoted in Jonathan Culler, "Commentary," *New Literary History* 6, no. 1 (1974): 223.

10. Charles W. Mills, "Non-Cartesian Sums: Philosophy and the African-American Experience," in *Blackness Visible: Essays on Philosophy and Race* (Ithaca, NY: Cornell University Press, 1998), 6.

11. Ernesto Laclau, "Articulation and the Limits of Metaphor," in *A Time for the Humanities: Futurity and the Limits of Autonomy*, ed. Tim Dean, James S. Bono, and Ewa Olonowska-Ziarek (New York: Fordham University Press, 2008).

12. Gerald Posselt, "The Tropological Economy of Catachresis," *Critical Studies* 25 (2005). In chapter 3 I touch on Thomas Keenan's understanding of the commodity form as catachresis, which has greatly inspired my own desire to think about catachresis as an aesthetic category as well. See Thomas Keenan, "The Point is to (Ex) Change It: Reading *Capital* Rhetorically," in *Fetishism as Cultural Discourse*, ed. Emily Apter and William Pietz (Ithaca, NY: Cornell University Press, 1993).

13. For the queerness of catachresis see Viviane K. Namaste, "The Use and Abuse of Queer Tropes: Metaphor and Catachresis in Queer Theory and Politics," *Social Semiotics* 9, no. 2 (1999); Lee Edelman, *Transmemberment of Song*; Lee Edelman, *Homographesis: Essays in Gay Literary and Cultural Theory* (New York: Routledge, 1994); Amy Villarejo, *Lesbian Rule: Cultural Criticism and the Value of Desire* (Durham, NC: Duke University Press, 2003).

14. Bruno Latour, *We Have Never Been Modern* (Cambridge, MA: Harvard University Press, 1993).

15. As Paul de Man summarizes: "We have no way of defining, of policing the boundaries that separate the name of one entity from the name of another; tropes are not just travellers, they tend to be smugglers and probably smugglers of stolen goods at that. What makes matters even worse is that there is no way of finding out whether

they do so with criminal intent or not." Paul de Man, "The Epistemology of Metaphor," *Critical Inquiry* 5, no. 1 (1978): 19.

16. Paul de Man, "The Epistemology of Metaphor," 21.

17. As he clarifies, "in its most restricted sense, prosopopeia makes accessible to the senses, in this case the ear, a voice which is out of earshot because it is no longer alive. In its most inclusive and also its etymological sense, it designates the very process of *figuration as giving face to what is devoid of it*" (emphasis added). Paul de Man, "The Epistemology of Metaphor," 26.

18. Foucault, *This Is Not a Pipe*, 47. He concludes: "Magritte's painting doubtless rests here, where thought in the mode of resemblance and things in relations of similitude have just vertically intersected."

19. My concept of facialization is loosely inspired by Gilles Deleuze and Félix Guattari, *A Thousand Plateaus: Capitalism and Schizophrenia*, trans. Brian Massumi (Minneapolis: University of Minnesota Press, 1987).

20. Kathryn Bond Stockton, *The Queer Child, or Growing Sideways in the Twentieth Century* (Durham, NC: Duke University Press, 2009). I am grateful to Kristopher Cannon for introducing me to Stockton's work and the concept of sideways growth.

21. Here, I again refer to the idea that concepts such as DuBois's notion of double-consciousness and Fanon's idea of the "triple person" indicate the reflexive position that is afforded to the black subject for the simple fact of being subjected to having to see oneself through the eyes of others.

22. Vivian Sobchack, "What My Fingers Knew: The Cinesthetic Subject, or Vision in the Flesh," in *Carnal Thoughts: Embodiment and Moving Image Culture* (Berkeley and Los Angeles: University of California Press, 2004).

23. Sobchack, "What My Fingers Knew," 73. Emphasis in original.

24. Luchina Fisher, "Why Some Blacks Prefer 'Blind Side' to 'Precious,'" *ABC News*, December 2009; Armond White, "Pride and Precious," *New York Press*, November 4, 2009; A. O. Scott, "Two Films, Two Routes from Poverty," *New York Times*, November 22, 2009; Ron Wynn, "*Precious* and *the Blind Side* Renew the Debate: Where Does an Honest Portrayal of Black Lives Stop, and Exploitation Start?," *Nashville Scene*, November 19, 2009. For a rich discussion of *Precious* see the special issue of *Black Camera* 14, no. 1 (2012) devoted to the film.

25. Demetria Irwin, "Gabourey Sidibe Is Sweet but Not 'Precious,'" *New York Amsterdam News*, November 12, 2009.

26. Richard Corliss, "*The Blind Side*: What's All the Cheering About?," *Time*, December 3, 2009.

27. For the concept of pornotroping see Hortense J. Spillers, "Mama's Baby, Papa's Maybe: An American Grammar Book," *Diacritics* 17, no. 2 (1987); Alexander G. Weheliye, "Pornotropes," *Journal of Visual Culture* 7, no. 1 (2008).

28. Interestingly this is noted in the *New York Amsterdam News* review mentioned

in note 25: "The fact that Gabby can be seen in countless magazines (and on at least one cover), television interviews and red-carpet events is truly remarkable. This is noteworthy not just because "Precious" is Gabby's first professional acting role, but also because of how Gabby looks. In an entertainment industry of size zeros, colored contacts and an emphasis on "exotic" or racially ambiguous beauty, Gabby is definitely a stand out. She has dark, ebony skin that radiates the warmth of her African ancestors, and her plump, round figure is not the type often found on magazine covers." Irwin, "Gabourey Sidibe Is Sweet but Not 'Precious.'"

29. See Henry Louis Gates Jr., *The Signifying Monkey: A Theory of African-American Literary Criticism* (New York: Oxford University Press, 1988).

30. For a discussion of the integrationist imagination see my essay "A Necessary Signifier: The Body as Author and Text in *the Jackie Robinson Story*," *Adaptation: A Journal of Literature on Screen Studies* 1, no. 2 (2008), where I examine the process of visual accommodation of mainstream visual culture following Jackie Robinson's integration of baseball.

31. The chiasm, as Sobchack explains drawing on Merleau-Ponty, is the place where the intentional movement of the spectator toward the screen is reversed and brought back to an awareness of the spectator's own sensible body. See Sobchack, "What My Fingers Knew."

32. I discuss this structure in *Shadowboxer* in my "Shadowboxing: Lee Daniels's Non-Representational Cinema," in *Contemporary Black American Cinema: Race, Gender, and Sexuality at the Movies*, ed. Mia Mask (New York: Routledge, 2012), where I emphasize how, considered together, the two films both address and overcome the representational approach to black cinema.

33. As Sobchack explains, the term "cinesthetic" is meant to comprise the way in which the cinematic experience triggers and relies on both synaesthesia (or intersensoriality) and coenaesthesia (the perception of a person's whole sensorial being). At stake is the possibility to explain how meaning emerges from the conjunction of the spectator's bodies and cinematic representation. Sobchack, "What My Fingers Knew," 67.

34. The cinesthetic subject, Sobchack writes, is the one that "feels his or her literal body as only one side of *an irreducible and dynamic relational structure of reversibility and reciprocity* that has as its other side the figural objects of bodily provocation on the screen." Sobchack, "What My Fingers Knew," 79. Emphasis in original.

35. Charles Johnson, "A Phenomenology of the Black Body," *Michigan Quarterly Review* 32, no. 4 (1993): 606.

36. Chris Lee, "Mariah Carey Shows Her Ugly Side in 'Precious.' Yes, That's the Pop Diva — Deglammed and with Facial Hair — Playing the Dowdy Caseworker," *Los Angeles Times*, November 6, 2009.

37. Lee Daniels, "A Precious Ensemble," in featurette for the film *Precious: Based on the Novel "Push" by Sapphire* (Santa Monica, CA.: Lionsgate, 2009), DVD.

38. Jeanne Wolf, "Mariah Carey: 'Music Is Always Where My Heart Is,'" www. parade.com/celebrity/celebrity-parade/2009/1102-mariah-carey-precious.html.

39. Richard Powell, *Cutting a Figure: Fashioning Black Portraiture* (Chicago: University of Chicago Press, 2009).

40. For a discussion of the trope of the canvas see Kimberly Lamm, "Visuality and Black Masculinity in Ralph Ellison's *Invisible Man* and Romare Bearden's Photomontages," *Callaloo* 26, no. 3 (2003), 813–35.

41. Kobena Mercer, "Romare Bearden, 1964: Collage as Kunstwollen," in *Cosmopolitan Modernisms*, ed. Kobena Mercer (Cambridge, MA: MIT Press, 2005).

42. Powell begins his investigation of cutting from the use of the term *sharp* to indicate how an ostentatiously stylish person can "stand out" and be a "cut above" everybody else. Powell, *Cutting a Figure: Fashioning Black Portraiture*, 4, 14. For another compelling elaboration on the cut see Kathryn Bond Stockton, *Beautiful Bottom, Beautiful Shame: Where "Black" Meets "Queer"* (Durham, NC: Duke University Press, 2006). Stockton describes the cut in relation to Barthes's notion of the aesthetic wound, as the effect of a compelling detail, which has the ability to attract our attention, trigger our flight of fantasy, and to function as the holding pen for repressed histories.

43. Mercer, "Romare Bearden, 1964: Collage as Kunstwollen."

44. Lamm, "Visuality and Black Masculinity," 821.

45. Johnson, "Phenomenology of the Black Body," 606.

46. This statement is in response to the question posed by Gerald Matt, "You portray almost exclusively black women. To what extent are your figures 'abstract self-depictions'?" See Gerald Matt, "Wangechi Mutu in Conversation with Gerald Matt," in Wangechi Mutu, Angela Stief, and Gerald Matt, eds., *Wangechi Mutu: In Whose Image?* (Wien: Kunsthalle, 2009), 37.

47. See Kristopher Cannon's discussion of the cut in "Cutting Race Otherwise: Imagining Michael Jackson," *Spectator* 30, no. 2 (2010).

48. Mutu says she works alone, hands on. Cutting the pieces of the collages takes time and allows her to reflect. She does not like the Internet as an image database because she is interested in magazines for "the physical presence of the picture: the tactile quality of the paper, the aging processes of the material, the print quality." The end result, as Pierre de Weck notes, is "auratically" charged, if anything, by her labor. See Wangechi Mutu, Deutsche Guggenheim Berlin, and Deutsche Bank, *Wangechi Mutu, Artist of the Year 2010: My Dirty Little Heaven* (Ostfildern: Hatje Cantz, 2010).

49. Mutu, Stief, and Matt, *Wangechi Mutu: In Whose Image?*, 41.

50. Emphasis added. Isolde Brielmeier, "Interview with Wangechi Mutu Part I: The Body," in *Wangechi Mutu a Shady Promise*, ed. Douglas Singleton (Bologna, Italy: Damiani, 2008), 21.

51. "The only way to keep around this body that is society is by mutating," she

claims. "That's where these chimeras, these creatures, these women warriors come from — they're not me, per se, they're human conditions." Interview with Barbara Kruger, quoted in Klaus Ottmann, "The Human Form Divine: Wangechi Mutu's "Enceptual" Art," in Mutu, Guggenheim Berlin, and Deutsche Bank, *Wangechi Mutu, Artist of the Year 2010*, 64.

52. Wangechi Mutu in conversation with Barbara Kruger, *Interview*, April 2007, quoted in Mutu, Guggenheim Berlin, and Deutsche Bank, *Wangechi Mutu, Artist of the Year 2010*, 60.

53. Pierre de Weck, in Mutu, Guggenheim Berlin, and Deutsche Bank, *Wangechi Mutu, Artist of the Year* 2010, 18.

54. Here I use this formalist concept in a materialist sense and wonder what is the material substance of collage. How can we describe it, characterize it?

55. Angela Stief, "Images of Triumph and Transgression," in Mutu, Stief, and Matt, *Wangechi Mutu: In Whose Image?*, 15.

56. Fatimah Tobing Rony, *The Third Eye: Race, Cinema, and Ethnographic Spectacle* (Durham, NC: Duke University Press, 1996), 6.

57. Philippe Ricord, "Traité Complet Des Maladies Vénériennes: Clinique Iconographique De L'hopital Des Vénériens Recueil D'observations, Suivies De Considérations Pratique, Sur Les Maladies Qui Ont Été Traitées Dans Cet Hopital," ed. Just Rouvier (Paris: 1851).

58. Tobing Rony, *The Third Eye*, 17.

59. There are at least two other frameworks that are very relevant to understand Mutu's work that, however, I am not pursuing here. One is post-humanism: see, for example, Nicole R. Smith, "Wangechi Mutu Feminist Collage and the Cyborg" (master's thesis, Georgia State University, 2009); and the other is Afrofuturism (already mentioned in the introduction), even though Mutu rejects the label because she resents the suggestion that the ideas of "Africa" and "future" would be considered an oxymoron.

60. Jennifer González, "Flesh in the Machine: She's Egungun Again," in *Wangechi Mutu: This You Call Civilization?*, ed. David Moos, Wangechi Mutu, and Art Gallery of Ontario (Toronto: Art Gallery of Ontario, 2010), 72.

61. See for example "The Cinderella Curse" — an installation with dripping bottles and felt: Wangechi Mutu, *The Cinderella Curse*, 2007, Savannah College of Art and Design-Atlanta.; or "Exhuming Gluttony," where upside down bottles are wrapped with rabbit fur: Wangechi Mutu, *Exhuming Gluttony: A Lover's Requiem,* 2006, Installation, Salon 94.

62. Saidiya V. Hartman, *Scenes of Subjection: Terror, Slavery, and Self-Making in Nineteenth-Century America* (New York: Oxford University Press, 1997).

63. Consider, for instance, *A Fake Jewel in the Crown,* 2007; *The Bride Who Married A Camel's Head*, 2009; *Fallen Heads,* 2010.

64. "In the hybrids of Wangechi Mutu, the human and animal are collaged as

a tactic for defying the tyrannical, taxonomical order of seeing, that most violent imposition onto the bodies of those made into specimen." Brielmeier, "Interview with Wangechi Mutu," 146. My understanding of hybridity in this case comes from Bruno Latour's work, specifically in Latour, *We Have Never Been Modern*.

65. This argument about the temporality of catachresis is developed in Posselt, "The Tropological Economy of Catachresis."

66. M. M. Bakhtin, "Forms of Time and of the Chronotope in the Novel," in *The Dialogic Imagination: Four Essays* ed. Michael Holquist (Austin: University of Texas Press, 1981); Robert Stam, *Subversive Pleasures: Bakhtin, Cultural Criticism, and Film* (Baltimore: Johns Hopkins University Press, 1989).

67. Lauri Firstenberg, "'Perverse Anthropology: The Photomontage of Wangechi Mutu. A Conversation with the Artist,'" in Mutu, Guggenheim Berlin, and Deutsche Bank, *Wangechi Mutu, Artist of the Year 2010*, 42.

68. Okwui Enwezor, "Weird Beauty: Ritual Violence and Archaeology of Mass Media in Wangechi Mutu's Work," in Mutu, Guggenheim Berlin, and Deutsche Bank, *Wangechi Mutu, Artist of the Year 2010*, 28.

69. Carol Thompson, "Sticks and Stones Will Break Your Bones, but Words Can Also Hurt You: Don't Let Sleeping Heads Lie," in *Wangechi Mutu: This You Call Civilization?*, ed. David Moos, Wangechi Mutu, and Art Gallery of Ontario (Toronto: Art Gallery of Ontario, 2010), 48.

70. Emphasis in original. Michael E. Veal, "Enter Cautiously," in *Wangechi Mutu: A Shady Promise*, ed. Douglas Singleton (Bologna, Italy: Damiani, 2008), 10.

71. Henry M. Sayre, "Scars: Painting, Photography, Performance, Pornography, and the Disfigurement of Art," *Performing Arts Journal* 16, no. 1 (1994).

72. This photograph is part of *The Ballad of Sexual Dependence*, a photographic diary of Nan Goldin's immediate community of friends. It is one of the only two photographs in the book that sever the human figure and do not indicate the subject's name in their title. For a discussion of the community-making nature of Goldin's photography see Louis Kaplan, "Photography and the Exposure of Community. Sharing Nan Goldin and Jean-Luc Nancy," *Angelaki*, 6, no. 3 (2001).

73. Henry M. Sayre, "Scars: Painting, Photography, Performance, Pornography, and the Disfigurement of Art," 65.

74. Hartman develops this specific notion of empathy in reading abolitionist literature, particularly that of John Rankin. There she discovers that "in order to convince the reader of the horrors of slavery, Rankin must volunteer himself and his family for abasement [in an imagined scene of whipping]. Yet if this violence can become palpable and indignation can be fully aroused only through the masochistic fantasy, then it becomes clear that empathy is double-edged, for in making the other's suffering one's own, this suffering is occluded by the other's obliteration." Hartman, *Scenes of Subjection*, 19.

75. *Mining the Museum* is the first installation Fred Wilson had the opportunity to create within a public museum at the Maryland Historical Society jointly sponsored by the Contemporary Museum, Baltimore, in which he was given access to the historical society's permanent collection. The word "mining," as Judith Stein observes, indicated "excavating the collections to extract the buried presence of racial minorities, planting emotionally explosive historical material to raise consciousness and effect institutional change, and finding reflections of himself within the museum." Judith Stein, "Sins of Omission," *Art in America* (1993): 110; quoted in Jennifer A. González, *Subject to Display: Reframing Race in Contemporary Installation Art* (Cambridge, MA: MIT Press, 2008), 83. The dates 1820 and 1960 refer, respectively, to the Missouri Compromise, which annexed Missouri as a slave state, and Maine as a free state and to the Civil Rights Voting Act of 1960.

76. A spectacle for which, they seemingly argue, there is still too much tolerance. See Christina Elizabeth Sharpe, *Monstrous Intimacies: Making Post-Slavery Subjects*, Perverse Modernities (Durham, NC: Duke University Press, 2010).

77. Darby English, *How to See a Work of Art in Total Darkness* (Cambridge, MA: MIT Press, 2007), 165.

78. González, *Subject to Display*, 10.

79. González, *Subject to Display*, 91–92.

80. González, *Subject to Display*, 10. See Robin Bernstein, "Dances with Things: Material Culture and the Performance of Race," *Social Text* 27, no. 4 (2009). Following Diana Taylor, Bernstein observes how interactions are codified in repertoires and things carry the memory of their past usage. Diana Taylor, *The Archive and the Repertoire: Performing Cultural Memory in the Americas* (Durham, NC: Duke University Press, 2003).

81. Philip Fisher, *Making and Effacing Art: Modern American Art in a Culture of Museums* (New York: Oxford University Press, 1991); quoted in Bernstein, "Dances with Things," 82.

THREE **THE MONEY OF THE REAL**

1. Dick Gregory, *From the Back of the Bus* (New York: Avon Books, 1962), 48.

2. Nicholas Mirzoeff, "The Shadow and the Substance: Race, Photography, and the Index," in *Only Skin Deep: Changing Visions of the American Self*, ed. Coco Fusco and Brian Wallis (New York: International Center of Photography, 2003).

3. Cheryl I. Harris, "Whiteness as Property," *Harvard Law Review* 106, no. 8 (1993).

4. Emphasis in original. Gayatri Chakravorty Spivak, "Some Concept Metaphors of Political Economy in Derrida's Texts," *Leftwright/Intervention* 20 (1986); Peter Stallybrass, "Marx's Coat," in *Border Fetishisms: Material Objects in Unstable Spaces*, ed. Patricia Spyer (New York: Routledge, 1998), 183.

5. The title, of Mirzoeff's essay is taken from the caption for a *carte-de-visite* produced and circulated by emancipated slave Sojourner Truth: "I sell the shadow to support the substance," which comments precisely on this dynamic of exchange. "Here the emancipated woman," observes Mirzoeff, "makes her image the object of financial exchange in place of the substance, her whole person, which had once been for sale," Mirzoeff, "The Shadow and the Substance," 117.

6. Jean-Louis Comolli, "Machines of the Visible," in *The Cinematic Apparatus*, ed. Teresa de Lauretis and Stephen Heath (New York: St. Martin's Press, 1980); Allan Sekula, "The Traffic in Photographs," in *Only Skin Deep: Changing Visions of the American Self*, ed. Coco Fusco and Brian Wallis (New York: International Center of Photography, 2003); Fredric Jameson, *Postmodernism, or, the Cultural Logic of Late Capitalism* (Durham, NC: Duke University Press, 1991). In more recent film studies, there are at least three crucial titles: Jonathan Beller, *The Cinematic Mode of Production: Attention Economy and the Society of the Spectacle* (Hanover, NH: University Press of New England, 2006); Sean Cubitt, *The Cinema Effect* (Cambridge, MA: MIT Press, 2004); Steven Shaviro, "Post-Cinematic Affect: On Grace Jones, *Boarding Gate,* and *Southland Tales*," *Film-Philosophy* 14, no. 1 (2010). Influential in my early thinking about this subject has been also Matthew Tinkcom, *Working Like a Homosexual: Camp, Capital, Cinema* (Durham, NC: Duke University Press, 2002).

7. Sekula, "The Traffic in Photographs," 82.

8. Said differently, I conceive of these last two chapters as a way to look at photography as the passage of the image through race and capital, a claim that I address in two steps. Firstly, this chapter examines race as a form of appearance of capital. Secondly, chapter 4 discusses photography as a form of appearance of race.

9. Giovanni Arrighi, *The Long Twentieth Century: Money, Power, and the Origins of Our Times* (New York: Verso, 1994); Fredric Jameson, "Culture and Finance Capital," *Critical Inquiry* 24, no. 1 (1997).

10. The "Black Atlantic" is a geographical and historiographical cultural unit instituted by the transatlantic slave trade, which has been employed in Cultural Studies and Art History, as well as more widely, to conduct a global, yet nuanced, examination of the arts and culture of the African diaspora. See Paul Gilroy, *The Black Atlantic: Modernity and Double Consciousness* (Cambridge, MA: Harvard University Press, 1993); Tanya Barson and Peter Gorshluter, eds. *Afro Modern: Journeys through the Black Atlantic* (Liverpool, England: Tate Publishing, 2010).

11. Baucom's synthesis: "[the book's] historiography partially corresponds to what is sometimes called the New British history and sometimes Atlantic history. Its cultural theory emerges from a range of recent works in black-Atlantic, trans-Atlantic, and circum-Atlantic cultural studies. Its philosophy of history . . . derives from Benjamin. Its time consciousness is hauntological. . . . And Liverpool is one of [the Long Twentieth Century's] capitals, the voyage of the *Zong* one of its 'arcades,' the *Zong*'s

insurance contract one of its allegories." Ian Baucom, *Specters of the Atlantic: Finance Capital, Slavery, and the Philosophy of History* (Durham, NC: Duke University Press, 2005), 31.

12. Lyndon Barrett, *Blackness and Value: Seeing Double* (Cambridge and New York: Cambridge University Press, 1999). He writes, "*Seeing Double* is a suggestive subtitle for this study for several reasons. First, duality suggests the binarism by which the concept of value most routinely attempts to present itself. To 'see' value is in some sense to 'see' double. Another sense of the phrase 'seeing double' implies a state of impaired, unreliable, or faulty perception, and this sense of the phrase is captured by the yoking of racial blackness with the concept of value. [I]n U.S. cultural logic the abstract entities 'value' and 'race' keenly reflect one another, even to the point at which they might be considered isomorphic" (1). Barrett continues a reflection on value which began in Barbara Herrnstein Smith, *Contigencies of Value: Alternative Perspectives for Critical Theory* (Cambridge, MA: Harvard University Press, 1988). And, of course, Jean Baudrillard, *The Mirror of Production*, trans. Mark Poster (St. Louis: Telos Press, 1975); Jean Baudrillard, *For a Critique of the Political Economy of the Sign* (St. Louis: Telos Press, 1981).

13. A similar idea is pursued also by the recent by book George Yancy, *Look, a White!: Philosophical Essays on Whiteness* (Philadelphia: Temple University Press, 2012).

14. "The wealth of those societies in which the capitalist mode of production prevails appears as a 'monstrous collection of commodities,' the commodity as its elemental form." Karl Marx, *Capital: Volume 1: A Critique of Political Economy*, trans. Ben Fowkes (New York: Penguin Classics, 1990), 125; see Thomas Keenan, "The Point Is to (Ex)Change It: Reading *Capital*, Rhetorically," in *Fetishism as Cultural Discourse*, ed. Emily Apter and William Pietz (Ithaca, NY: Cornell University Press, 1993).

15. Emphasis added. Marx, *Capital*, 138–39.

16. Marx, *Capital*, 163–64.

17. Stallybrass, "Marx's Coat."

18. According to Keenan's close reading of the tropological structure of *Capital*'s first chapter exchange entails first a synecdochical reduction of the commodity to its elementary components in order to show what it has in common with other commodities so that it can be exchanged and, second, an abstraction, which shows that what is congealed in each and every commodity is human labor, that humanity is abstracted and yet still spectrally present in each and every commodity. Keenan argues that the exchangeability of the commodity is fundamentally a catachrestic process because it ultimately entails that the sphere of the human exchanges for nothing in return. Keenan, "Reading *Capital*, Rhetorically," 181.

19. It is this pivotal function of form that enables Marx to begin *Capital* from the analysis of the commodity form; that is, with the confidence that the entire structure

of capitalism can be read in the commodity. It is the structure of embodiment of the commodity — again its *form* — that creates, as it attempts to resolve, one of *Capital*'s fascinating but also challenging hermeneutic questions: how does the commodity reflect/represent the entire system? This is ultimately possible because the commodity form is the germ of the money form, which, in turn, is the locus of generalization of capital's logic of exchange.

20. Marx, *Capital*, 143. Ernst Hartwig Kantorowicz, *The King's Two Bodies: A Study in Mediaeval Political Theology* (Princeton, NJ: Princeton University Press, 1997). For Kantorowicz, the medieval doctrine of political theology that he described as the "King's Two Bodies" developed to explain the continuity of kingship beyond the mortality of individual kings. Because the natural (biological) body of the king is constitutively inadequate to represent his kingship, it had to be supplemented by another, immortal, and sublime body, not subjected to biological deterioration. According to this doctrine, which in turn is a repurposing of St. Paul's notion of the *corpus Christi* into a more flexible concept of the *corpus mysticum*, for the king to "function as the general equivalent of subjects in his realm . . . his being had to undergo, as if by some necessity in the logic of symbolic authority, a kind of doubling or '*germination*'" resulting in the production of the "abstract physiological fiction of a sublime, quasi-angelic body, a body of immortal flesh that was thereby seen to enjoy both juridical and medical immunity, to stand above the laws of men and the laws of perishable nature" (emphasis added). Eric L. Santner, *The Royal Remains: The People's Two Bodies and the Endgames of Sovereignty* (Chicago: Chicago University Press, 2011), 35. Jameson too points out how Marx's language anticipates Kantorowicz's work. He describes this moment as a "political mirror stage." Jameson, *Representing Capital: A Commentary on Volume One* (London and New York: Verso, 2011), 37.

21. Igor Kopytoff, "The Cultural Biography of Things: Commoditization as Process," in *The Social Life of Things: Commodities in Cultural Perspective*, ed. Arjun Appadurai (Cambridge: Cambridge University Press, 1986).

22. In *The Fugitive's Properties*, Stephen Best traces the afterlife of slavery in the aesthetics of legal representation and, in particular, the continued presence of slavery's ontological scandal in the systematic confusion between person and property. Stephen Best, *The Fugitive's Properties: Law and the Poetics of Possession* (Chicago: University of Chicago Press, 2004).

23. For a discussion of the relationship between political and visual representation in the *Leviathan* see Horst Bredekamp, "Thomas Hobbes's Visual Strategies," in *The Cambridge Companion to Hobbes's Leviathan*, ed. Patricia Springborg (Cambridge: Cambridge University Press, 2007); Eric Alliez, "Body without Image: Ernesto Neto's Anti-Leviathan," *Radical Philosophy*, no. 156 (2009). On representations of the body politic see also Nicholas Mirzoeff, *Bodyscape: Art, Modernity and the Ideal Figure*

(London and New York: Routledge, 1995). For a reading the Leviathan in relation to race and citizenship see Danielle S. Allen, *Talking to Strangers: Anxieties of Citizenship after Brown V. Board of Education* (Chicago: University of Chicago Press, 2004).

24. Jacques Derrida, *Specters of Marx: The State of Debt, the Work of Mourning, and the New International*, trans. Peggy Kamuf (New York and London: Routledge, 2006). In *Capital*'s chapter on the working day Marx attempts to counteract the abstractive logic of capital by "showing the workers" with his prose. This attempt, Ann Cvetkovich argues, is at the root of his employment of the gothic imaginary and the sensationalist language of the Victorian novel. His display of the deformed worker's body is made to carry, to poetically mirror, the weight of Marx's critique of equation. Ann Cvetkovich, *Mixed Feelings: Feminism, Mass Culture, and Victorian Sensationalism* (New Brunswick, NJ: Rutgers University Press, 1992). See also Jameson, *Representing Capital*, 25.

25. Gayatri Chakravorty Spivak, "Scattered Speculations on the Question of Value," *Diacritics* 15, no. 4 (1985).

26. "The table continues to be wood, an ordinary, sensuous thing. But as soon as it emerges as a commodity, it changes into a thing which transcends sensuousness. It not only stands with its feet on the ground, but, in relation to all other commodities, it stands on its head, and evolves out of its wooden brain grotesque ideas, far more wonderful than if it were to begin dancing of its own free will." Marx, *Capital*, 163–64.

27. Fred Moten, *In the Break: The Aesthetics of the Black Radical Tradition* (Minneapolis: University of Minnesota Press, 2003), 1–24. Moten focuses on Aunt Hester's scream as an example of aural resistance of/from the object that Marx was able to imagine only in the subjunctive mode ("if these commodities could talk, they would say . . . "). "The speaking commodity thus cuts Marx; but the shrieking commodity [i.e. Aunt Hester's scream] cuts Saussure, thereby cutting Marx doubly: this by way of an irruption of phonic substance that cuts and augments meaning with a phonographic, rematerializing inscription" (14).

28. Bill Brown, "The Tyranny of Things (Trivia in Karl Marx and Mark Twain)," *Critical Inquiry* 28, no. 2 (2002), 454.

29. Gyorgy Markus, "Walter Benjamin Or: The Commodity as Phantasmagoria," *New German Critique*, no. 83 (2001).

30. Walter Benjamin, "Central Park," *New German Critique* 34 (1985): 42. Stephen Best's discussion of this passage first brought it to my attention. Best, *The Fugitive's Properties*, 2.

31. *A Narrative of the Most Remarkable Particulars in the Life of James Albert Ukawsaw Gronniosaw, An African Prince, As Related by Himself.* The trope of the Talking Book assumes various forms and expresses different readings of the linguistic economy of slavery in the different slave narratives Gates examines, written between 1770 and 1865. Henry Louis Gates Jr., *The Signifying Monkey: A Theory of African-*

American Literary Criticism (New York: Oxford University Press, 1988). See also the seminal Houston Baker, Jr., *Blues, Ideology, and Afro-American Literature: A Vernacular Theory* (Chicago: University of Chicago Press, 1984).

32. Gates, *Signifying Monkey*, 137.

33. Commodity fetishism works in two different directions here: the book and the slave are both speaking commodities, but the former is so as a result of commodity fetishism, understood as the animation and personification of the commodity, while the latter is so as a consequence of a commodification of the person. While the book possesses a merely phantasmatic persona, the slave, as Kopytoff points out, is literally a commodity with a biography. Kopytoff, "Cultural Biography of Things."

34. Charles W. Mills, "Non-Cartesian Sums: Philosophy and the African-American Experience," in *Blackness Visible: Essays on Philosophy and Race* (Ithaca, NY: Cornell University Press, 1998), 9.

35. Jameson, *Representing Capital*.

36. Jacques Derrida and F. C. T. Moore, "White Mythology: Metaphor in the Text of Philosophy," *New Literary History* 6, no. 1; Allen Hoey, "The Name on the Coin: Metaphor, Metonymy, and Money," *Diacritics* 18, no. 2 (1988), 35.

37. Baucom, *Specters of the Atlantic*, 31.

38. This is Kant's terminology developed in "An Old Question Raised Again: Is the Human Race Constantly Progressing?" which Baucom also adopts. Baucom, *Specters of the Atlantic*, 116.

39. Baucom, *Specters of the Atlantic*, 139.

40. Bill Brown, "Reification, Reanimation, and the American Uncanny," *Critical Inquiry* 32 (2006).

41. See also Robyn Wiegman, *American Anatomies: Theorizing Race and Gender* (Durham, NC: Duke University Press, 1995).

42. Charles W. Mills, "European Specters," in *From Class to Race: Essays in White Marxism and Black Radicalism* (Lanham, MD: Rowman & Littlefield, 2003).

43. My thinking about blackface has been informed by Eric Lott, *Love and Theft: Blackface Minstrelsy and the American Working Class* (New York: Oxford University Press, 1993); Michael Rogin, *Blackface, White Noise: Jewish Immigrants in the Hollywood Melting Pot* (Berkeley and Los Angeles: University of California Press, 1996); Susan Gubar, *Racechanges: White Skin, Black Face in American Culture* (New York and Oxford: Oxford University Press, 1997); W. T. Lhamon Jr., *Raising Cain: Blackface Performance from Jim Crow to Hip Hop* (Cambridge, MA: Harvard University Press, 1998). And obviously Ralph Ellison, "Change the Joke and Slip the Yoke," in *The Collected Essays of Ralph Ellison* (New York: Modern Library, 1995). See also Tavia Nyong'o, *The Amalgamation Waltz: Race, Performance, and the Ruses of Memory* (Minneapolis: University of Minnesota Press, 2009).

44. Minstrelsy, Lott argues, is born from an act of fascination with what is perceived

to be black culture and gesture at the same time as it effects an expropriation of the markers and cultural trappings of blackness itself. See Lott, *Love and Theft*, especially chapter 2.

45. As Susan Gubar similarly points out, "Not simply mimetic, racechange is an extravagant aesthetic construction that functions self-reflexively to comment on representation in general." Gubar, *Racechanges*, 10.

46. Emphasis added. Dick Gregory, *Nigger* (E. P. Dutton, 1964), 144.

47. Among the publications from this period there are two biographies, two photo books, a political campaign book and two books of political analysis: Dick Gregory, *Nigger*; Gregory, *Up from Nigger* (New York: Fawcett, 1977); Gregory, *From the Back of the Bus*; Gregory, *What's Happening?* (New York: E. P. Dutton, 1965); Gregory, *Write Me In!* (New York: Bantam Books, 1968); Gregory, *The Shadow That Scares Me* (Pocket Books, 1968); Richard Claxton Gregory, *No More Lies: The Myth and the Reality of American History* (New York: Harper & Row, 1971). Important is also his more recent memoir, Dick Gregory and P. Moses Sheila, *Callous on My Soul: A Memoir* (Atlanta: Longstreet Press, 2000).

48. For a discussion of the relationship between Gregory's comedy, his dietary philosophy, and political views see Doris Witt, *Black Hunger: Food and the Politics of U.S. Identity* (New York and Oxford: Oxford University Press, 1999)..

49. Here, I am obviously referring to Stuart Hall's influential claim that race is a free-floating signifier made at a lecture at Goldsmiths' College, New Cross, London, in 1997.

50. I discuss the counterfactual as a legal form underlying the doctrine of separate but equal in chapter 4.

51. Attention should be given to Gregory's astute use of visual and material culture. Not only was he never segregated as a stand-up comedian, but he also consistently published photo books in which his jokes laid alongside photographic images of him either playing in clubs or performing a series of black-on-black impersonations. For this last idea see Gubar, *Racechanges*.

52. The idea of the nightclub as an abject space comes from John Limon, *Stand-up Comedy in Theory, or, Abjection in America* (Durham, NC: Duke University Press, 2000).

53. "When the white man steps behind the mask of the trickster," he wrote, "his freedom is circumscribed by the fear that he is not simply *miming* a personification of his disorder and chaos, but *that he will become in fact that which he intends only to symbolize.*" Emphasis added. Ellison, "Change the Joke," 107.

54. Markus, "Commodity as Phantasmagoria"; Walter Benjamin, "Paris, the Capital of the Nineteenth Century. 1935," in *The Arcades Project* (Cambridge, MA: Belknap Press, 1999); Margaret Cohen, "Walter Benjamin's Phantasmagoria," *New German Critique*, no. 48 (1989).

55. Tom Gunning, "Illusions Past and Future: The Phantasmagoria and Its Specters,"

MediaArtHistoriesArchive, 2004, http://hdl.handle.net/10002/296; Laurent Mannoni and Richard Crangle, *The Great Art of Light and Shadow: Archaeology of the Cinema* (Exeter, England: University of Exeter Press, 2000); Marina Warner, *Phantasmagoria: Spirit Visions, Metaphors, and Media into the Twenty-First Century* (Oxford and New York: Oxford University Press, 2008). For a discussion of the connection between racial encounters, permeable bodies, and racially unstable ontology and its connection to the minstrel show see Daphne A. Brooks, *Bodies in Dissent: Spectacular Performances of Race and Freedom, 1850–1910* (Durham, NC: Duke University Press, 2006).

56. As a second-degree racial signifier, blackface makeup was the expression of minstrelsy's claim to be imitative of black culture even though early minstrel acts, as Eric Lott writes, participated in "an exchange system of cultural signifiers that both produced and continually marked the inauthenticity of their "blackness"; their ridicule asserted the difference between counterfeit and currency even as they disseminated what most audiences believed were black music, dance, and gesture." Eric Lott, "Love and Theft: The Racial Unconscious of the Blackface Minstrelsy," *Representations* no. 39 (1992): 39. Similarly, Ralph Ellison claimed that the counterfeiting of the black image is the result of "America's Manichean fascination with the symbolism of blackness and whiteness," and, therefore, its referent is not black and white people, but rather the process of signification of race itself. Ellison, "Change the Joke," 103.

57. See Lawrence Weschler, *Boggs: A Comedy of Values* (Chicago: University of Chicago Press, 1999).

58. Weschler, *Boggs: A Comedy of Values*, 23.

59. The defetishization of the commodity money (that is, the realization that its value resides only in the transaction it allows), though, is only a temporary stage within a cycle of value production which culminates in a refetishization of the transaction that dismantled money's fetishism in the first place, once its material traces and their representations are put on sale in the art market. Money, as a system of representation, is only temporarily freed, slowed down.

60. U.S. Code Section 474 and 475 of Title 18, cited in Weschler, *Boggs*, emphasis in original. Weschler chronicles a number of run-ins with the law. Since the book was published in 1999, however, more than ten years of legal troubles are unaccounted for.

61. Kara Keeling argues that the show's stars' puzzled and disappointed reaction to the animated puppets mirrors the earlier reaction to the 1940s film footage and, therefore, suggests retroactively that the black image was always already an animation. Kara Keeling, "Passing for Human: *Bamboozled* and Digital Humanism," *Women & Performance: A Journal of Feminist Theory* 29, no. 15 (2005). The puppets share a similar invitation to tactile engagement that Jennifer Barker describes in relation to *Toy Story*. Except that here the Fisher Price toy quality of the puppets brings the spectator to realize, on the one hand, a desire to touch the "cool and smooth" skin of the film but, on the other, to disavow its content and reject its racism. Jennifer M. Barker, *The*

Tactile Eye: Touch and the Cinematic Experience (Berkeley and Los Angeles: University of California Press, 2009), 45.

62. *Bamboozled* has been read also in relation to its strategic and subversive employment of stereotypes with a focus on its generic status in between tragedy and satire, by leveraging minstrelsy as an allegory of exploitative relations of blackness in the entertainment industry, the commerce of blackness, as raising questions about the ownership and self-definition of blackness, as an example of the aesthetics of the grotesque, as a reflection on post-humanism and so on. See "Living Color: Race, Stereotype, and Animation in Spike Lee's *Bamboozled*," in W. J. T. Mitchell, *What Do Pictures Want? The Lives and Loves of Images* (Chicago: University of Chicago Press, 2005); Brown, "Reification, Reanimation"; Keeling, "Passing for Human"; Harry J. Elam, Jr., "Spike Lee's *Bamboozled*," in *Black Cultural Traffic Crossroads in Global Performance and Popular Culture*, ed. Harry J. Elam Jr. and Jackson Kennell (Ann Arbor: University of Michigan Press, 2005); Beretta Smith-Shomade, "'I Be Smakin' My Hoes': Paradox and Authenticity in *Bamboozled*," in *The Spike Lee Reader*, ed. Paula J. Massood (Philadelphia: Temple University Press, 2007); Tavia Nyong'o, "Racial Kitsch and Black Performance," in *The Spike Lee Reader*; Susan Gubar, "Racial Camp in *The Producers* and *Bamboozled*," *Film Quarterly* 60, no. 2 (2006); Gregory Laski, "Falling Back into History: The Uncanny Trauma of Blackface Minstrelsy in Spike Lee's *Bamboozled*," *Callaloo* 33, no. 4 (2010); Ed Guerrero, "*Bamboozled*: In the Mirror of Abjection," *Black Contemporary American Cinema: Race, Gender and Sexuality at the Movies,* ed. Mia Mask (New York: Routledge, 2012).

63. For another focus on the recursive historical temporality of the film as well as the idea of uncanny trauma of slavery see the already-cited essay by Laski, "Falling Back into History.."

64. Brown, "Reification, Reanimation," 185.

65. Mitchell, *What Do Pictures Want?*, specifically chapter 14, "Living Color: Race, Stereotype, and Animation in Spike Lee's *Bamboozled*." For Homi Bhabha, in turn, the stereotype can only be disempowered when regarded not as the object of desire, but its setting; not as an ascription of a priori identities, but rather their production. The stereotype is a scene of subject formation and, more to the point, it operates like a fetish. It responds to multiple desires — to make present, to make visible, to make knowable, and to fixate. Homi Bhabha, "The Other Question: Stereotype, Discrimination and the Discourse of Colonialism," in *The Location of Culture* (New York: Routledge, 1994).

66. Brown, "Reification, Reanimation," 197.

67. Brown, "Reification, Reanimation," 200.

68. For an insightful discussion of Levinthal's photographs of Sambo art see Manthia Diawara, "The Blackface Stereotype," in David Levinthal and Manthia Diawara, *Blackface* (Santa Fe, NM: Arena Editions, 1999). See also W. T. Lhamon Jr.,

"Optic Black: Naturalizing the Refusal to Fit," in *Black Cultural Traffic: Crossroads in Global Performance and Popular Culture*, ed. Harry J. Elam Jr. and Kennell Jackson (Ann Arbor: University of Michigan Press, 2005).

69. Emphasis added. Lhamon, "Optic Black," 115, 113.

70. This could be possibly read as an instance of "rude aesthetics." See Hugh S. Manon, "Rude Aesthetics in the Digital Mainstream," (paper presented at the World Picture Conference, Oklahoma State University, October 24–25, 2008).

71. Keeling, "Passing for Human," 244.

72. Blackness, Keeling points out, is involved in passing, whether it is commodity circulation or capital's financial flows. Keeling, "Passing for Human," 248.

73. Schudson, "Advertising as Capitalist Realism." *Advertising & Society Review* 1, no.1 (2000), 53.

74. Schudson, "Advertising as Capitalist Realism," 11.

75. Rene de Guzman, "Nothing Better," in *Pitch Blackness*, ed. Hank Willis Thomas (New York: Aperture, 2008), 95–96.

76. Rene de Guzman, "Nothing Better."

77. Benjamin, "Central Park," 42.

78. For the idea of the metaphysical stillness of racial images see James Snead, *White Screens, Black Images: Hollywood from the Dark Side* (New York and London: Routledge, 1994).

79. The logbook of the *Zong* does not survive, but other ships' logbooks do. Baucom reprints one of them (recording the purchase and trading of slaves in exchange for rum and gold, as well as a host of corollary transactions involving food, water, and firewood), but, before doing so, he sets the terms under which this document needs to be encountered. He asks the reader to resist the list's "reiterative predictability" and its flattening pathos, which solicits "indulgence for horror banalized, horror catalogued." He urges: "So, I ask, do not skim, read." See Baucom, *Specters of the Atlantic*, 11.

80. Jacques Derrida, "Différance," in *Margins of Philosophy*, transl. Alan Bass (Chicago: The University of Chicago Press, 1982). The adoption of the Derridean notion of *différance* to understand the (literary) writing of race is due to Henry Louis Gates Jr.'s book, *Signifying Monkey*.

81. For the "matter" of the visual see the special issue of *Representations*, edited by Huey Copeland and Krista Thompson, "Perpetual Returns: New World Slavery and the Matter of the Visual," *Representations* 113, no. 1 (2011). There are various accounts of the history of the term *postblack*, initially employed by Robert Farris Thompson and then popularized by Thelma Golden in occasion of the 2001 exhibition *Freestyle* at the Studio Museum of Harlem. See Robert Farris Thompson, "Afro Modernism," *Artforum* 30 (1991); Thelma Golden et al., *Freestyle* (New York: The Studio Museum in Harlem, 2001); Barson, *Afro Modern*; Mary Schmidt Campbell, "African American Art in a Post-Black Era," *Women & Performance: a journal of feminist theory* 17, no. 3

(2007); Paul Taylor, "Post-Black, Old Black," *African American Review* 41, no. 4 (2007). See also Darby English, *How to See a Work of Art in Total Darkness* (Cambridge, MA: MIT Press, 2007); Derek Conrad Murray, "Hip-Hop vs. High Art: Notes on Race as Spectacle," *Art Journal* 63, no. 2 (2004); April J. Sunami, "Transforming 'Blackness': 'Post-Black' and Contemporary Hip-Hop in Visual Culture" (master's thesis, Ohio University, 2008); Cathy Byrd, "Is There a 'Post-Black' Art?," *Art Papers Magazine* 26, no. 6 (2002).

82. Mills, "European Specters," 168–69.

83. Marcus Wood, *Blind Memory: Visual Representations of Slavery in England and America 1780–1865* (New York: Routledge, 2000), 16–40.

84. Michael Kaplan, "Iconomics: The Rhetoric of Speculation," *Public Culture* 15, no. 3 (2003).

85. Furthermore, the logo, Coombe claims, is a signature of authenticity. Through the logo, the emotional attachment and the loyalty to the brand are congealed in the exchange value of the sign. Rosemary J. Coombe, *The Cultural Life of Intellectual Properties: Authorship, Appropriation and the Law* (Durham, NC: Duke University Press, 1998), 175.

86. The idea of tasting the other is vividly discussed in bell hooks, "Eating the Other," in *Black Looks: Race and Representation* (Cambridge, MA: South End Press, 1992).

87. Sara Ahmed, *The Cultural Politics of Emotions* (New York: Routledge, 2004), 1.

88. The idea of the advertising tableau is explored in Roland Marchand, *Advertising the American Dream: Making Way for Modernity, 1920–1940* (Berkeley and Los Angeles: University of California Press, 1985).

89. The work's title ventriloquizes advertising rhetoric but introverts its mode of address. Rather than pitching the product to the consumer, it provocatively asks if she is "right" for it. The "it," in turn, condenses the instability of the picture because its many possible referents effect what "right woman" might mean in this context.

90. Harry J. Elam Jr., "Changes Clothes and Go. A Postscript to Postblackness," in *Black Cultural Traffic. Crossroads in Global Performance and Popular Culture,* ed. Harry J. Elam Jr. and Kennell Jackson (Ann Arbor: University of Michigan Press, 2005); Jennifer A. González, "The Face and the Public: Race, Secrecy, and Digital Art Practice," *Camera Obscura* 70, no. 24 (2009); Coco Fusco, "All Too Real: The Tale of an on-Line Black Sale. Coco Fusco Interviews Keith Townsend Obadike," 2001, www.blacknetart.com/coco.html. Keith and Mendi Obadike, "The Black. Net.Art Actions: *Blackness for Sale* (2001), *The Interaction of Coloreds* (2002), and *The Pink of Stealth* (2003)," in Mary Flanagan and Austin Booth, eds. *re:skin* (Cambridge, MA: MIT Press, 2006).

91. "Because ayo invites people to wish for her object status without actually delivering herself as such . . . ayo is the object-less art piece, but the audience,

rendered vulnerable once they expose a desire to appropriate blackness that goes unconsummated in the relationship ayo establishes, become objectified by their lack of agency. [T]he resistance to psychic and socioeconomic violence emerges . . . from the inversion of the ways in which the subject/object relationship is traditionally racialized, both in the realm of the arts and in everyday social experience." Brandi Wilkins Catanese, "'How Do I Rent a Negro?': Racialized Subjectivity and Digital Performance Art," *Theater Journal* 75 (2005): 704. Obadike's tenth warning ironically addresses these fantasies: "The Seller does not recommend that this Blackness be used by whites looking for a wild weekend."

92. González, "The Face and the Public," 57.

93. Fusco, "All Too Real." Ultimately, as Jennifer Gonzalez argues, Obadike's failure to sell his blackness shows that race is not a property but rather a *"relation of public encounters"* taking place under the *form* of a commodity. Emphasis in original. González, "The Face and the Public," 56.

94. Elam, "Change Clothes and Go," 386.

95. Elam, "Change Clothes and Go," 386.

FOUR **THE LONG PHOTOGRAPHIC CENTURY**

1. Seshadri-Crooks offers a Lacanian reading of the film that has partly informed my thinking. Kalpana Seshadri-Crooks, "Looking Alike: Or the Ethics of Suture," in *Desiring Whiteness: A Lacanian Analysis of Race* (New York and London: Routledge, 2000).

2. The controversy initiated by Betye Saar is summarized in Gwendolyn DuBois Shaw, *Seeing the Unspeakable: The Art of Kara Walker* (Durham, NC: Duke University Press, 2004). It is also the impetus behind the recent publication of Howardena Pindell, *Kara Walker-No, Kara Walker-Yes, Kara Walker-?* (New York: Midmarch Arts Press, 2009). Discussion of controversial work such as Walker's necessarily raises ethical questions: the charge of obscenity, in fact, expresses moral concerns with the propriety, efficacy, and ownership of a certain racial imagery. These issues are made all the more acute by the extraordinary success she has had with white collectors. The impossibility to determine the proper affective response to her work (pain, pleasure, shock, outrage, and so on) in fact, importantly foregrounds how such affects carry different ethical repercussions along racial lines. The approach I adopt here is to regard her as a visual theorist of the foundational role of blackness in the ontology of the image.

3. As previously mentioned I derive the idea of the "historical ontology of slavery" and its relationship with the American uncanny from Bill Brown, "Reification, Reanimation, and the American Uncanny," *Critical Inquiry* 32 (2006). I will cite as appropriate from most supporters of Walker's work, but for now here are some key publications: Robert Reid-Pharr, Annette Dixon, and Thelma Golden, eds., *Kara*

Walker: Pictures from Another Time (Ann Arbor: University of Michigan Museum of Art and D.A.P.P., 2002); Ian Berry et al., eds., *Kara Walker: Narratives of a Negress*, 2nd ed. (New York: Rizzoli, The Frances Young Tang Teaching Museum and Art Gallery at Skidmore College, Williams College Museum of Art, 2007); Philippe Vergne, ed. *Kara Walker: My Complement, My Enemy, My Oppressor, My Love*, 1st ed. (Minneapolis: Walker Art Center, 2007); Kara Elizabeth Walker, *Kara Walker: After the Deluge* (New York: Rizzoli, 2007); Joan Copjec, "Moses the Egyptian and the Big Black Mammy of the Antebellum South: Freud (with Kara Walker) on Race and History," in *Imagine There's No Woman: Ethics and Sublimation* (Cambridge, MA: MIT Press, 2002); Psyche A. Williams-Forson, "Flying the Coop with Kara Walker," in *Building Houses out of Chicken Legs* (Chapel Hill: University of North Carolina Press, 2006).

4. For Best and Marcus, the idea of pursuing surface readings is intended to provide an alternative to the still hegemonic practice of symptomatic readings. Here are some notions of surface their special issue addresses: surface as materiality; surface as the intricate verbal structure of literary language; embracing surface as an affective and ethical stance; attention to surface as practice of critical description; surface as location of patterns that exist within and across texts; surface as literal meaning. Stephen Best and Sharon Marcus, "Surface Reading: An Introduction," *Representations* 108 (2009).

5. For background on the film see Roy Grundmann's interview with the filmmakers, which early on inspired me to think about face value in relation to race. Roy Grundmann, "Identity Politics at Face Value," *Cineaste* 20 (1994).

6. Manthia Diawara, "Noir by Noirs: Toward a New Realism in Black Cinema," in *Shades of Noir*, ed. Joan Copjec (London: Verso, 1993); Eric Lott, "The Whiteness of Film Noir," *American Literary History* 9, no. 3 (1997); Dan Flory, "Black on White: Film Noir and the Epistemology of Race in Recent African American Cinema," *Journal of Social Philosophy* 31, no. 1 (2000); Dan Flory, *Philosophy, Black Film, Film Noir* (University Park: Pennsylvania State University Press, 2008). My understanding of the relationship between blackness and film noir is profoundly influenced by Michael Boyce Gillespie, "Significations of Blackness: American Cinema and the Idea of a Black Film" (PhD diss., New York University, 2007), especially chapter 3, "Darker Than Blue: *Deep Cover* and the Noir Modal of Blackness."

7. Brian Price, "Color, the Formless, and Cinematic Eros," in *Color: The Film Reader*, ed. Brian Price and Angela Dalle Vacche (New York: Routledge, 2006), 78.

8. Shawn Michelle Smith, among many others, connects the advent of photography and specifically of the photographic archive alongside disciplines such as criminology, racial biology, phrenology, and eugenics, to a new nineteenth-century focus on the body that created this split model of subjectivity: "If interiority was the essence imagined to be stable as external signs fluctuated, it was stabilized only through the proliferation of *surface signs*, of representations of the body, called upon to make such essences *readable*, apparent, knowable. The photographic sign invited one to

participate in a *leap of faith* whereby the body might serve as *index* to an imagined essence. And by the same leap of faith, by the same process of *metonymy*, individuals could imagine themselves linked to others similarly represented, and thereby mutually affirm an imagined essence." Emphasis added. Shawn Michelle Smith, *American Archives: Gender, Race, and Class in Visual Culture* (Princeton, NJ: Princeton University Press, 1999), 5.

9. Annie Howell, personal conversation with the filmmakers, 2005.

10. Marcie Frank, "The Camera and the Speculum: David Cronenberg's *Dead Ringers*," *PMLA* 106, no. 3 (1991), 459.

11. Susan Elizabeth Earle and Renée Ater, *Aaron Douglas: African American Modernist* (New Haven, CT: Yale University Press, 2007). See also Amy Kirschke, *Aaron Douglas: Art, Race, and the Harlem Renaissance* (Jackson: University Press of Mississippi, 1995). I thank Eddie Chambers for having discussed with me some of these ideas about Aaron Douglas.

12. Among the rich literature on passing, consider at least Lauren Berlant, "National Brands/ National Body: Imitation of Life," in *Comparative American Identities: Race, Sex, and Nationality in the Modern Text*, ed. Hortense J. Spillers (New York and London: Routledge, 1991); P. Gabrielle. Foreman, "Who's Your Mama?: 'White' Mulatta Genealogies, Early Photography, and Anti-Passing Narratives of Slavery and Freedom," *American Literary History* 14, no. 3 (2002); Susan Gubar, *Racechanges: White Skin, Black Face in American Culture* (New York and Oxford: Oxford University Press, 1997).

13. I refer to Michael Harris's discussion of Motley in Michael D. Harris, *Colored Pictures: Race and Visual Representation* (Chapel Hill: University of North Carolina Press, 2003).

14. Ellen McBreen, "Biblical Gender Bending in Harlem: The Queer Performance of Nugent's Salome," *Art Journal* 57, no. 3 (1998); Seth Clark Silberman, "Lighting the Harlem Renaissance Afire!!: Embodying Richard Bruce Nugent's Bohemian Politic," in *The Gratest Taboo: Homosexuality in Black Communities*, ed. Deloy Constantine-Simms (Los Angeles: Alyson Books, 2001). See also Amy Kirschke, *Art in Crisis: W.E.B. Du Bois and the Struggle for African American Identity and Memory* (Bloomington: Indiana University Press, 2007).

15. As Lyndon Barrett puts it, the "perplexity" of value is the "impossibility to determining "whether value is understood primarily in regard to the dynamics of *distinction* or of *exchange*." Lyndon Barrett, *Blackness and Value: Seeing Double* (Cambridge and New York: Cambridge University Press, 1999), 12.

16. Yet, underneath the film's surface, Clay's body is phenomenologically fleshed out. The film strives to fashion for him a coherent living body that experiences things and objects independently from his "racial" identity. When Dr. Shinoda takes Clay home from the hospital, he tells him: "Try to feel what it is like to be home. Help your body to remember." He mentions staying open and receptive to the "free association

of body and memory." "There are triggers here. Memory triggers . . . Your memory is here. I promise you." The idea is that the body will find its soul (its conscience and identity, in this case) by experiencing its relationship to objects and that the skin is not just a chromatically marked surface but also the border that feels — the site at which the body interacts with the social space and becomes conscious of itself. The film is in keeping with the phenomenology of the surface of psychoanalysis, described by Lippit as a search for depth on the surface of things. Akira Mizuta Lippit, *Atomic Light (Shadow Optics)* (Minneapolis: University of Minnesota Press, 2005). Deprived of memory and continuity, Clay has to re-create the ground on which his experiences are going to land, the pad in which they will be written. Dr. Shinoda's Freudianism does not only manifest itself in his therapeutic strategies — free association, dream analysis, and so on — and in his quotes ("dreams appear like a coded puzzle," he tells Clay), but also visually: the surface (of the dream, of the body, of the film image) is presented as a Rorschach test, samples of which hang from walls in Dr. Shinoda's office.

17. Stephen Best, *The Fugitive's Properties: Law and the Poetics of Possession* (Chicago: University of Chicago Press, 2004), 210–11.

18. Best, *The Fugitive's Properties*, 227.

19. For the idea of whiteness as property see the seminal essay by Cheryl I. Harris, "Whiteness as Property," *Harvard Law Review* 106, no. 8 (1993).

20. Emphasis in original. Amy Robinson, "Forms of Appearance of Value: Homer Plessy and the Politics of Privacy," in *Performance and Cultural Politics*, ed. Elin Diamond (London and New York: Routledge, 1996), 248.

21. "A statute which implies merely a legal distinction between the white and the color races — a distinction which is founded in the color of the two races and which must always exist so long as white men are distinguished from the other race by color — has no tendency to destroy the legal equality of the two races. . . . " Justice Henry Billings Brown, "Majority Opinion in *Plessy V. Ferguson*," in *Desegregation and the Supreme Court*, ed. Benjamin Munn Ziegler (Boston: D.C. Heath and Company, 1958). Quoted in Coco Fusco, "Racial Time, Racial Marks, Racial Metaphors," in *Only Skin Deep: Changing Visions of the American Self*, ed. Brian Wallis and Coco Fusco (New York: International Center of Photography, 2003), 15.

22. Quoted in Robinson, "Forms of Appearance of Value: Homer Plessy and the Politics of Privacy," 223–24.

23. Harris, "Whiteness as Property."

24. Best, *The Fugitive's Properties*, 228.

25. Christian Metz, *Film Language: A Semiotics of the Cinema*, trans. Michael Taylor (New York: Oxford Univerdity Press, 1974), and *The Imaginary Signifier: Psychanalysis and the Cinema* (Bloomington: Indiana University Press, 1981).

26. Christina Sharpe notices how white critics tend to recognize, identify and describe in gritty details, only the recognizably black characters; how the blackness

of the silhouettes is often imagined to refer only to diegetically and stereotypically recognizable black characters, while the white ones — who are never really shown in these types of contexts, compromising situations and certainly have no recognizable stereotype belonging to the same sociohistorical context — go unnoticed. This is an acute commentary on white disavowal, of course, but also on the ontological audacity of Walker's silhouettes, who, by coating everybody in black, gains the ability to equalize their treatment and therefore prod deep seated and disavowed scenes of monstrous intimacies. Sharpe also notices that Walker has increasingly begun to make silhouettes in different color, possibly in order to address this profound critical imbalance. Christina Elizabeth Sharpe, *Monstrous Intimacies: Making Post-Slavery Subjects* (Durham, NC: Duke University Press, 2010).

27. I owe this observation to Eddie Chambers. Personal conversation.

28. John P. Bowles continues: "Walker creates quasi-cinematic scenes in which perpetrators are the victims of their own fantasies. . . . Her figures are apparitions who resemble the normative white subject but who are instead difference itself made manifest. They represent, on some level, who white viewers fear they might be. . . . They seem credible but are fantasy, and they are too horrible to be real." John P. Bowles et al., "Blinded by the White: Art and History at the Limits of Whiteness," *Art Journal* 60, no. 4 (2001): 39.

29. Noël Burch, *Life to Those Shadows,* trans. Ben Brewster (Berkeley and Los Angeles: University of California Press, 1990).

30. DuBois Shaw, *Seeing the Unspeakable.*

31. This is the criticism summarized in Pindell, *Kara Walker-No.* Against this position, very recently W. J. T. Mitchell praised her work alongside Spike Lee's *Bamboozled* for bringing back the plantation as the setting through which to reassess contemporary U.S. history. W. J. T. Mitchell, *Seeing through Race* (Cambridge, MA: Harvard University, 2012).

32. Steven Shaviro, "Post-Cinematic Affect: On Grace Jones, *Boarding Gate* and *Southland Tales,*" *Film-Philosophy* 14, no. 1 (2010), 5–6.

33. Anne M. Wagner, "Kara Walker: 'The Black-White Relation,'" in *Kara Walker: Narratives of a Negresse,* ed. Ian Berry, Darby English, Vivian Patterson, and Mark Reinhardt (New York: Rizzoli, 2007), 94.

34. On the isomorphism between fetish and stereotype see the already cited essay by Homi Bhabha, "The Other Question: Stereotype, Discrimination and the Discourse of Colonialism," in *The Location of Culture* (New York: Routlledge, 1994).

35. Joann Caspar Lavater, *Essay on Physiognomy for the Promotion of the Knowledge and the Love of Mankind,* vol. II, 90, quoted in John B. Lyon, "'The Science of Sciences': Replication and Reproduction in Lavater's Physiognomics," *Eighteenth-Century Studies* 40, no. 2 (2007), 262.

36. This paradigm continues into the twentieth century as evidenced by studies

such as Ida McLearn, G. M. Morant, and Karl Pearson, "On the Importance of the Type Silhouette for Racial Characterisation in Anthropology," *Biometrika* 20B, no. 3–4 (1928). The study's conclusion places Englishmen and Africans at opposite extremes of the Great Chain of Being, with English women occupying a middle position. Or consider a 1930 study in the *American Journal of Psychology* to determine: (1) what relation exists between the silhouetted features of a man's face and the judgment of observers as to his character? (2) What qualities of character are usually linked together in the judgments of an observer? (3) Are certain features of the silhouette perceived more clearly than others? The underlining idea is the possibility of using the silhouette to measure like and dislike. R. K. White and Carney Landis, "Perception of Silhouettes," *American Journal of Psychology* 42, no. 3 (1930). For a discussion of Walker's critical engagement with the paradigm of the social sciences see Mark Reinhardt, "The Art of Racial Profiling," in *Kara Walker: Narratives of a Negresse*, ed. Ian Berry, Darby English, Vivian Patterson, and Mark Reinhardt (New York: Rizzoli, 2007), 108–29.

37. "Primitive" is one of the terms Walker uses to evoke a female persona, modeled after Josephine Baker's exotic *sauvage*, which sometimes she adopts for herself to underscore the expectations of her patronage.

38. Homi Bhabha, "Remembering Fanon: Self, Psyche, and the Colonial Condition," in *Rethinking Fanon: The Continuing Dialogue*, ed. Nigel Gibson (New York: Humanity Books, 1999), 186; Allan Sekula, "The Body and the Archive," *October* 39 (1986).

39. Bhabha, "Remembering Fanon."

40. Victor Stoichita, *A Short History of the Shadow* (London: Reaktion Books, 1997), 27.

41. The relationship to landscape painting is specifically addressed by Darby English in "This Is Not About the Past: Silhouettes in the Work of Kara Walker," in *Kara Walker: Narratives of a Negresse*, ed. Ian Berry, Darby English, Vivian Patterson, and Mark Reinhardt (New York: Rizzoli, 2007); Darby English, *How to See a Work of Art in Total Darkness* (Cambridge, MA: MIT Press, 2007).

42. Wagner, "Black-White Relation," 95.

43. David Rodowick, *The Virtual Life of Film* (Cambridge, MA: Harvard University Press, 2007).

44. Metz, *The Imaginary Signifier*.

45. See Jonathan Auerbach, *Body Shots: Early Cinema's Incarnations* (Berkeley and Los Angeles: University of California Press, 2007). In particular, consider the reference to Marey's practice of dressing people in black to emphasize the recording of movement. See also Mary Ann Doane, *The Emergence of Cinematic Time: Modernity, Contingency, the Archive* (Cambridge, MA: Harvard University Press, 2002).

46. Trond Lundemo, "The Colors of Haptic Space," in *Color: The Film Reader*, ed. Brian Price and Angela Dalle Vacche (New York: Routledge, 2006).

47. See Jennifer M. Barker, *The Tactile Eye: Touch and the Cinematic Experience* (Berkeley and Los Angeles: University of California Press, 2009), 157–61; Auerbach, *Body Shots: Early Cinema's Incarnations*.

48. Best, *The Fugitive's Properties*: 228–37. Briefly, the plot: a white woman travels on a train with her black maid. A white man sitting behind her initiates a flirtatious series of exchanges. Then the train enters a tunnel (signified by a fade to black) and as it exits the tunnel, the white woman and the maid have exchanged seats so that the white man, who had taken advantage of the darkness to make his move, discovers he had been kissing the maid. The two women laugh, amused by the success of their scheme and the film ends. On *What Happened in the Tunnel* see also Jane Gaines, *Fire and Desire: Mixed-Race Movies in the Silent Era* (Chicago: University of Chicago Press, 2001). The duck-rabbit effect of Walker's silhouettes can be said to invoke similar counterfactual stakes.

49. Akira Lippit has the following to say about X-ray photographs: "With the appearance of the X-ray, the subject was forced to concede the limits of the body. Erasing one limit against which it claimed to be outside, the X-ray image, with its simultaneous view of the inside and outside, turned the vantage point of the spectator-subject inside out. The point of view established by the x-ray image is both inside and out." Lippit, *Atomic Light*, 42.

50. English, "Not About the Past," 156.

51. Emphasis in original. Barker, *The Tactile Eye*, 136. See also Vivian Sobchack, "Animation and Automation, or, the Incredible Effortfulness of Being," *Screen* 50, no. 4 (2009). The argument that digital cinema indicates a move toward animation is made by Lev Manovich, "What is Digital Cinema?," in *The Visual Culture Reader*, ed. Nicholas Mirzoeff (New York: Routledge, 2002), and Sean Cubitt, *The Cinema Effect* (Cambridge, MA: MIT Press, 2004).

52. Robert Storr, "Spooked," in *Kara Walker: My Complement, My Enemy, My Oppressor, My Love*, ed. Philippe Vergne (Minneapolis: Walker Art Center, 2007), 65.

53. Storr, "Spooked," 65.

54. David Marriott, *Haunted Life: Visual Culture and Black Modernity* (New Brunswick, NJ: Rutgers University Press, 2007), 4.

55. This is a social ontology that for Osborne has become now more visible with digital images, where "digital" for him describes first and foremost the form in which images exist and circulate. Peter Osborne, "Infinite Exchange: The Social Ontology of the Photographic Image," *Philosophy of Photography* 1, no. 1 (2010).

56. Think about the difference it would make to see one of these images hanging on a gallery wall, projected on a classroom screen, seen at a bus stop, printed on photographic paper and held in our hands, or worn on a T-shirt. In this last case especially, one would become keenly aware of one's own raced embodiment. How does it feel to wear it? Who can wear it? When and where?

57. For a similar way of discussing blackness as a form of rendering see Nicole

R. Fleetwood, *Troubling Vision: Performance, Visuality, and Blackness* (Chicago: University of Chicago Press, 2011).

58. Sybille Krämer, "Was Eigentlich Ist Eine Spur," (paper presented at Spurenlesen: Zur Genealogie von Kulturtechniken, Humboldt-Universität, Berlin, February 10–12, 2005); quoted in Peter Geimer, "Image as Trace: Speculations About an Undead Paradigm," *differences* 18, no. 1 (2007): 16.

59. See Laura U. Marks, *Touch: Sensuous Theory and Multisensory Media* (Minneapolis: University of Minnesota Press, 2002).

60. In other words, part of the photochemical imagination relies on the phantasy that the world can be touched through a photographic image. Part of the digital imagination constructs a world of code, of translatability, circulation, equalization. For an account of this phantasy of translatability see Drew Ayers, "Vernacular Posthumanism: Visual Culture and Material Imagination" (PhD diss., Georgia State University, 2012).

61. Emphasis added. Brian Massumi, *Parables for the Virtual: Movement, Affect, Sensation* (Durham. NC: Duke University Press, 2002), 138, 143.

62. On the cut, see again Richard Powell, *Cutting a Figure: Fashioning Black Portraiture* (Chicago: University of Chicago Press, 2009). See also Kristopher L. Cannon, "Cutting Race Otherwise: Imagining Michael Jackson," *Spectator* 30, no. 2 (2010).

CONCLUSION **IN THE SHADOW**

1. Fred Moten, "The Case of Blackness," *Criticism* 50, no. 2 (2008); David Marriott, *Haunted Life: Visual Culture and Black Modernity* (New Bruswick, NJ: Rutgers University Press, 2007).

2. This is in reference to Fanon's famous claim that the black man "has no ontological resistance in the eyes of the white man. [. . .] For not only must the black man be black; he must be black in relation to the white man." Frantz Fanon, *Black Skin, White Masks*, trans. Richard Philcox (New York: Grove Press, 2008), 90.

3. Emphasis added. Toni Morrison, *Playing in the Dark: Whiteness and the Literary Imagination* (New York: Vintage Books, 1992), 10.

4. "Excess flesh" is Nicole Fleetwood's term in her *Troubling Vision: Performance, Visuality, and Blackness* (Chicago: University of Chicago Press, 2011).

BIBLIOGRAPHY

Abel, Elizabeth. "Black Writing, White Reading: Race and the Politics of Feminist Interpretation." *Critical Inquiry* 19, no. 3 (1993): 470–98.

———. "Shadows." *Representations* 84 (2004): 166–99.

Agamben, Giorgio. *Homo Sacer: Sovereign Power and Bare Life*. Stanford, CA: Stanford University Press, 1998.

Ahmed, Sara. *Strange Encounters: Embodied Others and Post-Coloniality*. London and New York: Routledge, 2000.

———. *The Cultural Politics of Emotions*: New York: Routledge, 2004.

Allen, Danielle S. *Talking to Strangers: Anxieties of Citizenship after Brown V. Board of Education*. Chicago: University of Chicago Press, 2004.

Allen, James. *Without Sanctuary: Lynching Photography in America*. Santa Fe, NM: Twin Palms Publishers, 2000.

Alliez, Eric. "Body without Image. Ernesto Neto's Anti-Leviathan." *Radical Philosophy*, no. 156 (2009): 23–34.

Andrew, Dudley. "The Economies of Adaptation." In *True to the Spirit: Film Adaptation and the Question of Fidelity*, edited by Colin MacCabe, Kathleen Murray, and Rick Warner. 27–39. Oxford and New York: Oxford University Press, 2011.

Andrews, Stephen. "Glenn Ligon: In Conversation." In *Glenn Ligon: Some Changes*, edited by Glenn Ligon, Darby English, and Stephen Andrews. 171–85. Toronto: Power Plant, 2005.

Apel, Dora. "On Looking: Lynching Photographs and Legacies of Lynching after 9/11." *American Quarterly* 55, no. 3 (2003): 457–78.

———. *Imagery of Lynching: Black Men, White Women, and the Mob*. New Brunswick, NJ: Rutgers University Press, 2004.

Apel, Dora, and Shawn Michelle Smith. *Lynching Photographs*. Berkeley and Los Angeles: University of California Press, 2008.

Arrighi, Giovanni. *The Long Twentieth Century: Money, Power, and the Origins of Our Times*. New York: Verso, 1994.

Auerbach, Jonathan. *Body Shots: Early Cinema's Incarnations*. Berkeley and Los Angeles: University of California Press, 2007.

Ayers, Drew. "Humans without Bodies: DNA Portraiture and Biocybernetic Reproduction." *Configurations* 19, no. 2 (2011): 287–321.

———. "Vernacular Posthumanism: Visual Culture and Material Imagination." PhD diss., Georgia State University, 2012.

Baker, Houston Jr. *Blues, Ideology, and Afro-American Literature: A Vernacular Theory*. Chicago: University of Chicago Press, 1984.

Bakhtin, M. M. "Forms of Time and of the Chronotope in the Novel." In *The Dialogic Imagination Four Essays*, edited by Michael Holquist. Austin: University of Texas Press, 1981.

Barker, Jennifer M. *The Tactile Eye: Touch and the Cinematic Experience*. Berkeley and Los Angeles: University of California Press, 2009.

Barrett, Lyndon. *Blackness and Value: Seeing Double*. Cambridge and New York: Cambridge University Press, 1999.

Barson, Tanya, and Peter Gorshluter, eds. *Afro Modern: Journeys through the Black Atlantic*. Liverpool, England: Tate Publishing, 2010.

Barthes, Roland. *Camera Lucida: Reflections on Photography*. New York: Hill and Wang, 1981.

———. "The Photographic Message." In *Image-Music-Text*, translated by Stephen Heath. New York: Hill & Wang, 1977.

———. "The Reality Effect." In *The Rustle of Language*, 141–48. New York: Hill & Wang, 1986.

Batchen, Geoffrey, ed. *Photography Degree Zero: Reflections on Roland Barthes's Camera Lucida*. Cambridge, MA: MIT Press, 2009.

Baucom, Ian. *Specters of the Atlantic: Finance Capital, Slavery, and the Philosophy of History*. Durham, NC: Duke University Press, 2005.

Baudrillard, Jean. *The Mirror of Production*. Translated by Mark Poster. St. Louis: Telos Press, 1975.

———. *For a Critique of the Political Economy of the Sign*. St. Louis: Telos Press, 1981.

Bazin, André. *What Is Cinema?*, vol. 1. Translated by Hugh Gray. Berkeley and Los Angeles: University of California Press, 1967.

Beller, Jonathan. *The Cinematic Mode of Production: Attention Economy and the Society of the Spectacle*. Hanover, NH: University Press of New England, 2006.

Bellour, Raymond. "The Double Helix." In *Electronic Culture: Technology and Visual Representation*, edited by Timothy Druckrey, 173–99. New York: Aperture, 1996.

———. "Concerning 'the Photographic.'" In *Still Moving: Between Cinema and Photography*, edited by Karen Beckman and Jean Ma, translated by Chris Darke, 153–276. Durham, NC: Duke University Press, 2008.

Benjamin, Walter. "Central Park." *New German Critique* 34 (1985).

———. "Paris, the Capital of the Nineteenth Century. 1935." In *The Arcades Project*, 3–13. Cambridge, MA: Belknap Press, 1999.

Berlant, Lauren. "National Brands/National Body: Imitation of Life." In *Comparative American Identities: Race, Sex, and Nationality in the Modern Text*, edited by Hortense J. Spillers, 110–40. New York: Routledge, 1991.

Bernstein, Patricia. *The First Waco Horror: The Lynching of Jesse Washington and the Rise of the NAACP*. College Station: Texas A&M University Press, 2005.

Bernstein, Robin. "Dances with Things. Material Culture and the Performance of Race." *Social Text* 27, no. 4 (2009): 67–94.

Berry, Ian, Darby English, Vivian Patterson, and Mark Reinhardt, eds. *Kara Walker: Narratives of a Negress*. 2nd ed. New York: Rizzoli, The Frances Young Tang Teaching Museum and Art Gallery at Skidmore College, Williams College Museum of Art, 2007.

Best, Stephen. *The Fugitive's Properties: Law and the Poetics of Possession*. Chicago: University of Chicago Press, 2004.

Best, Stephen, and Sharon Marcus. "Surface Reading: An Introduction." *Representations* 108 (2009): 1–21.

Bhabha, Homi. "Signs Taken for Wonders." In *Race, Writing, and Difference*, edited by Henry Louis Gates Jr., 163–84. Chicago: University of Chicago Press, 1985.

———. *The Location of Culture*. New York: Routledge, 1994.

———. "Remembering Fanon: Self, Psyche, and the Colonial Condition." In *Rethinking Fanon: The Continuing Dialogue*, edited by Nigel Gibson, 179–96. New York: Humanity Books, 1999.

Bowles, John P., Olu Oguibe, Karen Stevenson, Maurice Berger, Ellen Fernandez-Sacco, and Adrian Piper. "Blinded by the White: Art and History at the Limits of Whiteness." *Art Journal* 60, no. 4 (2001): 38–67.

Bredekamp, Horst. "Thomas Hobbes's Visual Strategies." In *The Cambridge Companion to Hobbes's Leviathan*, edited by Patricia Springborg, 29–60. Cambridge: Cambridge University Press, 2007.

Brielmeier, Isolde. "Interview with Wangechi Mutu Part I: The Body." In *Wangechi Mutu a Shady Promise*, edited by Douglas Singleton. Bologna, Italy: Damiani, 2008.

Brooks, Daphne A. *Bodies in Dissent: Spectacular Performances of Race and Freedom, 1850–1910*. Durham, NC: Duke University Press, 2006.

Brown, Bill. "The Tyranny of Things (Trivia in Karl Marx and Mark Twain)." *Critical Inquiry* 28, no. 2 (Winter 2002): 442–69.

———. "Reification, Reanimation, and the American Uncanny." *Critical Inquiry* 32 (2006): 175–207.

Brown, Henry Billings. "Majority Opinion in *Plessy V. Ferguson*." In *Desegregation and the Supreme Court*, edited by Benjamin Munn Ziegler. Boston: Heath and Company, 1958.

Bryant, Antony, and Griselda Pollock. *Digital and Other Virtualities: Renegotiating the Image*. London and New York: I. B. Tauris, 2010.

Burch, Noël. *Life to Those Shadows*. Translated by Ben Brewster. Berkeley and Los Angeles: University of California Press, 1990.

Byrd, Cathy. "Is There a 'Post-Black' Art?" *Art Papers Magazine* 26, no. 6 (2002).

Calhoon, Kenneth S. "Personal Effects: Rilke, Barthes, and the Matter of Photography." *MLN* 113, no. 3 (1998): 612–34.

Cannon, Kristopher L. "Cutting Race Otherwise: Imagining Michael Jackson." *Spectator* 30, no. 2 (2010): 28–36.

Casetti, Francesco. "Sutured Reality: Film, from Photographic to Digital." *October* no. 138 (2011): 95–106.

Cavell, Stanley. *The World Viewed: Reflections on the Ontology of Film*. Cambridge, MA: Harvard University Press, 1979.

Cheng, Anne Anlin. *Second Skin: Josephine Baker and the Modern Surface*. Oxford: Oxford University Press, 2011.

Cohen, Margaret. "Walter Benjamin's Phantasmagoria." *New German Critique*, no. 48 (1989): 87–107.

Coleman, Beth. "Race as Technology." *Camera Obscura* 24, no. 1 (2009): 176–207.

Comolli, Jean-Louis. "Machines of the Visible." In *The Cinematic Apparatus*, edited by Teresa de Lauretis and Stephen Heath. New York: St. Martin's Press, 1980.

Coombe, Rosemary J. *The Cultural Life of Intellectual Properties: Authorship, Appropriation and the Law*. Durham, NC: Duke University Press, 1998.

Copeland, Huey. "Glenn Ligon and Other Runaway Subjects." *Representations* 113, no. 1 (2011): 73–110.

Copeland, Huey, and Krista Thompson. "Perpetual Returns: New World Slavery and the Matter of the Visual." *Representations* 113, no. 1 (2011): 1–15.

Copjec, Joan. "Moses the Egyptian and the Big Black Mammy of the Antebellum

South: Freud (with Kara Walker) on Race and History." In *Imagine There's No Woman: Ethics and Sublimation*, 82–107. Cambridge, MA: MIT Press, 2002.

Corliss, Richard. "*The Blind Side*: What's All the Cheering About?" *Time*, December 3, 2009.

Cubitt, Sean. *The Cinema Effect*. Cambridge, MA: MIT Press, 2004.

Culler, Jonathan. "Commentary." *New Literary History* 6, no. 1 (1974): 219–29.

Cvetkovich, Ann. *Mixed Feelings: Feminism, Mass Culture, and Victorian Sensationalism*. New Brunswick, NJ: Rutgers University Press, 1992.

Daniels, Lee. "A Precious Ensemble." In featurette for the film *Precious: Based on the Novel "Push" by Sapphire*. Directed by Lee Daniels. Santa Monica, CA: Lionsgate, 2009. DVD.

de Guzman, Rene. "Nothing Better." In *Pitch Blackness*, edited by Hank Willis Thomas. New York: Aperture, 2008.

De Lauretis, Teresa. "Difference Embodied: Reflections on *Black Skin, White Masks*." *Parallax* 8, no. 2 (2002): 54–68.

de Man, Paul. "The Epistemology of Metaphor." *Critical Inquiry* 5, no. 1 (1978).

Del Rio, Elena. "The Body as Foundation of the Screen: Allegories of Technology in Atom Egoyan's *Speaking Parts*." *Camera Obscura* 37–38 (1996).

———. "Body Transformations in the Films of Claire Denis: From Ritual to Play." *Studies in French Cinema* 3, no. 3 (2003): 185–97.

del Río, Elena. *Deleuze and the Cinemas of Performance: Powers of Affection*. Edinburgh: Edinburgh University Press, 2008.

Deleuze, Gilles, and Félix Guattari. *A Thousand Plateaus: Capitalism and Schizophrenia*. Translated by Brian Massumi. Minneapolis: University of Minnesota Press, 1987.

Derrida, Jacques, and F. C. T. Moore. "White Mythology: Metaphor in the Text of Philosophy." *New Literary History* 6, no. 1 (1974): 5–74.

Derrida, Jacques. "Différance." In *Margins of Philosophy*. Translated by Alan Bass. Chicago: University of Chicago Press, 1982.

———. *Specters of Marx. The State of Debt, the Work of Mourning, and the New International*. Translated by Peggy Kamuf. New York: Routledge, 2006.

Diawara, Manthia. "The Blackface Stereotype." In *Blackface*, David Levinthal and Manthia Diawara, 7–17. Santa Fe, NM: Arena Editions, 1999.

———. "Noir by Noirs: Toward a New Realism in Black Cinema." In *Shades of Noir*, edited by Joan Copjec, 261–78. London: Verso, 1993.

Didi-Huberman, Georges. "The Index of the Absent Wound (Monograph on a Stain)." *October* 29 (Summer 1984): 63–81.

Dinerstein, Joel. *Swinging the Machine: Modernity, Technology, and African American Culture between the World Wars*. Amherst: University of Massachusetts Press, 2003.

Doane, Mary Ann. *The Emergence of Cinematic Time. Modernity, Contingency, the Archive*. Cambridge, MA: Harvard University Press, 2002.

———. "The Indexical and the Concept of Medium Specificity." *differences* 18, no. 1 (2007): 128–52.

———. "Indexicality: Trace and Sign: Introduction." *differences* 18, no. 1 (2007): 1–6.

Dray, Philip. *At the Hands of Persons Unknown: The Lynching of Black America*. New York: Random House, 2002.

DuBois, W. E. B., *The Souls of Black Folks*. New York: Modern Library, 1996.

DuBois Shaw, Gwendolyn. *Seeing the Unspeakable: The Art of Kara Walker*. Durham, NC: Duke University Press, 2004.

Earle, Susan Elizabeth, and Renée Ater. *Aaron Douglas: African American Modernist*. New Haven, CT: Yale University Press, 2007.

Edelman, Lee. *Transmemberment of Song: Hart Crane's Anatomies of Rhetoric and Desire*. Stanford, CA: Stanford University Press, 1987.

———. *Homographesis: Essays in Gay Literary and Cultural Theory*. New York: Routledge, 1994.

Edwards, Elizabeth, and Janice Hart, eds. *Photographs Objects Histories: On the Materiality of Images*. London and New York: Routledge, 2004.

Elam, Harry J., Jr. "Spike Lee's *Bamboozled*." In *Black Cultural Traffic: Crossroads in Global Performance and Popular Culture*, edited by Harry J. Elam Jr. and Kennell Jackson, 346–62. Ann Arbor: University of Michigan Press, 2005.

———. "Change the Clothes and Go: A Postscript to Postblackness." In *Black Cultural Traffic: Crossroads in Global Performance and Popular Culture,* edited by Harry J. Elam Jr. and Kennell Jackson. 379–88. Ann Arbor: University of Michigan Press, 2005.

Ellison, Ralph. *Invisible Man*. New York: Random House, 1982.

———. "Change the Joke and Slip the Yoke." In *The Collected Essays of Ralph Ellison*, 100–112. New York: Modern Library, 1995.

English, Darby. "Glenn Ligon: Committed to Difficulty." In *Glenn Ligon: Some Changes*, edited by Glenn Ligon, Darby English, and Stephen Andrews, 31–77. Toronto: Power Plant, 2005.

———. *How to See a Work of Art in Total Darkness*. Cambridge, MA: MIT Press, 2007.

———. "This Is Not About the Past: Silhouettes in the Work of Kara Walker." In *Kara Walker: Narratives of a Negresse*, edited by Ian Berry, Darby English, Vivian Patterson, and Mark Reinhardt, 141–67. New York: Rizzoli, 2007.

Eshun, Kodwo. "Further Considerations of Afrofuturism." *CR: The New Centennial Review* 3, no. 2 (2003): 287–302.

Fanon, Frantz. *Black Skin, White Masks*. Translated by Richard Philcox. New York: Grove Press, 2008.

Fisher, Luchina. "Why Some Blacks Prefer 'Blind Side' to 'Precious.'" *ABC News*, December 7, 2009.

Fisher, Philip. *Making and Effacing Art: Modern American Art in a Culture of Museums*. New York: Oxford University Press, 1991.

Flanagan, Mary, and Austin Booth, eds. *re:skin*. Cambridge, MA: MIT Press, 2006.

Fleetwood, Nicole R. *Troubling Vision: Performance, Visuality, and Blackness*. Chicago: University of Chicago Press, 2011.

Flory, Dan. "Black on White: Film Noir and the Epistemology of Race in Recent African American Cinema." *Journal of Social Philosophy* 31, no. 1 (2000): 82–116.

———. *Philosophy, Black Film, Film Noir*. University Park: Pennsylvania State University Press, 2008.

Fontanier, Pierre. *Les Figures Du Discours*. Paris: Flammarion, 1977.

Foreman, P. Gabrielle. "Who's Your Mama? 'White' Mulatta Genealogies, Early Photography, and Anti-Passing Narratives of Slavery and Freedom." *American Literary History* 14, no. 3 (2002): 505–39.

Fossati, Giovanni. *From Grain to Pixel: The Archival Life of Film in Transition*. Amsterdam: Amsterdam University Press, 2009.

Foucault, Michel. *The Order of Things. An Archaeology of the Human Sciences*. New York: Random House, 1970.

———. *This Is Not a Pipe*. Translated by James Harkness. Berkeley and Los Angeles: University of California Press, 1983.

Frank, Marcie. "The Camera and the Speculum: David Cronenberg's *Dead Ringers*." *PMLA* 106, no. 3 (1991): 459-70.

Fusco, Coco. "All Too Real: The Tale of an on-Line Black Sale. Coco Fusco Interviews Keith Townsend Obadike." blacknetart.com/coco.html, 2001.

Fusco, Coco, and Brian Wallis, eds. *Only Skin Deep: Changing Visions of the American Self*. New York: International Center of Photography, 2003.

Gaines, Jane. *Fire and Desire: Mixed-Race Movies in the Silent Era*. Chicago: University of Chicago Press, 2001.

Gates, Henry Louis, Jr. "Criticism in the Jungle." In *Black Literature and Literary Theory*, edited by Henry Louis Gates Jr. and Sunday Ogbonna Anozie, 1–24. New York: Methuen, 1984.

———. *The Signifying Monkey: A Theory of African-American Literary Criticism*. New York: Oxford University Press, 1988.

Geimer, Peter. "Image as Trace: Speculations About an Undead Paradigm." *differences* 18, no. 1 (2007): 7–28.

Gillespie, Michael Boyce. "Significations of Blackness: American Cinema and the Idea of a Black Film." PhD diss., New York University, 2007.

Gilroy, Paul. *The Black Atlantic: Modernity and Double Consciousness*. Cambridge, MA: Harvard University Press, 1993.

Giroux, Henry. "Violence, Katrina, and the Biopolitics of Disposability." *Theory, Culture & Society* 24, no. 7–8 (2007): 305–9.

Golden, Thelma, et al. *Freestyle*. New York: The Studio Museum in Harlem, 2001.

Goldsby, Jacqueline. *A Spectacular Secret: Lynching in American Life and Literature*. Chicago: University of Chicago Press, 2006.

González, Jennifer A. *Subject to Display: Reframing Race in Contemporary Installation Art*. Cambridge, MA: MIT Press, 2008.

———. "The Face and the Public: Race, Secrecy, and Digital Art Practice." *Camera Obscura* 70, no. 24 (2009): 36–65.

———. "Flesh in the Machine: She's Egungun Again." In *Wangechi Mutu: This You Call Civilization?*, edited by David Moos, Wangechi Mutu, and Art Gallery of Ontario. 72-75. Toronto: Art Gallery of Ontario, 2010.

Gregory, Dick. *From the Back of the Bus*. New York: Avon Books, 1962.

———. *Nigger*. New York: E. P. Dutton, 1964.

———. *What's Happening?* New York: E. P. Dutton, 1965.

———. *The Shadow That Scares Me*. New York: Pocket Books, 1968.

———. *Write Me In!* New York: Bantam Books, 1968.

———. *Up from Nigger*. New York: Fawcett, 1977.

Gregory, Dick, and P. Moses Sheila. *Callous on My Soul: A Memoir*. Atlanta: Longstreet Press, 2000.

Gregory, Richard Claxton. *No More Lies: The Myth and the Reality of American History*. New York: Harper & Row, 1971.

Grundmann, Roy. "Identity Politics at Face Value." *Cineaste* 20 (1994): 3.

Gubar, Susan. *Racechanges: White Skin, Black Face in American Culture*. New York and Oxford: Oxford University Press, 1997.

———. "Racial Camp in *The Producers* and *Bamboozled*." *Film Quarterly* 60, no. 2 (2006).

Guerrero, Ed. "*Bamboozled*: In the Mirror of Abjection." In *Black Contemporary American Cinema: Race, Gender and Sexuality at the Movies*, edited by Mia Mask. New York: Routledge, 2012.

Gunning, Tom. "Illusions Past and Future: The Phantasmagoria and Its Specters." In *MediaArtHistoriesArchive*. http://hdl.handle.net/10002/296, 2004.

———. "What's the Point of an Index? Or, Faking Photographs." *Nordicom Review* 25, no. 1–2 (2004): 39–49.

———. "Moving Away from the Index: Cinema and the Impression of Reality." *differences* 18, no. 1 (2007): 29–52.

Hainge, Greg. "Unfixing the Photographic Image: Photography, Indexicality, Fidelity and Normativity." *Continuum: Journal of Media & Cultural Studies* 22, no. 5 (2011): 715–30.

Hall, Stuart. "The after-Life of Frantz Fanon: Why Fanon? Why Now? *Why Black Skins, White Masks?*" In *The Fact of Blackness*, edited by Alan Read, 12–37. Seattle: Bay Press, 1996.

Harris, Cheryl I. "Whiteness as Property." *Harvard Law Review* 106, no. 8 (June 1993): 1707–91.

Harris, Michael D. *Colored Pictures: Race and Visual Representation*. Chapel Hill: University of North Carolina Press, 2003.

Hartman, Saidiya V. *Scenes of Subjection: Terror, Slavery, and Self-Making in Nineteenth-Century America*. New York: Oxford University Press, 1997.

Heidegger, Martin. "The Age of the World Picture." In *Off the Beaten Track*, translated by Julian Young and Kenneth Haynes, 57–85. New York: Cambridge University Press, 2002.

Hoey, Allen. "The Name on the Coin: Metaphor, Metonymy, and Money." *Diacritics* 18, no. 2 (1988): 26–37.

hooks, bell. "Eating the Other." In *Black Looks: Race and Representation*, 21–39. Cambridge, MA: South End Press, 1992.

Irwin, Demetria. "Gabourey Sidibe Is Sweet but Not 'Precious.'" *New York Amsterdam News*, November 12, 2009.

Jameson, Fredric. *Postmodernism, or, the Cultural Logic of Late Capitalism*. Durham, NC: Duke University Press, 1991.

——— . "Culture and Finance Capital." *Critical Inquiry* 24, no. 1 (Autumn 1997): 246–65.

——— . *Representing Capital: A Commentary on Volume One*. London and New York: Verso, 2011.

JanMohamed, Abdul R. *The Death-Bound-Subject: Richard Wright's Archaeology of Death*. Durham, NC: Duke University Press, 2005.

Johnson, Charles. "A Phenomenology of the Black Body." *Michigan Quarterly Review* 32, no. 4 (1993): 599–614.

Kantorowicz, Ernst Hartwig. *The King's Two Bodies: A Study in Mediaeval Political Theology*. Princeton, NJ: Princeton University Press, 1997.

Kaplan, Louis., "Photography and the Exposure of Community. Sharing Nan Goldin and Jean-Luc Nancy." *Angelaki*, 6, no. 3 (2001): 7–30.

Kaplan, Michael. "Iconomics: The Rhetoric of Speculation." *Public Culture* 15, no. 3 (2003): 477–93.

Keeling, Kara. "In the Interval: Frantz Fanon and the 'Problems' of Visual Representation." *Qui Parle* 13, no. 2 (2003): 91–117.

——— . "Passing for Human: Bamboozled and Digital Humanism." *Women & Performance: A Journal of Feminist Theory* 29, no. 15 (2005): 237–50.

——— . *The Witch's Flight: The Cinematic, the Black Femme, and the Image of Common Sense*. Durham, NC: Duke University Press, 2007.

Keenan, Thomas. "The Point Is to (Ex)Change It: Reading *Capital*, Rhetorically." In *Fetishism as Cultural Discourse*, edited by Emily Apter and William Pietz, 152–85. Ithaca, NY: Cornell University Press, 1993.

Kessler, Frank. "What You Get Is What You See: Digital Images and the Claim on the Real." In *Digital Material: Tracing New Media in Everyday Life and Technology*, edited by Marianne van den Boomen, Sybille Lammes, Ann-Sophie Lehmann, Joost Raessens, and Mirko Tobias Schäfer, 187–97. Amsterdam: Amsterdam University Press, 2009.

Kirschke, Amy. *Aaron Douglas: Art, Race, and the Harlem Renaissance*. Jackson: University Press of Mississippi, 1995.

———. *Art in Crisis: W.E.B. Du Bois and the Struggle for African American Identity and Memory*. Bloomington: Indiana University Press, 2007.

Kopytoff, Igor. "The Cultural Biography of Things: Commoditization as Process." In *The Social Life of Things: Commodities in Cultural Perspective*, edited by Arjun Appadurai, 64–91. Cambridge: Cambridge University Press, 1986.

Krämer, Sybille, "Was Eigentlich Ist Eine Spur." Paper presented at Spurenlesen: Zur Genealogie von Kulturtechniken Conference, Humboldt-Universität, Berlin, February 10–12, 2005.

Krauss, Rosalind. "Notes on the Index: Seventies Art in America." *October* 3 (1977): 68–81.

Laclau, Ernesto. "Articulation and the Limits of Metaphor." In *A Time for the Humanities: Futurity and the Limits of Autonomy*, edited by Tim Dean, James S. Bono, and Ewa Olonowska-Ziarek. 61–83. New York: Fordham University Press, 2008.

Lamm, Kimberly. "Visuality and Black Masculinity in Ralph Ellison's *Invisible Man* and Romare Bearden's Photomontages." *Callaloo* 26, no. 3 (2003): 813–35.

Laski, Gregory. "Falling Back into History. The Uncanny Trauma of Blackface Minstrelsy in Spike Lee's *Bamboozled*." *Callaloo* 33, no. 4 (2010): 1093–1115.

Latour, Bruno. *We Have Never Been Modern*. Cambridge, MA: Harvard University Press, 1993.

Lee, Chris. "Mariah Carey Shows Her Ugly Side in 'Precious.' Yes, That's the Pop Diva—Deglammed and with Facial Hair—Playing the Dowdy Caseworker." *Los Angeles Times*, November 6, 2009.

Lhamon, W. T. Jr. *Raising Cain: Blackface Performance from Jim Crow to Hip Hop*. Cambridge, MA: Harvard University Press, 1998.

Lhamon, W.T., Jr.,. "Optic Black: Naturalizing the Refusal to Fit." In *Black Cultural Traffic: Crossroads in Global Performance and Popular Culture*, edited by Harry J. Elam Jr. and Kennell Jackson, 111–40. Ann Arbor: University of Michigan Press, 2005.

Ligon, Glenn, Darby English, Stephen Andrews, and Power Plant Art Gallery. *Glenn Ligon: Some Changes*. Toronto: Power Plant, 2005.

Limon, John. *Stand-up Comedy in Theory, or, Abjection in America*. Durham, NC: Duke University Press, 2000.

Lippit, Akira Mizuta. *Atomic Light (Shadow Optics)*. Minneapolis: University of Minnesota Press, 2005.

Lorde, Audre. "Eye to Eye: Black Women, Hatred, and Anger." In *Sister Outsider*, 145–75. New York: Ten Speed Press, 2007.

Loren, Scott, and Jörg Metelmann. "What's the Matter: Race as Res." *Journal of Visual Culture* 10, no. 3 (2011): 397–405.

Lott, Eric. "Love and Theft: The Racial Unconscious of Blackface Minstrelsy." *Representations*, no. 39 (1992): 23–50.

———. *Love and Theft. Blackface Minstrelsy and the American Working Class.* New York: Oxford University Press, 1993.

———. "The Whiteness of Film Noir." *American Literary History* 9, no. 3 (1997): 542–66.

Lundemo, Trond. "The Colors of Haptic Space." In *Color: The Film Reader*, edited by Brian Price and Angela Dalle Vacche, 88–101. New York: Routledge, 2006.

Lyon, John B. "'The Science of Sciences': Replication and Reproduction in Lavater's Physiognomics." *Eighteenth-Century Studies* 40, no. 2 (2007): 257–77.

Mannoni, Laurent, and Richard Crangle. *The Great Art of Light and Shadow: Archaeology of the Cinema.* Exeter, England: University of Exeter Press, 2000.

Manon, Hugh S., "Rude Aesthetics in the Digital Mainstream." Paper presented at the World Picture Conference, Oklahoma State University, October 24–25, 2008.

Manovich, Lev. "What Is Digital Cinema?" In *The Visual Culture Reader*, edited by Nicholas Mirzoeff, 405–16. London and New York: Routledge, 2002.

Marchand, Roland. *Advertising and the American Dream: Making Way for Modernity, 1920–1940.* Berkeley and Los Angeles: University of California Press, 1985.

Marks, Laura U. *The Skin of the Film: Intercultural Cinema, Embodiment, and the Senses.* Durham, NC: Duke University Press, 2000.

———. *Touch: Sensuous Theory and Multisensory Media.* Minneapolis: University of Minnesota Press, 2002.

———. *Enfoldment and Infinity: An Islamic Genealogy of New Media Art.* Cambridge, MA: MIT Press, 2010.

Markus, Gyorgy. "Walter Benjamin Or: The Commodity as Phantasmagoria." *New German Critique*, no. 83 (Spring–Summer 2001): 3–42.

Marriott, David. *Haunted Life: Visual Culture and Black Modernity.* New Brunswick, NJ: Rutgers University Press, 2007.

Marx, Karl. *Capital: Volume 1: A Critique of Political Economy.* Translated by Ben Fowkes. New York: Penguin Classics, 1990.

Massood, Paula J. *The Spike Lee Reader.* Philadelphia: Temple University Press, 2007.

Massumi, Brian. "The Future Birth of the Affective Fact. The Political Ontology of Threat." In *The Affect Theory Reader*, edited by Melissa Gregg and Gregory J. Seigworth, 52–70. Durham, NC: Duke University Press, 2010.

———. *Parables for the Virtual: Movement, Affect, Sensation.* Durham, NC: Duke University Press, 2002.

Maurice, Alice. "What the Shadow Knows: Race, Image, and Meaning in *Shadows* (1922)." *Cinema Journal* 47, no. 3 (2007): 66–89.

Mavor, Carol. "Black and Blue: The Shadows of *Camera Lucida*." In *Photography Degree Zero: Reflections on Camera Lucida*, edited by Geoffrey Batchen, 211–41. Cambridge, MA: MIT Press, 2009.

McBreen, Ellen. "Biblical Gender Bending in Harlem: The Queer Performance of Nugent's Salome." *Art Journal* 57, no. 3 (1998): 22–28.

McLearn, Ida, G. M. Morant, and Karl Pearson. "On the Importance of the Type Silhouette for Racial Characterisation in Anthropology." *Biometrika* 20B, no. 3–4 (1928): 389–400.

Mercer, Kobena. "Busy in the Ruins of a Wretched Phantasia." In *Frantz Fanon: Critical Perspectives*, edited by Anthony Alessandrini, 195–218. London and New York: Routledge, 1999.

———. "Skin Head Sex Thing: Racial Difference and the Homoerotic Imaginary." In *The Masculinity Studies Reader*, edited by Rachel Adams and David Savran, 169–210. Malden, MA: Blackwell, 2002.

———. "Romare Bearden, 1964: Collage as Kunstwollen." In *Cosmopolitan Modernisms*, edited by Kobena Mercer, 124–45. Cambridge, MA: MIT Press, 2005.

Mercer, Kobena, and Isaac Julien. "De Margin and De Center." *Screen* 29, no. 4 (1988): 2–11.

Metz, Christian. *Film Language: A Semiotics of the Cinema*. Translated by Michael Taylor. New York,: Oxford University Press, 1974.

———. *The Imaginary Signifier: Psychanalysis and the Cinema*. Bloomington: Indiana University Press, 1981.

Mills, Charles W. "European Specters." In *From Class to Race: Essays in White Marxism and Black Radicalism*. Lanham, MD: Rowman & Littlefield, 2003.

———. "Non-Cartesian Sums: Philosophy and the African-American Experience." In *Blackness Visible: Essays on Philosophy and Race*. Ithaca, NY: Cornell University Press, 1998.

Mirzoeff, Nicholas. *Bodyscape: Art, Modernity and the Ideal Figure*. London and New York: Routledge, 1995.

———. "The Shadow and the Substance: Race, Photography, and the Index." In *Only Skin Deep: Changing Visions of the American Self*, edited by Coco Fusco and Brian Wallis, 111–28. New York: International Center of Photography, 2003.

———. "On Visuality." *Journal of Visual Culture* 5, no. 1 (2006): 53–79.

———. "The Sea and the Land: Biopower and Visuality from Slavery to Katrina." *Culture, Theory and Critique* 50, no. 2 (2009): 289–305.

———. *The Right to Look: A Counterhistory of Visuality*. Durham NC: Duke University Press, 2011.

Mitchell, W. J. T. *Seeing through Race*. Cambridge, MA: Harvard University Press, 2012.

———. "Playing the Race Card with Lacan." *Journal of Visual Culture* 10, no. 3 (2011): 405–9.

———. *What Do Pictures Want? The Lives and Loves of Images*. Chicago: The University of Chicago Press, 2005.

———. *Picture Theory: Essays on Verbal and Visual Representation*. Chicago: University of Chicago Press, 1994.

Morley, Simon. *Writing on the Wall: Word and Image in Modern Art*. Berkeley and Los Angeles: University of California Press, 2003.

Morrison, Toni. *Playing in the Dark: Whiteness and the Literary Imagination*. New York: Vintage Books, 1992.

Moten, Fred. "The Case of Blackness." *Criticism* 50, no. 2 (2008): 177–218.

———. *In the Break: The Aesthetics of the Black Radical Tradition*. Minneapolis: University of Minnesota Press, 2003.

Mulvey, Laura. *Death 24x a Second: Stillness and the Moving Image*. Chicago: University of Chicago Press, 2006.

Muñoz, Josè. "Photographies of Mourning: Melancholia and Ambivalence in Van Der Zee, Mapplethorpe, and *Looking for Langston*." In *Race and the Subject of Masculinities*, edited by Harry Uebel and Michael Stecopoulos, 337–58. Durham, NC: Duke University Press, 1997.

Munster, Anna. *Materializing New Media: Embodiment in Information Aesthetics*. Hanover, NH: Dartmouth College Press, 2006.

Murray, Derek Conrad. "Hip-Hop vs. High Art: Notes on Race as Spectacle." *Art Journal* 63, no. 2 (2004): 5–19.

Murray, Timothy. *Digital Baroque: New Media Art and Cinematic Folds*. Minneapolis: University of Minnesota Press, 2008.

Mutu, Wangechi, Deutsche Guggenheim Berlin, and Deutsche Bank. *Wangechi Mutu, Artist of the Year 2010: My Dirty Little Heaven*. Ostfildern: Hatje Cantz, 2010.

Mutu, Wangechi, Angela Stief, and Gerald Matt, eds. *Wangechi Mutu: In Whose Image?* Wien: Kunsthalle, 2009.

Namaste, Viviane K. "The Use and Abuse of Queer Tropes: Metaphor and Catachresis in Queer Theory and Politics." *Social Semiotics* 9, no. 2 (1999): 213–34.

Nelson, Alondra. "Afrofuturism: A Special Issue of Social Text." *Social Text* 20, no. 2 (2002).

Nyong'o, Tavia. *The Amalgamation Waltz: Race, Performance, and the Ruses of Memory*. Minneapolis: University of Minnesota Press, 2009.

Olin, Margaret. "Touching Photographs: Roland Barthes's 'Mistaken'" Identification." In *Photography Degree Zero: Reflections on Camera Lucida*, edited by Geoffrey Batchen, 75–89. Cambridge, MA: MIT Press, 2009.

Osborne, Peter. "Infinite Exchange: The Social Ontology of the Photographic Image." *Philosophy of Photography* 1, no. 1 (2010): 59–68.

Peirce, Charles S. *The Essential Peirce: Selected Philosophical Writings*. Edited by Nathan Houser and Christian J.W. Kloesel. Bloomington: Indiana University Press, 1992.

Perry, Sam. "Competing Image Vernaculars in the Anti-Lynching Movement of the 1930s." PhD diss., Georgia State University, 2011.

Pindell, Howardena. *Kara Walker-No, Kara Walker-Yes, Kara Walker-?* New York: Midmarch Arts Press, 2009.

Posselt, Gerald. "The Tropological Economy of Catachresis." *Critical Studies* 25 (2005): 81–94.

Powell, Richard. *Cutting a Figure. Fashioning Black Portraiture*. Chicago: University of Chicago Press, 2009.

Prettyman Beverly, Michele. "Phenomenal Bodies: The Metaphysical Possibilities of Post-Black Film and Visual Culture." PhD diss. Georgia State University, 2012.

Price, Brian. "Color, the Formless, and Cinematic Eros." In *Color: The Film Reader*, edited by Brian Price and Angela Dalle Vacche, 76–87. New York: Routledge, 2006.

Rabaté, Jean-Michel. *Writing the Image after Roland Barthes*. Philadelphia: University of Pennsylvania Press, 1997.

Raengo, Alessandra. "A Necessary Signifier: The Body as Author and Text in *The Jackie Robinson Story*." *Adaptation: A Journal of Literature on Screen Studies* 1, no. 2 (2008).

———. "Shadowboxing: Lee Daniels's Non-Representational Cinema." In *Contemporary Black American Cinema: Race, Gender, and Sexuality at the Movies*, edited by Mia Mask, 200–216. New York: Routledge, 2012.

———. "Reification, Reanimation, and the Money of the Real." *World Picture Journal* 7 (2012). http://www.worldpicturejournal.com/WP_7/Raengo.html.

Raiford, Leigh. "The Consumption of Lynching Images." In *Only Skin Deep: Changing Visions of the American Self*, edited by Coco Fusco and Brian Wallis, 267–74. New York: International Center of Photography, 2003.

Rancière, Jacques. *The Politics of Aesthetics: The Distribution of the Sensible*. Translated by Gabriel Rockhill. New York: Continuum, 2004

———. *The Future of the Image*. Translated by Gregory Elliott. New York: Verso, 2007.

Reid-Pharr, Robert, Annette Dixon, and Thelma Golden, eds. *Kara Walker: Pictures from Another Time* Ann Arbor: University of Michigan Museum of Art, 2002.

Reinhardt, Mark. "The Art of Racial Profiling." In *Kara Walker: Narratives of a Negresse*, edited by Ian Berry, Darby English, Vivian Patterson, and Mark Reinhardt, 108–29. New York: Rizzoli, 2007.

Ricoeur, Paul. *The Rule of Metaphor*. Toronto: University of Toronto Press, 1977.

Ricord, Philippe. "Traité Complet Des Maladies Vénériennes: Clinique Iconographique De L'hopital Des Vénériens Recueil D'observations, Suivies De Considérations Pratique, Sur Les Maladies Qui Ont Été Traitées Dans Cet Hopital." Edited by Just Rouvier. Paris, 1851.

Robinson, Amy. "Forms of Appearance of Value: Homer Plessy and the Politics of Privacy." In *Performance and Cultural Politics*, edited by Elin Diamond, 237–61. London and New York: Routledge, 1996.

Rodowick, David. *The Virtual Life of Film*. Cambridge, MA: Harvard University Press, 2007.

Rogin, Michael. *Blackface, White Noise: Jewish Immigrants in the Hollywood Melting Pot*. Berkeley and Los Angeles: University of California Press, 1996.

Salamon, Gayle. "'The Place Where Life Hides Away': Merleau-Ponty, Fanon, and the Location of Bodily Being." *differences* 17, no. 2 (2006): 96–112.

Santner, Eric L. *The Royal Remains: The People's Two Bodies and the Endgames of Sovereignty*. Chicago: Chicago University Press, 2011.

Sayre, Henry M. "Scars: Painting, Photography, Performance, Pornography, and the Disfigurement of Art." *Performing Arts Journal* 16, no. 1 (1994): 64–74.

Schmidt Campbell, Mary. "African American Art in a Post-Black Era." *Women & Performance: A Journal of Feminist Theory* 17, no. 3 (2007): 317–30.

Schudson, Michael. "Advertising as Capitalist Realism." *Advertising & Society Review* 1, no. 1 (2000).

Scott, A. O. "Two Films, Two Routes from Poverty." *New York Times*, November 22, 2009.

Sekula, Allan. "The Body and the Archive." *October* 39 (1986): 3–64.

———. "The Traffic in Photographs." In *Only Skin Deep Changing Visions of the American Self*, edited by Coco Fusco and Brian Wallis, 79–110. New York: International Center of Photography, 2003.

Seshadri-Crooks, Kalpana. *Desiring Whiteness: A Lacanian Analysis of Race*. London and New York: Routledge, 2000.

Sexton, Jared. "People-of-Color-Blindness: Notes on the Afterlife of Slavery." *Social Text* 28, no. 2 (2010): 31–56.

———. "The Consequences of Race Mixture: Racialised Barriers and the Politics of Desire." *Social Identities* 9, no. 2 (2003): 241–75.

Sharpe, Christina Elizabeth. *Monstrous Intimacies: Making Post-Slavery Subjects*. Durham, NC: Duke University Press, 2010.

Shaviro, Steven. "Post-Cinematic Affect: On Grace Jones, *Boarding Gate* and *Southland Tales*." *Film-Philosophy* 14, no. 1 (2010): 1–102.

Shaw, Gwendolyn DuBois. *Seeing the Unspeakable: The Art of Kara Walker*. Durham, NC: Duke University Press, 2004.

Shawcross, Nancy M. *Roland Barthes on Photography: The Critical Tradition in Perspective*. Gainesville: University Press of Florida, 1997.

Shiff, Richard. "Cezanne's Physicality: The Politics of Touch." In *The Language of Art History*, edited by Salim Kemal and Ivan Gaskell, 129–80. Cambridge: Cambridge University Press, 1991.

Shohat, Ella, and Stam Robert. *Unthinking Eurocentrism: Multiculturalism and the Media*. London and New York: Routledge, 1994.

Silberman, Seth Clark. "Lighting the Harlem Renaissance Afire!!: Embodying Richard Bruce Nugent's Bohemian Politic." In *The Gratest Taboo: Homosexuality in Black Communities*, edited by Deloy Constantine-Simms, 254–73. Los Angeles: Alyson Books, 2001.

Smith, Barbara Herrnstein. *Contigencies of Value: Alternative Perspectives for Critical Theory*. Cambridge, MA: Harvard University Press, 1988.

Smith, Mark M. *How Race Is Made: Slavery, Segregation, and the Senses.* Chapel Hill: University of North Carolina Press, 2006.

Smith, Nicole R. "Wangechi Mutu Feminist Collage and the Cyborg." Master's thesis, Georgia State University, 2009.

Smith, Shawn Michelle. *American Archives: Gender, Race, and Class in Visual Culture.* Edited by Anonymous. Princeton, NJ: Princeton University Press, 1999.

——. *Photography on the Color Line: W.E.B. Du Bois, Race, and Visual Culture.* Durham, NC: Duke University Press, 2004.

——. "The Evidence of Lynching Photographs." In *Lynching Photographs*, edited by Dora Apel and Shawn Michelle Smith. Berkeley and Los Angeles: University of California Press, 2008.

——. "Race and Reproduction in *Camera Lucida*." In *Photography Degree Zero: Reflections on Camera Lucida*, edited by Geoffrey Batchen, 243–57. Cambridge, MA: MIT Press, 2009.

Snead, James. *White Screens, Black Images: Hollywood from the Dark Side.* Edited by Colin McCabe and Cornel West. New York: Routledge, 1994.

Sobchack, Vivian. *The Address of the Eye: A Phenomenology of Film Experience.* Princeton, NJ: Princeton University Press, 1992.

——. "The Insistent Fringe: Moving Images and Historical Consciousness." *History and Theory* 36, no. 4 (1997): 4–20.

——. *Carnal Thoughts: Embodiment and Moving Image Culture.* Berkeley and Los Angeles: University of California Press, 2004.

——. "Animation and Automation, or, the Incredible Efforfulness of Being." *Screen* 50, no. 4 (2009): 375–91.

Sontag, Susan. *On Photography.* New York: Farrar, Straus and Giroux, 1977.

——. *Regarding the Pain of Others.* New York: Picador, 2003.

Spillers, Hortense J. "Mama's Baby, Papa's Maybe. An American Grammar Book." *Diacritics* 17, no. 2 (1987): 65–81.

Spivak, Gayatri Chakravorty. "Scattered Speculations on the Question of Value." *Diacritics* 15, no. 4 (1985).

——. "Some Concept Metaphors of Political Economy in Derrida's Texts." *Leftwright/ Intervention* 20 (1986).

Stallybrass, Peter. "Marx's Coat." In *Border Fetishisms: Material Objects in Unstable Spaces*, edited by Patricia Spyer, 183–207. New York: Routledge, 1998.

Stam, Robert. *Subversive Pleasures: Bakhtin, Cultural Criticism, and Film.* Baltimore: Johns Hopkins University Press, 1989.

Stein, Judith. "Sins of Omission." *Art in America*, October 1993.

Stockton, Kathryn Bond. *Beautiful Bottom, Beautiful Shame: Where "Black" Meets "Queer."* Durham, NC: Duke University Press, 2006.

——. *The Queer Child, or Growing Sideways in the Twentieth Century.* Durham, NC: Duke University Press, 2009.

Stoichita, Victor. *A Short History of the Shadow*. London: Reaktion Books, 1997.

Storr, Robert. "Spooked." In *Kara Walker: My Complement, My Enemy, My Oppressor, My Love*, edited by Philippe Vergne, 62–73. Minneapolis: Walker Art Center, 2007.

Sunami, April J. "Transforming 'Blackness': 'Post-Black' and Contemporary Hip-Hop in Visual Culture." Master's thesis, Ohio University, 2008.

Sutton, Damian. *Photography, Cinema, Memory: The Crystal Image of Time*. Minneapolis: University of Minnesota Press, 2009.

Talbot, William Henry Fox. "A Brief Historical Sketch of the Invention of the Art." In *Classic Essays on Photography*, edited by Alan Trachtenberg, 27–36. New Haven, CT: Leete's Island Books, 1980.

Taylor, Diana. *The Archive and the Repertoire: Performing Cultural Memory in the Americas*. Durham, NC: Duke University Press, 2003.

Taylor, Paul. "Post-Black, Old Black." *African American Review* 41, no. 4 (2007).

Thompson, Carol. "Sticks and Stones Will Break Your Bones, but Words Can Also Hurt You: Don't Let Sleeping Heads Lie." In *Wangechi Mutu: This You Call Civilization?*, edited by David Moos, Wangechi Mutu, and Art Gallery of Ontario. Toronto: Art Gallery of Ontario, 2010.

Thompson, Robert Farris. "Afro Modernism." *Artforum* 30 (1991).

Tinkcom, Matthew. *Working Like a Homosexual: Camp, Capital, Cinema*. Durham, NC: Duke University Press, 2002.

Tobing Rony, Fatimah. *The Third Eye: Race, Cinema, and Ethnographic Spectacle*. Durham, NC: Duke University Press, 1996.

Veal, Michael E. "Enter Cautiously." In *Wangechi Mutu: A Shady Promise*, edited by Douglas Singleton, 9–10. Bologna, Italy: Damiani, 2008.

Vergne, Philippe, ed. *Kara Walker: My Complement, My Enemy, My Oppressor, My Love*. 1st ed. Minneapolis: Walker Art Center, 2007.

Villarejo, Amy. *Lesbian Rule: Cultural Criticism and the Value of Desire*. Durham, NC: Duke University Press, 2003.

Yancy, George. *Look, a White!: Philosophical Essays on Whiteness*. Philadelphia: Temple University Press, 2012.

Wagner, Anne M. "Kara Walker: 'The Black-White Relation.'" In *Kara Walker: Narratives of a Negress*, edited by Ian Berry, Darby English, Vivian Patterson, and Mark Reinhardt, 91–101. New York: Rizzoli, 2007.

Walker, Kara Elizabeth. *Kara Walker. After the Deluge*. New York: Rizzoli, 2007.

Warner, Marina. *Phantasmagoria: Spirit Visions, Metaphors, and Media into the Twenty-First Century*. Oxford and New York: Oxford University Press, 2008.

Weheliye, Alexander G. "Pornotropes." *Journal of Visual Culture* 7, no. 1 (2008): 65–81.

Weschler, Lawrence. *Boggs: A Comedy of Values*. Chicago: University of Chicago Press, 1999.

White, Armond. "Pride and Precious." *New York Press*, November 4, 2009.

White, R. K., and Carney Landis. "Perception of Silhouettes." *American Journal of Psychology* 42, no. 3 (1930): 431–35.

Wiegman, Robyn. *American Anatomies: Theorizing Race and Gender.* Durham, NC: Duke University Press, 1995.

Wilkins Catanese, Brandi. "'How Do I Rent a Negro?': Racialized Subjectivity and Digital Performance Art." *Theater Journal* 75 (2005): 699–714.

Williams-Forson, Psyche A. "Flying the Coop with Kara Walker." In *Building Houses out of Chicken Legs.* Chapel Hill: University of North Carolina Press, 2006.

Witt, Doris. *Black Hunger: Food and the Politics of U.S. Identity.* New York and Oxford: Oxford University Press, 1999.

Wittgenstein, Ludwig. *Philosophical Investigations.* Translated by G. E. M. Anscombe. New York: Macmillan, 1953.

Wolf, Jeanne. "Mariah Carey: 'Music Is Always Where My Heart Is.'" http://www.parade.com/celebrity/celebrity-parade/2009/1102-mariah-carey-precious.html.

Wood, Marcus. *Blind Memory: Visual Representations of Slavery in England and America 1780–1865.* New York: Routledge, 2000.

Wynn, Ron. "*Precious* and *The Blind Side* Renew the Debate: Where Does an Honest Portrayal of Black Lives Stop, and Exploitation Start?" *Nashville Scene.* November 19, 2009.

Zangrando, Robert L. *The NAACP Crusade against Lynching, 1909–1950.* Philadelphia: Temple University Press, 1980.

Zielinski, Siegfried. *Deep Time of the Media: Toward an Archaeology of Hearing and Seeing by Technical Means.* Translated by Gloria Custance. Cambridge, MA: MIT Press, 2006.

INDEX

Page numbers in *italics* indicate illustrations.

94–95, 99, 112–113, 117, 131, 142; figural, 50;
as indexical, 30; material culture, 84–86,
89–91, 95, 108–109, 159–161; pivoting, 20, 91,
95–96, 99–103, 120, 163; of the spectacle, 22;
subject-made-, 85, 91; visual, 10, 12–13, 27,
32, 34, 55, 70, 102, 120, 150, 156
Olin, Margaret, 46
ontology: of blackness, 102, 163, 168n8; of face
value, 11, 20, 104; historical ontology of
slavery, 49, 98, 108, 131; of the image, 3–4,
23, 31, 40, 59, 112, 116, 123, 132, 150, 162–163,
167n5; photographic, 16, 23, 32, 120, 144;
post-, 3; of race, 4, 167n5; social, 26, 56, 116,
157, 207n55; speculative, 128; of the visual,
3–4, 20
optic, 52, 77, 134; black, 110–112; white, 110,
124, 134
overembodiment, 17, 37, 53, 59, 62, 150

phantasmagoria, 18, 91, 102, 128, 146, 164
phantasmatic, 32, 36, 54, 113, 127, 159. See also
blackness; chiasm; index; mask; visuality
phenomenology, 53–55, 151; of the cinematic
experience, 59, 203–204n16; of the
photograph, 44, 144; of the raced body,
44, 144
photochemical imagination, 11, 16, 23, 27, 32,
37–38, 51, 89, 112, 131–132, 152, 156, 159–165,
208n60
photography: 44–50; as deferral, 16, 29, 51;
ectopography and, 18, 53–54, 69–70, 81–82,
85–86; as image state, 20, 32, 37–39, 44–45,
52–53, 68–70, 90, 131, 143–144, 159, 191n8; as
formal logic 30; materiality and, 26–27, 31,
33–34, 46, 49–50, 161; as a medium, 10, 38,
113, 151, 182–183n101; as the money of the
real, 19, 89–90, 131, 157; semiotic structure
of, 30–31, 32–35, 143; shadow and, 38–39,
41–42, 49; social uses of, 27, 135, 148, 159,
202n8; as surface, 36–37, 42–43, 152. See also
cut: ectopography; image state; money:
of the real; photochemical imagination;
referential
Plessy vs. Ferguson, 141, 153

postcolonial, 73, 80
pipe, 12–16, 13, 53–54, 61–62, 68–69, 130, 137,
143, 163
Powell, Richard, 68–69
PRECIOUS, 17, 60–71
Precious: Based on the Novel "Push" by
Sapphire, 17, 53, 60–67, 65, 67
Price, Brian, 134

Raiford, Leigh, 26
realism: capitalist, 113–116, 120, 161; theoretical,
97
reality a(e)ffect. See affect
reference, 4, 14, 32, 39, 69, 143
referential: affects, 11–13, 86, 171n32; closure, 13;
referentiality, 11–12, 16, 37, 104; self-, 112–113,
124. See also affect
representation(al): colonial, 56, 70, 76, 150;
of desire, 14, 16; economy of, 92–96, 119,
146–147; image, 80, 82, 89, 138, 159; racial, 4,
6, 9–10, 17, 61, 106, 164, 166; regime of, 98,
104, 116–117; theory of race, 4, 6–7, 12, 60,
151; of value, 103–104; of the visual, 12–13,
32, 54, 143–144
resemblance, 14, 31, 37, 53, 74, 137, 143, 158;
catachresis, 56–57, 70; icon, 40, 59, 88,
102–105, 116, 148–150; mirror, 40–41, 150
Ricoeur, Paul, 55
roach. See Lorde, Audre; Maggie
Robinson, Amy, 141
Rodowick, David, 27, 151

saying, seeing and, 11–14, 17, 53–54, 56, 59, 68,
130, 133
Sayre, Henry M., 82
Schudson, Michael, 112
Scourged Back, The, 120, 123, 158
screen: black, 111, 146, 152–153; body as, 36, 42,
59, 152, 156; cinematic, 36–37, 41, 65, 102,
144, 150–154; spectator and, 41, 65, 156
seeing as, 1, 10, 14–15, 55, 90, 132, 165
Sekula, Allan, 36, 148
Seshadri-Crooks, Kalpana, 133, 137, 183–184n7
shadow, 25, 33–42, 166. See also blackness;
figure; index; lynching; mirror; shifter